Transforming Your Mind:
Changing the Way You Think

By Larry Fox

Author Contact:
Fox Ventures
P.O. Box 2727
Chester, VA 23831-8542

www.xulonpress.com

Table of Contents

Introduction

S in has perverted every aspect of human nature, warping God's intent for man and causing man to be focused on himself rather than God. The "flesh" (often called sinful or carnal nature) includes a mindset oriented toward earthly human existence and motivated by self-centeredness. Self-centeredness is the predominant characteristic of sinful nature.

God has a plan to redeem mankind, buying us back from our enslavement to sin, replacing our sinful nature with godly nature, and restoring us to His image. God's plan of redemption is as extensive as the effects of sin, so it is relevant to our spirit, our mind and our body.

The "real you" is defined by what we call your character. Your spirit is most likely the source of your character traits and your mind affects the way you express them. It is reasonable to expect, therefore, that redemption should have a significant impact on the way you think, which is the subject of this study.

The underlying theme of every chapter in this book is repentance: changing the way you think. First, we will consider how you should change the way you think about yourself. We will examine such topics as forgiveness, thankfulness, success, integrity, judgment and feelings. Basically, what you think, how you feel and what attitudes you have, are your responsibility. There is no room in Christianity for victimization. But far from being a condemning message, this study shows that God has given you everything you need to be successful. There is hope! And in God's system, hope is not a "maybe someday it might possibly work out" kind of wishful thinking. The hope that God offers is a guarantee of results. And He will produce those results in you with your cooperation. What is the extent of your cooperation? Changing your mind to conform to God's system.

The second part of this book shows some of the ways you should change your thinking about God's kingdom. It is natural to think of the oppressive, dictatorial kings of history and project this image on God's kingdom. But there is no way you can understand the truth of God's kingdom by comparing it with the perversions of power and authority sin has caused in earthly kingdoms. We will examine God's values, your rights and responsibilities, and what it really means to be a part of his kingdom.

God has done absolutely everything He needs to do. He has defeated your enemy, Satan; He set you free from your enslavement to sin; He adopted you into His family, making you a legal heir; and He made His resources available to you. Therefore, the only barrier to your success as a believer is the one that figuratively exists between your ears.

I hope this demonstrates the importance of changing the way you think and I pray this Bible study will help you make that transition.

Part 1

Changing the Way
You Think
About Yourself

1

Changing Your Attitude

The Bible has much to say about the human mind, which provides such functions as awareness, thought, reflection and judgment. The New Testament often uses the Greek word *nous*, translated "mind," to represent these functions. The New Testament occasionally uses other words for mental processes—heart (*kardia*), soul (*psyche*), inner purpose (*ennoia*) and others—but these words are at times used interchangeably for man's spirit. Careful study shows, however, that the Greek words *nous* (mind) and *pneuma* (spirit) are not used interchangeably, so we could use these words to examine the differences between man's mind and spirit.

Not only does the New Testament attribute different functions to the mind and spirit, in a few places it makes a very clear distinction between them. For example, we find a reference to an "unspiritual mind" (Col. 2:18), which suggests a mind not oriented toward the spirit. In Paul's discussion of spiritual gifts, he contrasts his mind with his spirit: "For if I pray in a tongue, my spirit prays, but my mind is unfruitful. So what shall I do? I will pray with my spirit, but I will also pray with my mind; I will sing with my spirit, but I will also sing with my mind" (1 Cor. 14:14-15). The Bible does not specifically say the spirit reflects or thinks, although it is said to know the mind's thoughts so it clearly has awareness.

You can corrupt your mind and become depraved. The second half of Romans chapter 1 explains that God is revealing His wrath against godless and wicked men, allowing them to become depraved. In that passage we read that "since they did not think it worthwhile to retain the knowledge of God, he gave them over to a depraved mind, to do what ought not to be done" (Rom. 1:28). Elsewhere, we see a general reference to "men of corrupt mind" (1 Tim. 6:5). It is clear from these scriptures as well as from observation that the human mind can be degraded and perverted so that it becomes immoral.

Actually, sin has corrupted every human mind, including yours, but God intends for His people to do something about that. He not only makes it possible for you to do something about the way you think, He requires it of you.

Renewing Your Mind

"The man without the Spirit does not accept the things that come from the Spirit of God, for they are foolishness to him, and he cannot understand them, because they are spiritually discerned" (1 Cor. 2:14). Anyone who insists on understanding God before they commit their life to Him will wait a long time—too long. Using human intellect, you cannot fully understand spiritual matters because you cannot adequately explain them in terms your mind can grasp. In fact, some of the things God does seem downright foolish to many people because they judge God's actions on the basis of human experience.

Most people think Christians are simply foolish for what they believe and they think Christians have to rely on God because they're too weak to do otherwise. Even if by some weird quirk of logic they were right, God has chosen to use weak and foolish people to confound the strong and wise, so He alone will receive the glory. However, spiritual matters simply do not make sense to the mind of a non-Christian.

The Bible shows us that, in addition to failing to understand God, the mind of a non-Christian is hostile to God: "the sinful mind is hostile to God" (Rom. 8:7). A person absorbed by the world's standards and priorities is an enemy of God; that is how much sin has warped man's mind. In part, this means a non-Christian's natural inclination is always wrong because he's directed by his sinful nature. It may even be wise for you as a Christian to use this rule of thumb: Do the opposite of the natural human reaction. What are most people doing? Do the opposite. What do most non-Christians believe? Believe the opposite.

Christianity is not a supplement to normal life; you cannot add it to everything else you do, like a hobby. Christianity is an intimate relationship with God Almighty, the creator of the universe, who holds the universe together and keeps it running. Christianity permeates everything you do and influences every attitude and action. It is not a weekly social engagement on Sunday morning or a traditional prayer before meals that buys you a ticket to heaven. Christianity is at odds with the entire world system. It is at odds with human nature. It is at odds with normal human thinking and attitudes. That is why God insists that you change the way you think.

> *Therefore, I urge you, brothers, in view of God's mercy, to offer your bodies as living sacrifices, holy and pleasing to God—which is your spiritual worship. Do not conform any longer to the pattern of this world, but be transformed by the renewing of your mind. Then you will be able to test and approve what God's will is—his good, pleasing and perfect will* (Rom. 12:1-2).

Here we see a contrast between conforming and transforming. We have conformed all our lives to the pattern of this world, the spiritual and moral characteristics of our environment. We have had the same concerns as the world system and the same attitudes. We studied its wisdom and copied its fashions and mannerisms. But now is the time for us to stop. Instead of continuing to conform to the world system, we can and must be transformed, which literally means to experience metamorphosis. Metamorphosis must occur so we can change into another form. That transformation occurs as you renew your mind, adjusting the way you think.

What do people in the world think about? They think about themselves and how to get what they want. They compare themselves with others to measure their own worth.

The Book of Romans says you are to stop conforming to the world's patterns and be transformed by renewing your mind. In that context it continues: "Do not think of yourself more highly than you ought, but rather think of yourself with sober judgment, in accordance with the measure of faith God has given you" (v. 3). This addresses how you think of yourself, your self-image. It suggests that the only standard of judging yourself is that which God empowers you through faith to do. You cannot compare yourself with anyone else, as the world does. What is God's will for you? What has he given you faith to do? That is how you should judge yourself.

These verses actually are an introduction to a discussion of some basic aptitudes God gives people. We will not study those aptitudes now, but it is significant that you can only use your aptitudes properly if you change the way you think.

In Second Corinthians chapter 4, Paul describes some hardships he has suffered and discusses the hope of resurrection. Then he makes a significant statement:

Therefore we do not lose heart. Though outwardly we are wasting away, yet inwardly we are being renewed day by day. For our light and momentary troubles are achieving for us an eternal glory that far outweighs them all. So we fix our eyes not on what is seen, but on what is unseen. For what is seen is temporary, but what is unseen is eternal (2 Cor. 4:16-18).

How was he renewed daily in his inner nature? Did God increase his faith? Did God give Paul greater faith that he would take care of him? Possibly, but that would be a selfish use of faith if that were all.

There is another possibility. Notice the change in perspective that Paul describes. He contrasts what he calls light and momentary troubles with eternal glory. Elsewhere in this letter Paul lists some of his "light and momentary troubles": he was flogged five times, beaten with rods three times, stoned once and left for dead, and shipwrecked three times (2 Cor. 11:24-25). You and I would call any of these life-threatening experiences a catastrophe, yet Paul calls them all light and momentary troubles. He is not suggesting those experiences were painless or insignificant in themselves. His point is that they are earning for him "an eternal glory that far outweighs them all." The pain of those experiences was "light" compared to the glory he will experience. The years of suffering were "momentary" compared to eternity.

Paul's message is about priorities and perspective—how you think. Part of his inward renewal relates to the way he thought. The correct perspective tells you that what is eternal and unseen is more important than anything you experience in this life. Paul's response was to fix his eyes on what is unseen, which means eternal matters had become the center of his attention.

The Holy Spirit actively participates in the process of renewing your mind, as shown by the following scripture.

At one time we too were foolish, disobedient, deceived and enslaved by all kinds of passions and pleasures. We lived in malice and envy, being hated and hating one another. But when the kindness and love of God our Savior appeared, he saved us, not because of righteous things we had done, but because of his mercy. He saved us through the washing of rebirth and renewal by the Holy Spirit (Titus 3:3-5).

Foolishness, disobedience, deception, preoccupation with passions and desires, malice, envy and hatred all have to do with the way you thought before your salvation. You used to think just like the world, but you were reborn ("the washing of rebirth") and the Holy Spirit began to renew you. Your redemption began with the rebirth of your spirit, is continuing now through the renewing of your mind, and will be finalized with physical salvation when the Lord gives you a new body. The current phase is renewal by the Holy Spirit, which includes renewing your mind, and is a crucial part of your redemption.

"And we, who with unveiled faces all reflect the Lord's glory, are being transformed into his likeness with ever-increasing glory, which comes from the Lord, who is the Spirit" (2 Cor. 3:18). The word "transformed" is the same as in Romans 12:2, "transformed by the renewing of your mind." It is part of a process, because the verse says it is "with ever-increasing glory." The goal of the transformation is for you to have his "likeness," which means you will be like the Lord.

Does this suggest that you become like Jesus simply by controlling your thoughts or changing the way you think? Not at all. You cannot save yourself or develop godly character by your own efforts. However, your participation is vital to the process.

You are a free moral agent and God honors your choices. Prior to salvation, you were enslaved to sin and unable to exercise your will except to indulge in sin. But now the Son has set you free and you can choose between right and wrong. If you choose to serve yourself, God lets you. If you choose to let God do His work in you, then the Holy Spirit can develop God's nature in you. As we will see in Philippians chapter 2, you are to work out your own salvation, but God does the actual work in you. It is a joint effort.

Your role in this joint effort is to reprogram your mind. You need to change what you think about, change your attitudes, change your priorities and even change your standards. Hebrews 5:14 refers to those who have "trained themselves to distinguish good from evil." Because your previous sinful nature originally programmed your mind, you had a warped understanding of what is good and what is evil. Now you must change your standards of good and evil to conform to God's standards. You need to take an active role in changing your perception.

Here is another passage that discusses the renewal process:

You were taught, with regard to your former way of life, to put off your old self, which is being corrupted by its deceitful desires; to be made new in the attitude of your minds; and to put on the new self, created to be like God in true righteousness and holiness (Eph. 4:22-24).

"Put off . . . put on" means to choose to think and act differently. Both phrases, "put off" and "put on," are active so you are responsible for doing them yourself.

Between these two imperatives, however, we find a phrase that is not an imperative. It says you are to be made new in the attitude of your mind. The Greek word translated "made new" occurs only once in the New Testament, so we have no other biblical examples of the word to examine. The word means to renew, to make new again, to make young again, to receive strength again. I have been told that the verb form in verse 23 is the present infinitive, so the action is complete but is also a continuing process. We could translate the verse, "You were taught. . . to continuously renew your attitude," suggesting an unending process. Once you recognize the continuous bombardment of sinful attitudes the world system throws at you, you also recognize the need to continuously renew your attitude.

The part you are to make new is the attitude (literally, "spirit") of your mind. Does the "spirit of your mind" refer to the essential nature of your thinking, your basic attitude? It seems to.

Your attitude affects what you do and how well you do it. For example, when I was doing research on this material and preparing teaching notes, I was struggling with discouragement. I felt I really did not understand the material and what little I did understand was hardly worth teaching. As a result, it was extremely difficult for me to work on it. One morning God helped me realign my attitude (I renewed my mind) and suddenly I had much more understanding of these verses. My wrong attitude prevented me from doing my work and even understanding what the material meant.

In America, our Constitution and its Bill of Rights place great emphasis on individual liberties. As a result, in our culture individuality becomes sacred. You are entitled to your own opinion; you can say what you want as long as it doesn't injure someone; you can call or write any of your elected officials; some of our school systems encourage students to form their own opinions about classroom material; and so on. Our Western religious culture has much of the same flavor. You are entitled to your own opinion of God; you can interpret the Bible as you choose; you can worship God as you please. In our culture, these "religious rights" become almost sacred in themselves.

So anyone who suggests you should change your attitude or thinking immediately becomes suspect. How dare anyone say that your opinion is not acceptable? But that kind of reaction is the result of a sinful way of thinking. That normal human perspective, ultimately self-centered, values your opinion the most, protects your rights the most, indulges your desires the most, focuses your attention on yourself the most. The very suggestion that anything about you is wrong is a major attack on your self-image and your natural response is to leap to your own defense.

But we must recognize that the emphasis of Western culture is on the equality of man compared with other men, whereas the emphasis of the Bible is on the inferiority of man compared with God. If the issue is your opinion versus my opinion, then your opinion has as much legal validity and worth as mine. When you compare yourself to the eternal, all-powerful, all-knowing God, however, you must recognize your complete inferiority and the total worthlessness of your own opinion.

When another person speaks to you, it is okay to judge what they say to determine whether you agree or disagree; in fact, you should. When God speaks to you, however, you must first determine that it was, in fact, God who spoke, then your opinion must immediately become subservient. If what God says doesn't make sense, it is because of your inability to understand, not because God is foolish.

It is very difficult to operate in these two intellectual modes simultaneously—to critique on the one hand, to embrace without question on the other; to defend your position in one case, to abandon it in the other. With your worldly mindset demanding that you promote your own ideas and with so much in your culture defending your right to do so, it will take considerable effort to change. But you must change and you can change.

Imitating Christ's Attitude

Paul's letter to the Philippians contains some very important teaching about the importance of renewing your mind. Let us begin at chapter 2. "If you have any encouragement from being united with Christ, if any comfort from his love, if any fellowship with the Spirit, if any tenderness and compassion, then make my joy complete by being like-minded, having the same love, being one in spirit and purpose" (Phil. 2:1-2). By now, you can probably identify the main points.

Paul encourages them to be like-minded, which literally means "thinking the same thing." He says they should have the same "agape," probably emphasizing the need for unity and service to each other. They should think the same thing and love the same way. They were to be one in spirit, which relates to agreement, harmony and similarity in their attitude, judgment and view. They were also to be one in purpose. The Greek literally says, "the one thing thinking," to have the same way of thinking. Everything Paul said places great emphasis on their attitude, their viewpoint or perspective.

"Do nothing out of selfish ambition or vain conceit, but in humility consider others better than yourselves. Each of you should look not only to your own interests, but also to the interests of others" (vv. 3-4). The first forbidden motive he lists is selfish ambition, which is self-seeking, creates rivalry and is contentious. This motivation is energized by self-will and causes you to want to get ahead even if you must create problems for others.

Another forbidden motive listed in this verse is vain conceit. This refers to a conspicuous pride in your appearance or achievements. It encourages you to be vain, to boast and talk big. Selfish ambition and vain conceit both suggest self-promotion; these should never motivate your thoughts or actions.

Humility is closely related to agape, and here it is contrasted with selfish ambition and vain conceit. Humility will allow you to consider others better than yourself, which means to think more highly of others than you do of yourself. Humility is not debasing yourself or believing that you have no worth, but rather elevating others above yourself. Pushing yourself down is putting the emphasis on yourself. Raising others up emphasizes them, which is where your emphasis should be. Again, we are dealing with attitude.

This concept is reinforced in verse 4. "Each of you should look not only to your own interests, but also to the interests of others." The Greek word translated "interests" is a very common word translated many different ways, so there is no special significance to its use in this verse. This verse does not say you should ignore yourself, but instead says you should consider other people as well as yourself.

So the proper balance is to consider everyone, including yourself, but to place greater emphasis on others. Give others more consideration and higher priority than yourself. That is practical humility.

Romans 12:3 says, "Do not think of yourself more highly than you ought." Philippians 2:3-4 says that if you have more concern for yourself than for others, you are thinking more highly of yourself than you ought. First Corinthians contains some similar verses. In one place, Paul talks about offending someone by doing something they believe is wrong; specifically, eating food sacrificed to idols. In that context he says, "Nobody should seek his own good, but the good of others" (1 Cor. 10:24). Do not use your freedom to do something that would be harmful to someone else or cause them to violate their convictions. In another place, Paul is discussing the spiritual gifts of prophecy and tongues when he says, "Since you are eager to have spiritual gifts, try to excel in gifts that build up the church" (1 Cor. 14:12). These all reinforce the need to put others first, which requires a radical change in the way you think.

In the first four verses of Philippians chapter 2, Paul emphasizes the importance of a proper attitude. He stresses the need for the believers to think the same way or to have the same perspective, then describes that perspective as placing higher priority on others than on yourself. Then he states very specifically, "Your attitude should be the same as that of Christ Jesus" (Phil. 2:5). The Greek word translated "attitude" is the same word for "mind" that we have seen in other verses; it refers to the way you think, your general attitude.

Your attitude should be the same as Jesus'. He was uniquely qualified to obtain your salvation and He used His uniqueness to benefit you. Likewise, you should be willing to use your uniqueness to serve others. One purpose of this study is to help you understand who you are, but the goal is not to make you preoccupied with who you are, either proud or ashamed, depending on your focus. Instead, you are to use your abilities to serve others. That is the attitude Jesus had.

Let me give an extremely relevant analogy even if it appears offensive or undignified. Sexual activity has two purposes: to develop unity between a husband and wife, and to propagate the species. God designed humans so that sexual activity is extremely enjoyable, but people use pornography and masturbation to induce the pleasure artificially for entirely selfish reasons. Evidence tells us that these are widespread practices. The pleasure of sexual activity is to be a byproduct of the sex act, but people induce the pleasure for its own sake. They are abusing God's design simply to make themselves feel good.

Using your character for your own fulfillment and pleasure has the same effect. God designed you and equipped you to serve others effectively in certain ways, and when you do, you feel very satisfied and fulfilled. But when you use your strengths and abilities only for your own pleasure or benefit, you are abusing God's design. Using your God-given abilities to enjoy the pleasure they give you is a sin in the same category as pornography and masturbation.

Did the analogy offend you? Are you repulsed by pornography and masturbation? You should be. Do you think you offend God when you use your character strengths for your own pleasure? You can be certain He loves you but is repulsed by your self-centered attitudes.

Pleasure itself is not wrong or sinful. God designed you to enjoy pleasure and fulfillment, and you experience these when you do what you were created to do. But if I teach only because I enjoy teaching, I am abusing my gift and offending God. Every expression of self-centeredness repulses Him because it is the exact opposite of His nature.

I have heard people say such things as, "I love singing in the choir. I made sure I sang in all the churches I attended." If you sing in the choir primarily because you enjoy it, you are acting out of self-centeredness. It is the motivation for all sin, and every act committed in selfishness is a sin.

Your attitude should be the same as Jesus': using your qualities to serve and benefit others, even to the point of great personal loss. True agape is complete selflessness, a primary concern for the benefit of others.

Maybe you are thinking, "This Fox guy has gone off the deep end on this one. I can't accept this." Well, maybe you should consider the extent to which sin has affected your thinking. Carnal thinking will not accept the idea that self-indulgence is wrong—a sin and offensive to God!

Renewing your mind, changing your thinking, is extremely important. It is a critical part of your redemption and an essential part of your spiritual maturity.

> *Your attitude should be the same as that of Christ Jesus: Who, being in very nature God, did not consider equality with God something to be grasped, but made himself nothing, taking the very nature of a servant, being made in human likeness. And being found in appearance as a man, he humbled himself and became obedient to death—even death on a cross!* (Phil. 2:5-8).

These verses describe Jesus' attitude. It was His responsibility to come to earth and die for our sins, so He willingly gave up His deity and became a man. He did not grasp or clutch onto His equality with God, but served mankind and died the most torturous death devised by the people of that day. He went from one extreme (God), to the other (servant of man, executed as a criminal). He was willing to do it because it would benefit other people. That was His attitude. Notice the word "consider," which also relates to the way Jesus thought. All of these verses (2:1-8) are addressing the way we are to think.

This passage mentions Jesus' "equality with God"—or more literally, "equalities" (plural)—referring to the various ways the divine nature can exist and express itself. Jesus' equalities with God mean He had the same status and aptitudes. Yet He made himself nothing, or emptied Himself, laying aside His divine status and aptitudes. Hebrews 2:9 confirms that Jesus became "a little lower than the angels," so He definitely set aside His status. Hebrews 2:17 says that He became "like his brothers in every way," which means He discarded His divine aptitudes and became just like you and me.

Acts 1:8 reads, "you will receive power when the Holy Spirit comes on you," meaning that you can receive God's power through the Holy Spirit. Acts 10:38 says, "God anointed Jesus of Nazareth with the Holy Spirit and power," so Jesus was equipped the way you and I are, with the same Holy Spirit and the same power.

Jesus had God's nature because He was God, then He took on the nature of a servant. The word translated "nature" in Philippians 2 is used only of Jesus in the New Testament. Here it refers to the specific characteristics that are unique to God and essential to His being God, then those characteristics that are unique to and essential to being a servant. The two natures, God and servant, are opposites and cannot coexist in any way. So Jesus was completely and uniquely God, then became completely and uniquely a servant.

He laid aside (put off) the nature of God and picked up (put on) the nature of a servant. The Lord became the servant by putting off and putting on. Now He asks you to put off your sinful ways of thinking and put on the nature of a servant as He did. Jesus "humbled himself and became obedient to death—even death on a cross!" (v. 8). Jesus becoming obedient to death probably includes denying His human tendencies and aptitudes, not just His physical death on a cross since that is stated separately.

He was willing to lay aside His uniqueness, His equality with God, for the benefit of others. Likewise, you should be prepared to lay aside your uniqueness for the benefit of others. For example, God may ask you to do something that is "out of character" for you. So what if it is out of character? God equipped you with a certain character to operate naturally a certain way, so if He asks you to do something requiring a different character, you can expect Him to give you the ability to do so—we call it grace. Jesus completely abandoned His divine nature for the benefit of others, showing the extent to which you should use your abilities for the benefit of others. In fact, the purpose of your character is to serve others.

After describing what your attitude should be and how Jesus' attitude affected His actions, Paul says, "Therefore . . . ." I once had a pastor who said you always need to find out what the "therefore" is there for. Paul is about to show how you should respond to the "attitude" discussion we just examined. Consider carefully what he says:

Therefore, my dear friends, as you have always obeyed—not only in my presence, but now much more in my absence— continue to work out your salvation with fear and trembling, for it is God who works in you to will and to act according to his good purpose (Phil. 2:12-13).

"Continue to work out your salvation" refers to a personal salvation, rather than a general one. Other translations of the verse emphasize this by using the phrase, "your own salvation." While everyone's salvation will have common elements—all have sinned, deserve punishment, are helpless to save themselves, must have faith in Jesus' crucifixion—some of the details of your salvation are virtually unique.

Salvation means something a little different to each of us. For example, a fearful person must learn to take control in areas where he has responsibility, but an aggressive person must learn not to take control in all cases. Salvation has a continuing phase, in which you are bringing your attitudes into line with God's desire. So you are to continue working on this aspect of your salvation, as the verse says.

At first, the idea of fear and trembling seems incompatible with the continuing process of salvation. What could Paul's statement possibly mean? He is not thinking of the fear of man, because earlier in the same letter he says believers should not be frightened by those who oppose them (Phil. 1:28). He might be referring to fear of the Lord, which is certainly a scriptural concept (see Acts 9:31, 2 Cor. 7:1, Eph. 5:21). I think the context suggests, however, a fear of yourself. Considering Jesus' example, you should be terrified at the possibility of serving yourself instead of others. The thought of using your character for your own benefit should make you tremble with fear.

If the idea of serving yourself does not disturb you, you apparently do not understand how repulsive self-centeredness is to God, the one who will evaluate your every attitude and action when your life is over. Think about it. God is more concerned with your attitude than with your actions. You can do the right things for the wrong reasons and completely waste your life. Jesus said that some will come before Him who have done great things in His name, but He will "tell them plainly, 'I never knew you. Away from me, you evildoers!'" (Matt. 7:22-23).

In the statement, "I never knew you," the word "knew" is from the Greek word *ginosko*, which means to understand things as they really are by experiencing them. Jesus is saying something like, "I've never had any experience with you to get to know you." This is like saying that you are acquainted with someone, but you really do not know him. You get to know someone by spending time with him. The issue in Matthew 7:23 is that those people were doing things on their own; they did not spend enough time with God to get to know Him and find out what He wanted them to do.

Paul uses the analogy of gold, silver, costly stones, wood, hay or straw for the works people do, and says the "quality of each man's work" will be revealed with fire (1 Cor. 3:12-13). Could it be that those who have selfish motives even for doing God's work will be rejected or suffer great loss? I think so, and that is why you and I should be terrified at the prospect of abusing what God has given us. If you use your character for your own advantage, you are violating God's intent and the eternal consequences will be serious. If your life as a Christian does not pass the test, you will make it to heaven, "but only as one escaping through the flames" (1 Cor. 3:15). No reward, only eternal loss. Will a lifetime of self-centeredness be worth an eternity of loss? No.

"Continue to work out your salvation with fear and trembling, for it is God who works in you to will and to act according to his good purpose" (Phil. 2:12-13). God does the work in you, not yourself. You have a critical role in the process, but God does the actual work of salvation or redemption.

Now the question is, "Whose will and actions are according to God's good purpose in this verse?" It would be redundant or maybe even meaningless to state that God wills and acts according to His own good purpose, because God will not or cannot violate His own purpose. The only reasonable interpretation is that God's work in you permits you to will and act according to His good purpose. Those controlled by a worldly perspective cannot please God (see Rom. 8:8), but God's work frees you from carnal thinking so you can have the will and the ability to fulfill His purpose. His purpose for you includes using the character He gave you to serve others.

Pressing On

In the third chapter of Philippians, Paul continues to show how important it is to change the way you think.

> *If anyone else thinks he has reasons to put confidence in the flesh, I have more: circumcised on the eighth day, of the people of Israel, of the tribe of Benjamin, a Hebrew of Hebrews; in regard to the law, a Pharisee; as for zeal, persecuting the church; as for legalistic righteousness, faultless* (Phil. 3:4-6).

Paul is listing his credentials or personal qualifications. His accomplishments as an adult are very admirable, and he excelled in his work because of the person he was: zealous and disciplined. As he says, he had as much reason as anybody to be self-confident.

> *But whatever was to my profit I now consider loss for the sake of Christ. What is more, I consider everything a loss compared to the surpassing greatness of knowing Christ Jesus my Lord, for whose sake I have lost all things. I consider them rubbish, that I may gain Christ* (Phil. 3:7-8).

Look at the contrasts Paul uses: profit versus loss, loss versus greatness, rubbish versus gain. He is describing a radical change in his attitude and priorities: all his personal accomplishments (he had many) were rubbish. He is not describing hopelessness or pessimism, however. He has discarded these for something of greater value: "that I may gain Christ and be found in him, not having a righteousness of my own that comes from the law, but that which is through faith in Christ—the righteousness that comes from God and is by faith" (vv. 8-9). His goal is to gain righteousness through faith in Christ. He has discarded his personal righteousness, which he achieved by satisfying the law's requirements.

"I want to know Christ and the power of his resurrection and the fellowship of sharing in his sufferings, becoming like him in his death, and so, somehow, to attain to the resurrection from the dead" (vv. 10-11). What is Paul talking about?

Relationships are strengthened by shared experiences. Maybe Paul is continuing the contrast between what he used to value but now rejects, and the "surpassing greatness of knowing Christ Jesus my Lord." Relationship with God is the essence of Christianity. Paul's desire for relationship and intimacy with God was so great that he was willing to experience anything that would bring him closer to the Lord. Paul wanted the same daily victorious living as Jesus, overcoming temptations without sin or failure.

What were Jesus' sufferings that Paul wanted to share? Hebrews says Jesus was made "perfect through suffering" (Heb. 2:10) and He "suffered when he was tempted" (Heb. 2:18). Also, "Although he was a son, he learned obedience from what he suffered and, once made perfect, he became the source of eternal salvation for all who obey him" (Heb. 5:8-9).

The phrase, "once made perfect," is very important. Because He was born without sin, Jesus was perfect in the sense that He had no flaw. But something about His experience also caused Him to attain perfection. Until He faced every temptation and passed every test, He could not be perfect in the sense that He was complete. Jesus suffered when He was tempted, and that suffering made Him perfectly complete.

Did His suffering on the cross make Him perfect? No, He was perfected before He went to the cross because He could be the source of eternal salvation only after becoming perfect. The sufferings that perfected Him were the result of His remaining without sin in temptation — not a single failure in 33 years. This is more than "the three temptations of Christ."

Jesus was human and every moment of every day He experienced human desires: "I want people to believe me, to accept me. I know what I'm talking about, but they won't listen. They think I'm just a carpenter's son." Jesus the man wanted credibility and acceptance, just as you do. He was "tempted in every way, just as we are — yet was without sin" (Heb. 4:15). He had the same human needs and desires you do and His were as strong and persistent as yours.

When you want to do something that is wrong, do you suffer if you refuse to do it? If you have a strong desire and you deny it, you suffer. You give in to your desires because you don't want to suffer and would prefer the fulfillment of satisfying them. Jesus "learned obedience from what he suffered."

Paul said he wanted to share Jesus' sufferings and thereby become like Him in godly righteousness. Then he continued:

Not that I have already obtained all this, or have already been made perfect, but I press on to take hold of that for which Christ Jesus took hold of me. Brothers, I do not consider myself yet to have taken hold of it. But one thing I do: Forgetting what is behind and straining toward what is ahead, I press on toward the goal to win the prize for which God has called me heavenward in Christ Jesus. All of us who are mature should take such a view of things. And if on some point you think differently, that too God will make clear to you (Phil. 3:12-15).

Before Paul's conversion, he probably thought he had "arrived" because he had qualifications most people could never attain and his legalistic righteousness was "faultless" (v. 6). But now he has a very different perspective of himself. He has a new standard of perfection and he readily admits he has not obtained it or been made perfect.

What is his attitude? He is pressing on to gain or achieve what God intends, "to take hold of that for which Christ Jesus took hold of me." The phrase he uses, "take hold of," is very intense and means to seize or apprehend. The forcefulness of his commitment is demonstrated by other phrases as well: "press on" (used twice) and "straining."

What was it that Paul was so strongly committed to achieving? What did Jesus have in mind when He so forcefully took hold of Paul? We could go back to Paul's conversion experience, when God said, "This man is my chosen instrument to carry my name before the Gentiles and their kings and before the people of Israel. I will show him how much he must suffer for my name" (Acts 9:15-16). Is this the goal Paul said he was pressing and straining toward? Was

28

he trying to reach all the Gentiles and the people of Israel? Was he simply wanting to suffer so he could fulfill God's statement about him?

I don't think that is the goal Paul refers to in Philippians chapter 3. His main topic there is relationship with God and perfection before Him. He wrote that knowing Christ surpasses everything else. He said he wanted to "gain Christ," to be "found in him," to know Him and have the same experiences.

Having described the intensity of his efforts, Paul makes a very pointed statement that all mature believers "should take such a view of things." This phrase is a translation of the Greek word we have considered throughout this study, "mind," referring to the way you think and to your basic attitude.

Paul is saying that a mature believer should think the same way he does. And if he doesn't, God will make it clear to him that he should. Your attitude should be that an intimate relationship with God is more important than anything else, and that whatever you have to do to achieve it is worthwhile.

Paul wrote frequently about the importance of changing your priorities and the way you think. Colossians shows that doing so is a direct response to God setting you free from the bondage of sin and worldly principles. After explaining the worthlessness of human regulations, compared to life in Christ, Paul writes, "Since, then, you have been raised with Christ, set your hearts on things above, where Christ is seated at the right hand of God. Set your minds on things above, not on earthly things" (Col. 3:1-2).

Verse one in the Greek doesn't actually use the word, "heart," but instead says you should search for and try to discover the things above. Verse two says your general orientation should be toward things above, not on earthly things. These verses show how much you should be pondering, investigating, trying to understand heavenly matters. How does God view you? What is His plan for you? What does He expect of you? What does He want you to do?

Romans 12:1-2 gives a contrast: Don't conform to the world's patterns any longer, but be transformed by changing your outlook, the way you think, your priorities. Colossians 3:1-2 gives an identical contrast: change your thinking to heavenly matters (God's will), and stop being preoccupied with earthly things.

The surrounding verses give reason for this change and describe the correct response. You died to the world and should no longer live by its rules and standards (Col. 2:20). Therefore, you should put to death everything in you that belongs to this sinful world (Col. 3:5). This requires a radical change in priorities and your general outlook on life. It begins with what you think about and how you think.

You can only put your earthly perspective to death if you believe it is not as important as "things above." This explains why you struggle with sinful desires. If they are still important to you, you will take care of them and satisfy their demands. Change your mind!

Consider a couple of biblical examples of men who had changed the way they thought. Daniel is an Old Testament example of a spiritually minded man. He had a high executive position in the capital city, yet three times each day he stopped his work to pray. His relationship with God was more important to him than his work. In the New Testament you see Paul as an example of a spiritual man. His religious credentials were impeccable and he excelled in his work, but his appraisal of his accomplishments was that they were as worthless as a pile of manure. These men had changed their attitudes.

Jesus taught that if you make His kingdom and His righteousness your number one priority, then He will take care of your needs and you won't have to worry about them (Matt. 6:33). That is the exact opposite of the worldly way of thinking. Paul wrote that you should not think about how to gratify sinful desires (Rom. 13:14). Don't even think about it!

You probably do not realize how sinful your thinking is. The following thoughts are examples that spring from self-centered desires.

What do I feel like doing? What do I want to eat? If I could just tell him off! I can't believe what he did to me! What can I do to get that dress (or car, or stereo, or house)? Won't everyone be impressed when I wear this! If I were doing that job, it'd be done right! I wish he wouldn't ask me to do that;

he knows I don't like to do it. He makes me so mad when he says that! What can't he just leave me alone?

A friend of mine pointed out that we need to change our vocabulary. For example, I might say, "I tend to have a problem with impatience." Instead, I should admit that impatience is a sin and I am guilty. Stop playing down the severity of the problem. Maybe you feel you have a few problems but basically you are okay. You can deceive yourself very easily in this way when you compare yourself with people around you.

Paul said you should set your mind on heavenly things, where Jesus sits beside the Father and angels continuously declare His holiness. Is Jesus preoccupied with being in the Father's presence or with the multitude of angels around the throne? No, His attention is on you. Look at yourself from His perspective. How would you see yourself if you looked through Jesus' eyes? Would your attitudes still be acceptable? Compare yourself with Jesus, the one who lived a completely sinless life, because He is the only legitimate standard for comparison.

Clothe yourself with the Lord, put on His attributes, and don't even think about how to please yourself. This calls for a radical transformation in your attitude, your way of thinking and your general outlook on life. Renew your mind. Concentrate on building your relationship with God and fulfilling what He created you for. Put the world's ambitions behind you and press on toward godly character. Seize the kingdom of God forcefully. Let nothing prevent you from pleasing God. These statements require a complete transformation in the way you think, and nothing less is an appropriate response to God's redemptive plan.

Conclusion

You have lived like the world too long and need to be transformed, changed into an entirely different being. You have a vital role in that transformation because it can occur only as you renew your mind. This means to change how you think, what you think about, your attitudes, perspective, priorities and standards.

Personal Study

"Do not conform any longer to the pattern of this world, but be transformed by the renewing of your mind" (Rom. 12:2). "You were taught, with regard to your former way of life . . . to be made new in the attitude of your minds" (Eph. 4:22-23).

- What attitudes do you have that clearly conform to the world's pattern? How are these attitudes reinforced by advertising, entertainment or peer pressure? What habits or practices do you have that reinforce those attitudes?

- To renew your mind, or be made new in the attitude of your mind, implies completely changing the way you think. Since the best way to get rid of an undesirable attitude is to replace it with a desirable one, what desirable attitude can you form now that will change the way you think the rest of today?

- Which of your priorities and standards do you think displease God? What can you do to change them?

2

Repentance Is for Believers

Christians will probably all agree that for a person to become a child of God, he must repent of his sin and accept Jesus as his Lord and Savior. If someone does not repent, I seriously doubt that we can call him a Christian, because we consider repentance essential to salvation.

Unfortunately, many of us treat repentance as a once-in-a-lifetime event, a step in the process of converting from sinner to saint. It almost seems that repentance is no longer necessary once a person's sins are forgiven. However, that first act of repenting should set the pattern for an attitude of repentance.

This is not to suggest that we should continuously apologize to God for every human thing we do, although that might not be a bad idea at times. The biblical concept of repentance is much broader than that. The Greek word translated "repent" is the compound word *metanoeo*. The first part of the word (*meta-*) indicates a change or transformation and appears in many English words, such as "metamorphosis," which means a change in condition. The second part of *metanoeo* is from the root word *nous*, which we translate as "mind." So *metanoeo* literally means to change your mind, and by extension means to turn about, to express regret or adopt another view.

Whenever the Bible says you should repent or turn away from unrighteousness, its main emphasis is on your will, changing your mind or purpose. To turn to God you must understand the nature of sin and be aware of your personal guilt. The concepts of sin and righteousness are originally perceived spiritually, but understanding and awareness of them are functions of the mind. The fact that God demands repentance shows that it involves your mind; it is something you must choose to do.

Metanoeo suggests more than just rejecting your former position or attitude, and includes turning to and embracing a new one. It means to change your mind, not cease to have one. A Christian's mind plays a vital role in his relationship with God as he learns what God expects of him and chooses to please Him.

When you accepted Jesus as Savior, He erased the record of your sins, set you free from the law of sin and death and replaced your sinful nature with a righteous one. You became a new creature, your basic motivation changed and you were born again. You have only one nature, not two. Figuratively speaking, your sinful nature died with Jesus on the cross, so it is gone and no longer controls or even affects you. However, the results or by-products of your former sinful nature still remain: sinful attitudes, behaviors, desires, habits, instincts, perceptions, feelings, tendencies, memories and thoughts. Your task is to repent, to reject that sinful mindset and replace it with a righteous one.

Repenting is a process, not an isolated event. As you mature and become more like your Father (God), you will continue to discover things you need to change. Let me suggest an attitude you can change right now. Instead of viewing this as a frustrating, never ending struggle to make God happy, consider it an extended opportunity to get rid of those attitudes that cause you problems and prevent you from becoming more like God. As my pastor says, "Repentance is believers' territory." Let's examine the scriptures to see whether his statement is justified.

Jesus was teaching His disciples some basic principles of the kingdom when He said something that is tough to swallow. "If your brother sins, rebuke him, and if he repents, forgive him. If he sins against you seven times in a day, and seven times comes back to you and says, 'I repent,' forgive him" (Luke 17:3-4). This shocked the disciples because they responded, "Increase our faith!" (v. 5). Maybe you had the same reaction. I want to point out that Jesus was talking about "your brother," another Christian, sinning against you and repenting.

The word "repent" (*metanoeo*) occurs twice in these verses and it is something done by a believer. And now that we know what the word means, we can see that Jesus is talking about more than apologizing and asking someone to forgive you. For one thing, the other person's forgiveness is not what releases you from guilt; your repentance does. But to repent is to do more than apologize or be sorry; it requires a definite change.

Have you ever apologized for something you did and said you were sorry, but you had no desire to change? This probably happens frequently with children whose parents teach them to apologize. In most cases, the child probably regrets getting caught more than he regrets having offended someone, but he still needs to learn to apologize. More important, he needs to learn to repent, to decide to change his behavior. The purpose of punishment is to help him decide to change, because most of us would never learn to repent on our own.

Paul wrote the Book of Romans to the saints in Rome, whose "faith is being reported all over the world" (Rom. 1:8). He longed to see them so they "may be mutually encouraged by each other's faith" (v. 12). Yet Paul reprimanded them for showing "contempt for the riches of [God's] kindness, tolerance and patience, not realizing that God's kindness leads you toward repentance" (Rom. 2:4). We realize that God extends His tolerance and patience to sinners so they might repent and be saved, but this verse states that He treats us in a similar way so we might also repent. This verse also shows that He extends kindness to believers so they might repent, or change the way they think.

Think about that for a moment. God isn't kind to you because you deserve it, but in spite of the fact that you don't. He has forgiven your sins and is tolerant, patient and kind toward you so you will change your mind about sin.

Paul took a similar stand with the believers in Corinth. In one of the letters he wrote them, he tried to correct some of their attitudes that were resulting in jealousy, quarreling and tolerance of sexual immorality. In a follow-up letter, he expresses happiness that they had changed their attitudes. "I am happy, not because you were made sorry, but because your sorrow led you to repentance. For you became sorrowful as God intended and so were not harmed in any way by us" (2 Cor. 7:9). When Paul exposed their attitudes, they became sorrowful and repented; that is, they stopped their quarreling and they stopped tolerating the sexual immorality. Their repentance, or changed attitudes, changed their behavior.

There is a clear relationship between changed attitudes and changed behavior. What you do is not as important as who you are, because your attitudes determine your actions. It is clear from the Old Testament that doing all the right things and performing all the right ceremonies does nothing to change a person's attitudes. That is why the New Testament's emphasis is on your attitudes and character. John the Baptist told the Pharisees and Sadducees, "Produce fruit in keeping with repentance" (Matt. 3:8). Similarly, Paul said, "I preached that they should repent and turn to God and prove their repentance by their deeds" (Acts 26:20). Your actions are not only consistent with your attitude; they actually reveal your attitude. If you repent, your changed attitude will change your behavior.

If you want further evidence that God requires believers to repent, consider the opening chapters of the Book of Revelation, which are addressed to seven churches. "Remember the height from which you have fallen! Repent (*metanoeo*) and do the things you did at first. If you do not repent (*metanoeo*), I will come to you and remove your lampstand from its place" (Rev. 2:5). To another church he says, "Remember, therefore, what you have received and heard; obey it, and repent (*metanoeo*)" (Rev. 3:3). To still another church he says, "Those whom I love I rebuke and discipline. So be earnest, and repent (*metanoeo*)" (Rev. 2:16; 3:19). God tells four of the seven churches to repent.

One of these verses shows that believers will suffer the consequences if they do not repent: "If you do not repent, I will come to you and remove your lampstand from its place." God expects his people to repent, to change their attitude and outlook on life and then change their behavior.

A related word is *metanoia*, which usually is translated "repentance" or "conversion." It literally means your thinking has been converted. So if your thinking did not change significantly, you were not converted. This shows that changing your mind is crucial to your salvation.

Repentance is not mystical or mysterious. To repent simply means to change your way of thinking, which is virtually synonymous with renewing your mind. You can start with a sinful attitude and renew it, changing it with God's help to a godly attitude.

How to Repent

We read in Romans 1:21, "For although they knew God, they neither glorified him as God nor gave thanks to him, but their thinking became futile and their foolish hearts were darkened." And Ephesians 4:17 reads, "So I tell you this, and insist on it in the Lord, that you must no longer live as the Gentiles do, in the futility of their thinking."

Both verses refer to futile thinking by nonbelievers. "Futile" means serving no useful purpose, suggesting a preoccupation with insignificant matters. "Thinking" refers to more than just a person's ideas. "Futile thinking" means that what they think about is meaningless and that their priorities, standards and values are not worthwhile.

By whose standard is a nonbeliever's thinking worthless or futile? God's. He knows what is important and what is not. He considers their thinking futile because it is self-centered and therefore opposed to His kingdom. His kingdom is the ultimate reality and will prevail over everything else. Anything opposed to God's kingdom is futile.

Everyone is born with a sinful or carnal nature, which is inherently self-centered, so everyone's thinking originally is opposed to God's kingdom and is therefore futile. It is very natural for everyone's thinking to be self-centered and futile. Their carnal nature also reinforces that kind of thinking because it causes them to be concerned only with their own desires or what gratifies them. The more you satisfy your carnal nature, however, the more satisfaction it demands.

The entire world system is dominated by man's carnal nature. People experience peer pressure to conform to the prevalent groupthink of the moment, whether they are adults or children. Conforming to the current socially acceptable or politically correct way of thinking is futile not only because it arbitrarily changes but also because it consistently opposes God's position. Even advertising constantly appeals to sinful human nature, reinforcing its power and thereby encouraging people to preoccupy themselves with empty, futile thoughts.

Ephesians 4:17 says you should no longer live like that: "no longer live as the Gentiles do, in the futility of their thinking." So what does God want you to do instead? Repent. Change what you think about, your perspective, your standards, your values, your priorities, and so on. In other words, reprogram your mind.

Maybe you agree that you need to change your thinking, but how can you do it? Part of the answer is in Romans 13:14, which says not even to think about how to gratify sinful desires. What a radical thought for most Christians! Just like everyone else, we preoccupy ourselves with what we want and with schemes for making ourselves feel good. Listen to yourself talk. Consider how frequently you make statements like, "I want . . . or "I . . . need." As much as you might recoil at the thought, you need to stop thinking about how to please yourself.

It is very important to stop doing the wrong things, but that is not adequate by itself; you also must start doing the right things. That is why Paul wrote the following: "Finally, brothers, whatever is true, whatever is noble, whatever is right, whatever is pure, whatever is lovely, whatever is admirable—if anything is excellent or praise-worthy—think about such things" (Phil. 4:8). What standard can you use for true, noble, right, pure, lovely, admirable, excellent and praiseworthy? God's standard is the only legitimate one; any other standard is futile.

What practical steps can you take to change your thinking? First, you need to realize that your mind thinks about what you put in it. You are influenced by what you expose yourself to. If you subject yourself repeatedly to a certain environment or relationship, for example, it will affect you. Stop filling your mind with empty, useless, futile things, most of which comes from your entertainment. Obviously, you need recreation and entertainment, but not nearly as much as we get in America. Be more selective of your entertainment. You become like those you associate with and like the entertainment you consume. You absorb what you watch and listen to, so increase your intake of Scripture and of Christian music. Memorizing Scripture feeds your spirit, disciplines your mind, and gives your mind good material to think about.

I can almost hear you groan about memorizing Scripture. I am inclined to groan, too, but that reflects my worldly attitude. Memorizing Scripture has always been hard for me, maybe because I don't ordinarily think the way others do. I cannot make memorization become a pleasurable experience, but I can make it easier by changing my attitude about the material I memorize. Instead of viewing Scripture as God trying to impose on my life, I can see Scripture as precious, vital to my spiritual health and therefore highly desirable.

Another way to change your thinking is to control what you think about. When an undesirable thought pops into your mind, replace it. You cannot just get rid of it; you must replace it. This brings up a good use for memorized Scripture: replacing an undesirable thought with a scripture that directs your thinking to a more appropriate subject or attitude.

What can you do to help other believers change their thinking? Hebrews 3:13 says to "encourage one another daily, as long as it is called Today, so that none of you may be hardened by sin's deceitfulness." The Greek word translated "encourage" also means to exhort, urge or even beg. The same Greek word occurs later in Hebrews, where we read, "let us encourage one another—and all the more as you see the Day approaching" (Heb. 10:25). The same word appears in First Thessalonians, which includes a detailed description of the Lord's return for the saints followed by the statement, "Therefore encourage each other with these words" (1 Thess. 4:18). After explaining that believers do not need to be surprised by the day of the Lord and are not appointed to receive God's wrath, the writer says, "Therefore encourage one another and build each other up" (1 Thess. 5:11).

So when you see a believer getting tired or discouraged, encourage them and build them up; remind them the Lord is coming. If they are struggling with sin, "The Lord is coming!" If calamity overwhelms them and they feel like giving up, "The Lord is coming!" Encourage believers to stand firm, be courageous and strong in the Lord because He is coming soon.

You also can teach and correct other believers, but be sure to do it the way you would want to be treated. American culture places an extreme emphasis on individual rights and liberty, so we shy away from correcting others; we don't want to offend them or impose upon them. But no one is beyond correction. If I display a carnal attitude, correct me. If you correct me properly and I am offended by it, then I have two problems: my original sinful attitude and my unwillingness to receive correction.

The world system puts relentless pressure on you to keep you thinking like the world. You are bombarded with advertising propaganda, editorials masquerading as news broadcasts, and brazen sin masquerading as entertainment. People flaunt their unrighteousness. Most entertainment is brazenly sinful and frequently portrays anger, lust and selfish ambition. You are constantly exposed to it and it reinforces your old ways of thinking. "Because of the increase of wickedness, the *love of most will grow cold*" (Matt. 24:12, emphasis added). Do not be a victim of your environment! Do not let the wickedness around you and in your flesh cool your relationship with God!

Do you think like the world? Do you have similar priorities and standards? Do you want the same things? What do you think about in your spare time? What is the content of your prayers? Are most of them selfish?

You must take forceful action, not just bob around in the water hoping you don't drown before help arrives. Aggressively change your thinking until it conforms in every respect to God's thoughts. Every time you have a thought that violates God's nature, repent. Change the way you think until every thought conforms to His. As the Bible says, "we take captive every thought to make it obedient to Christ" (2 Cor. 10:5).

You have spent your entire life accepting the world's thinking and it is essential that you *repent*. Change your priorities. Change your standards. Change your perspective of life. Change what you put into your mind.

The Need for Repentance

The predominant characteristic of your former carnal nature was self-centeredness (pride). It caused you to be primarily concerned with your own thoughts, desires and needs. It caused you to act in what you believe is your own best interest, even at the expense of someone else.

Godly nature is motivated by humility, which is the exact opposite of self-centeredness. Humility is not a matter of having a poor opinion of yourself; rather, it is being more concerned for the needs and interests of others than your own. Humility does not cause you to abase yourself, because doing so focuses your attention on yourself, which is typical of self-centeredness.

As a Christian, you might not think of yourself as self-centered, but let me offer some evidences of self-centered thinking. Are your feelings hurt when someone speaks against you? Do you want to justify yourself when someone believes you were wrong? Do you notice yourself wanting to make your opinion known and wanting others to accept it? Are you disappointed when you don't get what you want?

"But that's just human nature." I agree completely; it is fallen human nature. It's natural for you to be self-centered. You have been self-centered all your life and it is difficult to see that you can or should be anything else. You may be thinking right now that there really is nothing wrong with being self-centered; that it is unreasonable to expect anything else; that it isn't humanly possible to be selfless; that someone who doesn't have a positive self-image needs psychiatric help. You may feel justified thinking this way, even trying to prove that you *need* to be self-centered and that unless you look out for yourself, others will take advantage of you, neglect you and even abuse you. Why would you respond so strongly this way? Because we are striking at the root of your old way of thinking.

Self-centeredness is such an integral part of sinful human nature that it is hard for you to realize you have it, even as a Christian. It was part of your nature when you were conceived, so you may never have experienced anything but self-centeredness and find it impossible to imagine having any other attitude. Its effects are so pervasive that it even influences your relationship with God and your understanding of Christianity.

Let me address an issue that demonstrates this problem. I object to what we could call the "strong man" concept of Christianity, which motivates such declarations as, "We are mighty warriors. God has given us power and authority over the works of Satan. God said for us to raise the dead, heal the sick and cast out devils. Nothing shall harm us." While such statements are clearly based on Scripture, there is a subtle shift in emphasis. The focus is on me, what I can do, and what I am. I become the center of attention.

Jesus said on several occasions that the absolutely greatest person in the entire kingdom of God is like an inadequate, insufficient, dependent little child. Humility is the key; it is the first and greatest value in God's kingdom and everything else is based on it. Consider Jesus' parables. Who was repeatedly portrayed in the role of leadership and authority? God. Who was repeatedly portrayed as servants or the needy? People, like you and me.

You can tell when a Christian's worldly thinking is perverting kingdom principles. The person becomes self-focused, self-assertive, domineering, critical of those who don't believe the same way, and enamored with attention. They emphasize what *they* are able to do in Christ: "I can do everything through him who gives me strength" (Phil. 4:13), with a big "I" and less emphasis on Christ. That is carnal Christianity, which is almost a contradiction of terms. It is as if they have simply switched to a different power supply, relying on God's power to make them successful where they used to fail. Because God will not share His glory, it seems likely that He will not use such a person for long, if at all.

Our focus must always be on God doing the work and we must consider it an honor that He does it through us. Jesus said all authority in heaven and on earth had been given to Him; therefore we are to go and do His work. In effect, He delegated authority to us to work in His behalf, relying on His power to do kingdom work, not our power doing our work. We must learn to think like servants: "I am an unworthy servant and I have done only what I was told to do" (see Luke 17:10). That dictates a radical change in how we think.

Changing your attitude and perspective may or may not change what you do, but it will certainly change your motive. Someone can preach the power of God with boldness because they enjoy being bold. Or they can preach the power of God with boldness because they have boldness resulting from their convictions. By watching them preach, you may not be able to tell what their motive is and you can misjudge them. Man looks at the external appearance, but God sees the person's attitude. You can be totally convinced that a person is being carnal and be completely wrong. Your opinion is simply an opinion, not necessarily the truth. Why is that person excited, laughing and jumping up and down as they pray for people? Is it because they like being the center of attention and being able to do powerful things? Or is it because it's a total blast to be on the scene when God does something? You don't know which it is.

You can't always properly judge a person by the way they talk about these matters. It is very common, for example, for people to talk about the authority we have in Christ; how God in us enables us to live a victorious life and do mighty works for God; how we should put on the armor of God and resist the enemy; how we should raise the dead, heal the sick and cast out devils. I agree that we are participants in God's work; that God has chosen to work through mankind rather than angels; that we are co-laborers with Christ. But it is possible for a very subtle change to occur in these kingdom truths when they take up residence in our minds, as mentioned earlier.

It is natural for you to assume credit for what God does and not even realize it. Self-centeredness makes you want the credit and glory at every opportunity. It is masterful at portraying itself as beneficial and even essential to your well-being. We speak of someone who needs to improve their self-image, for example; we consider low self-esteem as unhealthy. In reality, all self-focus is unhealthy, whether it is optimistic or pessimistic. Because self-focus is the foundation of an ungodly perspective, it is extremely natural to interpret kingdom principles in a way that makes you feel better about yourself. You want to feel good about your ability to do what you think needs to be done. On the other hand, God's servant submits all that he has to God; God then uses His own power to do His kingdom business through the submitted servant.

It is essential that you accept responsibility for what you think, for your attitudes and perspective. You must consciously and deliberately change your mind. I hear Christians say they don't have faith to do certain things. Or they are waiting for God to take away certain desires and attitudes; they are waiting for God to do it. I cringe when I hear such talk, then I grieve over the lost potential. If we wonder why God uses others but not us, we come dangerously close to accusing God of being unfair. Of course, God is sovereign, but He is not biased. Instead, He is wise in not using someone who is not prepared.

You must realize—that is, change your awareness—that God has already done everything He needs to do for you to be effective in His kingdom. The ball is now in your court. The issue is not whether God will do something else in you, but whether you will acknowledge what He has already done and respond appropriately.

I believe that is the key to what we call the baptism in the Holy Spirit, for example. You received the Spirit of God at salvation; the Spirit of adoption that testifies (confirms with us) that we are God's children. You don't need to receive "more" of the Holy Spirit, because you have already received Him in His entirety. I suggest that the baptism of the Holy Spirit is the release that occurs when you acknowledge His presence within you and permit Him to express Himself through you in whatever way He chooses. It is not a matter of receiving something new, but of changing the way you think of someone you already have received. He is the literal presence of God in you. You cannot receive more or less of God, but you can certainly regulate the degree of freedom He has to work through you.

As stated earlier, God does not need to give you anything else to work with. Your potential for success in the kingdom is directly related to your thinking. Have you chosen to believe you are his child and servant? That God is greater than Satan? That God has chosen to work through you? That success can only be defined in terms of kingdom values? If you have chosen to believe these points, you can also choose to believe that your thinking is the only hindrance. The New Testament repeatedly tells you to repent, put off and put on, to declare yourself God's servant, and so on. These all relate to how you think. The spiritual victory has already been won and the primary battlefield is now your mind: Do you believe what God has said and are you willing to act on it?

Sinners can be extremely successful when they decide to believe they have within themselves what it takes to be successful. That is why motivational seminars are effective; they convince people they can succeed. Conversely, a person will become a failure if he expects to be one. The world understands some of the power of the human mind. If only Christians weren't so naive about this potential! The effective child of God recognizes his inadequacies when faced with the significant matters of life and he recognizes that God in him is overwhelmingly sufficient. That understanding leads to real success. You must learn to rely on the absolute, unlimited power and authority of God, who lives within you, rather than relying on your personal abilities. This not only defines true success, but also produces it consistently. This requires changing the way you think; redefine success and recognize the source of success. True success results whenever you do what God wants, when and how He wants you to do it, and you rely on Him to do it through you.

"But I just don't see it happening. I can't believe that." Are other principles or laws invalid because you don't understand them or even believe they exist? Were the laws of science in operation before you learned about them in school? Of course, they were. And they continue to function and be available for your use.

Turning on a light is not a big deal for most of us, because we have accepted the concept of making a bulb shine by flipping a switch. You can observe others flipping a switch and believe that you will get the same results if you flip the same switch. Even if you have never used that particular switch before, you do not stand in front of it, gazing hopelessly at it, believing it will not work for you. You have chosen to believe you will get the same results others do and, in fact, would be totally surprised if you didn't. Why? Because you have chosen to expect certain results.

You can read God's statements in the Bible and hear good teaching for years, yet choose to believe that for some reason it does not apply to you. God's statements are true, however, regardless of whether you choose to believe them. What you believe is a matter of choice. You might believe, for example, that a certain person is angry with you. You will judge their words and actions on the basis of your belief. They can say something and you might react, "Aha! That proves they're angry with me," when in reality what they said had no such meaning.

You even respond to the Bible the same way. When you read something in the Bible, you interpret it in light of what you already believe. That is how it should be, but you need to recognize what is happening. You might read, "God is love," and you interpret the statement's meaning by using your biblical understanding of God and love. This shows how it is possible for each person to have his own insights to Scripture. It also shows how you can read something you have read numerous times before and suddenly gain new insight. Your understanding has changed since you read it before, so now you interpret it a little differently.

You might think God has shown you something new, but it is also possible He has been showing it to you for years and your understanding has finally allowed you to comprehend it. How many times and in how many ways do you have to explain something to someone before they finally grasp it? The truth of your statement has not changed and neither has your desire for them to understand it, but they have to condition their thinking to receive it. Similarly, you must condition your mind to believe what God says. It is up to you, and you must choose to do it.

Just as a worldly mindset is quick to accept glory for success, it quickly rejects responsibility for failure. "Passing the buck" began in the Garden of Eden, when Adam blamed both Eve and God for his failure: "It was the woman you gave me." Since then, every human has the tendency to point their finger at others. Even Christians point their finger at God by claiming they have done everything that can be expected of them and that it is now up to God.

"I don't know what else to do. It's in God's hands now." "God will have to give me [fill in the appropriate term], because I don't have what it takes." These and similar statements are only partially true. Their error lies in their rejection of responsibility. Looking at the situation from a carnal perspective causes you to judge by human standards. If you reprogrammed your mind to view the situation from God's perspective, you might reach an entirely different conclusion.

The key is repenting, changing the way you think. Maybe you cannot even imagine yourself thinking differently than you have all of your life. Let me offer an illustration that may help you see the potential.

Imagine a male child born with what we might call binary senses, senses that register only the presence or absence of a stimulus. He can see, but only black and white, not even any shades of gray. He cannot see the features on your face, for example, unless there are dark shadows. In low light levels, he cannot see you at all because everything looks black. As the light increases, he can see anything that appears white against a black background. As you turn your head, for example, your facial features magically appear and disappear as shadows define the features, then the shadows ultimately disappear. When the light gets bright enough, the shadows get softer until he can no longer see them, and everything becomes pure white. To him, everything looks like a polarized photograph, in which everything is black or white, with no colors or shades of gray.

His other senses are binary, too. He can hear, but he can only distinguish between the presence and absence of noise. He can hear no individual tones or differences in volume; he hears only noise or silence. His binary sense of taste tells him when something is in his mouth, but everything tastes exactly the same. The same is true of touch; he cannot distinguish between textures, between firmnesses, or between temperatures. His sense of smell tells him only that he can smell something, but everything smells exactly the same.

Imagine what this poor fellow is missing! The only way he can tell the difference between a tomato and a steak is by their shapes. To him, they have the same color, texture, feel, smell and taste. What's more, because he has only experienced binary sensations all his life, he cannot even imagine the sensual sensitivity the rest of us take for granted.

Let us further assume that a doctor has studied this young boy and knows how to correct the problems through operations and therapy. The operations will at times be very painful and the therapy extremely unpleasant. The boy will have to make a constant effort to develop his new senses and pay constant attention to them to understand his new abilities and learn to use them effectively.

Does the boy understand the value of what the doctor is offering him? No, he cannot, because he has never experienced anything other than binary senses. At some point he may have to say to himself, "I submit myself to the process, even though I have no idea what the results will be like, simply because I trust the doctor."

That is the commitment I am asking you to make. You probably have no realistic concept of what it means to be like Jesus, because you can only speculate on the basis of what you have seen in other people. But your Father tells you it is possible to live on an entirely different level—you can be like Him. From your current vantage point, you cannot even imagine what that would be like or how you would get there.

Now is the time to submit yourself to the process, even though you have no idea what the results will be like, simply because you trust your Father. The process of transformation will be difficult as you reject the ungodly motivations and desires you developed before you turned to Christ. You will need to be constantly vigilant to avoid indulging old attitudes and behavior. And for the rest of your life, you will continue learning to use your new nature more effectively.

That is the essence of repentance. You have only a slight understanding of what its results will be. But you can trust God, who tells you it will be more than worthwhile.

Conclusion

To repent is to change your mind. The New Testament's statements about repentance are mostly directed at believers, and it repeatedly encourages us to do so. The first step to changing your thinking is to realize that your mind thinks about what you put in it. If you stop filling your mind with things that reinforce ungodliness, and instead fill it with thoughts of God and the truths of the

Bible, you will have made a major step toward repenting. The world applies constant pressure to get you to accept its way of thinking. To offset this pressure, you must take forceful action and aggressively change your thinking until it conforms in every respect to God's thoughts.

Personal Study

It has been said that the first casualty in a conflict is truth. Imagine a conflict between two Christians, each of whom honestly believes the other is wrong.

- How might self-centeredness cause them to view the facts (truth) differently? Explain.

- What practical steps of repentance would help each person overcome self-centeredness in the conflict?

- If both parties repented, what results could they realistically expect?

- How could habitually practicing repentance prevent conflicts from occurring?

3

Believing by Choice

How do you decide whether to believe something you hear? You must decide whether the person who told you is credible, for one thing. Do you have confidence in them and are they a reliable source for the information they gave you? In addition to considering the source, you also evaluate what they said. Is the information itself believable? Is it compatible with what you already believe to be true, or does it violate what you think?

The point is this: You decide what you will believe. When someone says, "I don't believe that," they have chosen not to accept what they heard because it did not pass their credibility tests.

When you examine the Bible, you realize that God keeps urging you to believe certain things and not to believe others. He not only gave you the ability to choose what you will believe, He also holds you accountable for your beliefs.

The English word *believe* is a verb that means primarily to have a firm religious faith, or to accept something trustfully and on faith. The Greek word translated "believe" is actually the verb form of the noun "faith." This suggests that "faith" is what you have and "believe" is what you do with it. If you use your faith, you are believing, trusting or relying. If other people can place their faith in you, then you are faithful, trustworthy or reliable.

Consider another English word, *work*, which has both noun and verb forms. In the noun form, work is a task you have to do; in the verb form, to work is to do the task. It is the same word and the noun and verb forms are closely related in meaning. Similarly, the Greek words for "faith" and "to believe" are different grammatical forms of the same root word.

In our culture, we use "believe" very loosely. At times it means to have religious faith, but at other times it means nothing more than to think something is true. We say, "I believe he is coming tomorrow" to mean, "I'm sure he's coming." But the Greek and biblical meanings are much more forceful; to believe is to use your faith.

The Bible says you believe with your heart (Rom. 10:10), which probably represents your mind and spirit. We know that faith (or faithfulness) is a "fruit of the Spirit," so faith and believing somehow require the cooperation of your spirit. We have seen that believing also involves the mind, requiring you to evaluate and choose what you will believe. Therefore, we can conclude that believing is both a mental and spiritual activity, a cooperative effort of your mind and spirit.

Now let's consider what the Bible says about what you believe.

What Do You Believe?

When Jesus began His earthly ministry, His message was simple: "The time has come. The kingdom of God is near. Repent and believe the good news!" (Mark 1:15). He encouraged people to repent (change the way they think) and believe (use faith to accept what He says as true). The fact that He told them to repent and believe is proof that they could choose to do so.

Near the end of His ministry, Jesus was explaining the events that would precede His return and He said, "At that time if anyone says to you, 'Look, here is the Christ!' or, 'There he is!' do not believe it" (Matt. 24:23). It is clear that people can decide what to believe.

We have briefly shown from Scripture that you decide what you will or will not believe. Now let us consider how God responds to what you believe.

Jesus had some pretty stern words for the chief priests and elders who questioned His authority. They had asked, "By what authority are you doing these things? And who gave you this authority?" (Matt.

21:23). In reality they were challenging His credibility. They could prove their credibility because they were trained and acknowledged as religious leaders. But what credentials did Jesus offer? None they recognized, so they wanted to show that He was not credible and the people should not believe Him.

Jesus had no sympathy for the oppressive and self-protecting religious establishment, as His reply shows.

> *I tell you the truth, the tax collectors and the prostitutes are entering the kingdom of God ahead of you. For John came to you to show you the way of righteousness, and you did not believe him, but the tax collectors and the prostitutes did. And even after you saw this, you did not repent and believe him* (Matt. 21:31-32).

If anyone were to recognize the Messiah whom God had promised, you would expect it to be those trained in God's Word. Not only did they not recognize Him, they protected their religious establishment and challenged His credibility. What was Jesus' condemnation of them? They did not repent (change the way they thought) and believe (put their faith in what He said). They chose not to believe and He rebuked them for it.

You can probably understand His rebuking those who openly denounced His teaching, but how did Jesus respond to those who followed Him and were eager to learn from Him? As Jesus taught the crowd and His disciples about trusting God to provide for their basic needs, He referred to them as "you of little faith" (Matt. 6:30). When the disciples thought they were about to drown in a storm on a lake, how did Jesus address them? "You of little faith" (Matt. 8:26). When Peter walked on the water and began to sink, what did Jesus say? "You of little faith, why did you doubt?" (Matt. 14:31). When the disciples were concerned about not having enough bread? "You of little faith" (Matt. 16:8). He rebuked His followers for not believing, but He did it gently and encouraged them to believe in Him.

There is one incident, however, in which Jesus rebuked His disciples more forcefully. Jesus had told them He would be crucified and then would return from the dead. After He rose from the dead some women reported that His tomb was empty, two disciples confirmed His tomb was empty and two others reported having seen Jesus. "Later Jesus appeared to the Eleven as they were eating; he rebuked them for their lack of faith and their stubborn refusal to believe those who had seen him after he had risen" (Mark 16:14).

They stubbornly refused to believe because they had made up their minds. They had expected an earthly kingdom but Jesus had died and their hopes had shattered. Even when several people they trusted confirmed that Jesus was alive again as He had promised, they refused to believe.

What promises of God are you refusing to believe? Maybe those promises seem hollow when you look at the circumstances, and you just cannot believe they will come true. You may even need to ask God to remind you of some promises you have rejected and forgotten. It might be helpful for you to write them down.

"This is not my problem," you say. "I'm believing God to heal me" (or provide for you, or something else). The real question is: What is the object of your faith? God, or what He will do for you? If God never does anything else for you, He is still God and worthy of your praise and your faith. Even if you never see any evidence or the fulfillment of any of His promises, you can still believe.

Here are some pointers on how to believe God. Decide to believe that God is good. Decide to believe He loves you. Decide to believe He will always do whatever is right and whatever is best for you. Decide to have confidence in Him and trust Him. Decide to believe that God almighty knows what He is talking about. And compare what you think He is saying with what the Bible says.

The disciples had misdirected their faith. They believed that Jesus would set up a physical kingdom, rather than believe in Jesus Himself. You can easily fall into the same trap. If you choose to believe for what you expect to happen, you will become disappointed someday because your expectations are not always correct. But if you believe in God Himself, He will never disappoint you.

Believing is important, but it is more important to believe in the right things.

Belief or Consequences

Believing is a choice, as we have seen, and you will experience the consequences of your decision to believe. For example, we read about those who hear the gospel: "Whoever believes and is baptized will be saved, but whoever does not believe will be condemned" (Mark 16:16). We see a similar statement in John 3:18: "Whoever believes in him is not condemned, but whoever does not believe stands condemned already because he has not believed in the name of God's one and only Son." God does not treat disbelief lightly. Those who choose not to believe have condemned themselves.

Some acts of disbelief are less serious than rejecting the gospel message, but every refusal to believe has its consequences. When an angel appeared to Zechariah with the wonderful news that he and his wife would have an anointed son, even in their old age, Zechariah would not accept the news.

> *The angel answered, "I am Gabriel. I stand in the presence of God, and I have been sent to speak to you and to tell you this good news. And now you will be silent and not able to speak until the day this happens, because you did not believe my words, which will come true at their proper time"* (Luke 1:19-20).

Zechariah experienced the consequences of his disbelief: he was mute for nine months. Because he refused to believe what the angel said, he was unable to say anything until the angel's words came true. The consequences fit the offense.

While God holds you accountable for what you believe, He recognizes that sometimes you can easily misunderstand and He makes special provision for you. Jesus told His disciples that He would leave them soon, but the Father would send the Holy Spirit to be their Counselor in His place. Then He said something very interesting: "I have told you now before it happens, so that when it does happen you will believe" (John 14:29). This confirms our understanding of how we believe: Believing is a result of being convinced, and while believing is an application of faith, it becomes stronger with evidence.

So what should you do if you try to convince someone and they refuse to believe? We see an example of this in Scripture: "Paul entered the synagogue and spoke boldly there for three months, arguing persuasively about the kingdom of God. But some of them became obstinate; they refused to believe and publicly maligned the Way. So Paul left them" (Acts 19:8-9). Paul clearly gave the people opportunity to accept his message; he spoke boldly and argued persuasively for three months. Yet some of the people refused to believe him and began to openly criticize his teaching, so he left. When it becomes clear that people will not listen to you, go find someone who will.

God gave man a free will—the ability to choose—and He honors man's choices by allowing him to experience the results of them. Whereas He expects you to leave someone who refuses to believe, God does not respond so passively. The following verses are rather sobering: "They perish because they refused to love the truth and so be saved. For this reason God sends them a powerful delusion so that they will believe the lie and so that all will be condemned who have not believed the truth but have delighted in wickedness" (2 Thess. 2:10-12).

To love the truth is to embrace it as having great value. However, these people refused to embrace the truth; they made a choice, a firm decision. People will always believe something, so if they refuse to believe the truth, they will believe the lie. If they reject the truth, God will honor their choice and give them what they wanted by sending a powerful delusion. There will be no middle ground. God's action will not be cruel or unjust, because He will honor their free will. God will have a very clear reason for sending the delusion on them: everyone who rejects the truth will be condemned.

That earlier passage relates to the endtimes, when the man of lawlessness will appear, but God had also done this with another group of people. The following passage shows how God responded to the Jews' disbelief:

Even after Jesus had done all these miraculous signs in their presence, they still would not believe in him. This was to fulfill the word of Isaiah the prophet: "Lord, who has believed our message and to whom has the arm of the Lord been revealed?" For this reason they could not believe, because, as Isaiah says elsewhere: "He has blinded their eyes and deadened their hearts, so they can neither see with their eyes, nor understand with their hearts, nor turn—and I would heal them" (John 12:37-40).

God had a reason for hardening the hearts of the Jews who rejected Jesus: He wanted to spread the gospel to the Gentiles. Paul acknowledged God's plan when the Jews rejected His teaching: "We had to speak the word of God to you first. Since you reject it and do not consider yourselves worthy of eternal life, we now turn to the Gentiles" (Acts 13:46). Paul makes it clear in the Book of Romans, however, that once the full number of the Gentiles has come to Christ, God will remove the hardness from the Jews so they can be saved (Rom. 11:25-26).

Believing is an act of the will. If you are a parent, it is your responsibility to teach your children to submit their will to authority and, in a similar way, to choose to believe God and His Word. We see this in Paul's description of an elder's qualifications: "An elder must be blameless, the husband of but one wife, a man whose children believe" (Titus 1:6). An elder shall have taught his children and enabled them to believe, otherwise this requirement would be arbitrary and meaningless.

You can help others believe by convincing them of the truth of God's Word. Show them examples of God fulfilling the promises in the Bible, providing for you and helping you in difficult situations. Christians must tell each other what God has done for them because, by doing so, they build their faith or help them believe.

We saw earlier that Jesus rebuked His disciples for their lack of faith, and it is extremely important to God that you believe, too. The Book of Hebrews tells us, "without faith it is impossible to please God, because anyone who comes to him must believe that he exists and that he rewards those who earnestly seek him" (Heb. 11:6). It is impossible to please God if you do not believe (have faith). Because Christianity is a relationship with God and because He will eventually judge everything you do, pleasing Him should be a pretty high priority. Believing what He has said is a critical first step in pleasing Him.

There are many verses in the New Testament that associate your faith with receiving blessings from God. For example:

If any of you lacks wisdom, he should ask God, who gives generously to all without finding fault, and it will be given to him. But when he asks, he must believe and not doubt, because he who doubts is like a wave of the sea, blown and tossed by the wind. That man should not think he will receive anything from the Lord; he is a double-minded man, unstable in all he does (James 1:5-8).

There is a very clear sequence in these verses: 1) ask for wisdom, 2) believe God will give it, and 3) receive. What are you to believe? That God gives wisdom generously to all, even you, and will not withhold it because you did something to displease Him.

The Greek word for "doubt" in these verses does not suggest a weakness of faith; instead, it means to separate, to distinguish between, to decide. This type of doubting includes deciding that God will not keep His promises for you or in your situation. Doubting is believing that God will not do what He said, or believing the opposite of what He said. Anyone who doubts this way is vulnerable to his emotions and to circumstances, and he will vacillate between faith and disbelief. Such a person will not receive anything from the Lord, because without faith it is impossible to please God.

This contrast between faith and disbelief is very clear in the following verse: "Anyone who believes in the Son of God has this testimony in his heart. Anyone who does not believe God has made him out to be a liar, because he has not believed the testimony God has given about his Son" (1 John 5:10). If you do not believe God, you have decided that what He said is not true; therefore, you believe God lied.

The last few verses we examined show that believing God is something you choose to do; you don't accidentally believe or have faith suddenly forced on you. If believing were not voluntary, then God would be unjust to condemn or withhold anything from those who do not believe. Because God is just, however, he responds to those who choose to believe.

How serious is it when someone decides not to believe God? Consider Jude 5: "Though you already know all this, I want to remind you that the Lord delivered his people out of Egypt, but later destroyed those who did not believe." It's that serious.

You not only choose whether to believe, you also choose what you will believe. Faith is selective and you decide what or whom will be the object of your faith. If someone believes something that is not true, we say they are deceived. The Bible warns you not to believe everything you see or hear, because it is possible for you to be deceived. Consider John's warning, for example: "Dear friends, do not believe every spirit, but test the spirits to see whether they are from God, because many false prophets have gone out into the world" (1 John 4:1). It clearly is your responsibility to judge what you see and hear, then decide what you should believe.

Christians often accept a lack of faith or a lack of power as normal. We consider a powerful evangelist as unusual, for example, and people flock to see him. That is a wrong perception. It is normal for this world to be sinful, polluted and corrupted, but that is not God's intent. The world is going to hell but that is not God's desire. Most Christians today are spiritually anemic and full of doubt, but that is not God's intent either. How have we deceived ourselves into thinking that it is acceptable for us to doubt God?

Consider an analogy. It is not unusual for someone to call in sick at work when they simply do not feel like going to work that day. I have even joked, "Just thinking about going to work is enough to make me sick." If someone calls in sick repeatedly, however, they may eventually be confronted by their employer: "If you are not committed to this job, you need to find another one." Then they get to find another job to get sick over.

Many of us are off the clock most of the time as Christians. By preoccupying ourselves with our own activities, we essentially call in sick to God: "I'm not available right now." Somehow we cannot imagine God telling us not to report to work anymore because of our excessive absences. We have accepted spiritual laziness as normal and expect God to tolerate it, but He will not.

A virtual handful of people turned the world upside down in the first century, yet today's church is anemic and confused. Did God use up all of His energy in the first century? No! The problem is the church's attitudes: my attitudes and your attitudes. If you do not expect God to work through you, then repent and change your attitude. Choose to believe what God has said.

God usually honors your decisions, but at times He will help you change your mind. When Saul was on his way to arrest the believers in Damascus, the Lord knocked him down and temporarily blinded him to get his attention. God was rather persuasive and Paul changed his mind, later becoming a believer himself. Also, God stopped Jonah from running away and persuaded him to go to Ninevah. Having a sea creature swallow you and then vomit you onto a beach several days later can definitely change your mind.

Occasionally God even works through people in spite of their attitudes. I remember an incident years ago when someone asked me to pray for his elbow, which was in a lot of pain. I wanted to be alone because I was struggling with my own problems and aggravated with God about what He was doing in my life. I tried to persuade the person to have someone else pray for them, but they insisted that I do it. Going through the motions seemed to be the only way to get rid of the person. As I recall, the words I spoke barely qualified as a prayer and certainly were not full of faith, yet God healed their elbow instantly anyway.

I will always remember that occasionally God will work through me in spite of my attitude. The key word is "occasionally." That incident was an exception, as Saul and Jonah's experiences were exceptions. Even in those incidents, however, the people involved willingly cooperated with God eventually.

God gave you free will because He wants you to love and serve Him voluntarily. Sin has perverted your free will, causing you to think that what you want is good and what you choose is right.

Freedom of choice combined with sin becomes self-serving and self-fulfilling.

Free choice has become an end in itself, especially in Western culture, but it allows you to choose what you will believe. Your choice is critical because you will experience the consequences of what you choose. Choose to believe God, because that is the only way you can please Him.

Choosing Not to Believe

One of the ways God made man unique in creation was to give him moral freedom; God made man a free moral agent. As a result, you can make certain self-determining decisions and actions. Under sin, you were not inclined to obey God because sin had enslaved you, but now, in Christ, you are free to obey God if you choose.

Regardless of your spiritual condition, however, you are free to decide what you will believe. God gave you that ability and He honors it. Yet there are some places in the Bible that speak of God hardening people's hearts, or taking other actions that appear to violate men's free will. Let us examine some of these incidents to see what actually happened. We will see that God did in fact harden their hearts, but only after they had already made up their own minds and because God had a specific reason for doing so.

Let us begin with Israel's exodus from Egypt. It is a familiar story, so let us go straight to the issue of Pharaoh's ability to decide whether to release the Israelites. When God spoke to Moses from the burning bush, He said, "But I know that the king of Egypt will not let you go unless a mighty hand compels him. So I will stretch out my hand and strike the Egyptians with all the wonders that I will perform among them. After that, he will let you go" (Exod. 3:19-20).

God knew beforehand what Pharaoh's decision would be and God would use Pharaoh's refusal to display His power to both the Egyptians and Israelites. The Jews would talk about the experience for thousands of years as proof of God's existence and His love for them. The miracles and the exodus would mark a crucial moment in the history of the Jewish people and be an important symbol of the

Christians' deliverance from sin. Pharaoh's decision was that important and God knew what the decision would be.

Pharaoh was free to decide, yet God said, "I will harden his heart so that he will not let the people go" (Exod. 4:21). At what point would God harden Pharaoh's heart? The Bible shows us. The first time Moses presented God's message to Pharaoh, Pharaoh's response revealed his attitude. "Who is the Lord, that I should obey him and let Israel go? I do not know the Lord and I will not let Israel go" (Exod. 5:2). Instead of releasing the Israelites, Pharaoh increased their workload by requiring them to gather their own materials while maintaining their production quota (vv. 4-19).

That was Pharaoh's choice and the Bible does not say that God forced the decision on him. The Pharaohs believed they were the descendants of God and had God-given authority to rule, so why should this Pharaoh listen to someone else who claimed to speak for God? There was no reason he should, from his perspective.

Before Moses' second confrontation with Pharaoh, God again told him, "I will harden Pharaoh's heart, and though I multiply my miraculous signs and wonders in Egypt, he will not listen to you" (Exod. 7:3-4).

In Pharaoh's court, Moses threw his staff down and it became a snake, but the Egyptian magicians performed the same signs. "Yet Pharaoh's heart became hard and he would not listen to them, just as the Lord had said" (Exod. 7:13). We will see later where God hardened Pharaoh's heart, but this verse simply says Pharaoh's heart "became hard." Because this verse does not specifically credit God, we can conclude that Pharaoh hardened his own heart. Because his magicians could perform the same miracle, Pharaoh decided that Moses had no special authority.

We see the same response after Moses turned the water into blood. The "Egyptian magicians did the same things by their secret arts, and Pharaoh's heart became hard; he would not listen to Moses and Aaron, just as the Lord had said" (Exod. 7:22). Pharaoh hardened himself against Moses' demands.

After the plague of frogs, Pharaoh apparently softened. "Pharaoh summoned Moses and Aaron and said, 'Pray to the Lord to take the frogs away from me and my people, and I will let your people go to offer sacrifices to the Lord'" (Exod. 8:8). So Moses prayed and the plague stopped. "But when Pharaoh saw that there was relief, he hardened his heart and would not listen to Moses and Aaron, just as the Lord had said" (Exod. 8:15). Pharaoh clearly hardened his own heart.

After the fourth plague, "Pharaoh hardened his heart and would not let the people go" (Exod. 8:32). After the fifth plague, "his heart was unyielding" (Exod. 9:7). After the seventh plague, "He and his officials hardened their hearts" (Exod. 9:34). Yet two verses later, God said, "I have hardened his heart and the hearts of his officials" (Exod. 10:1). From that point on, the Bible says that God hardened Pharaoh's heart (Exod. 10:20, 27; 11:10; 14:4).

When a person's heart becomes hardened, his thinking and attitudes are firmly set. For a man to harden his heart does not mean he changes his mind; instead he defends or reinforces his position so he will not change. Pharaoh was free to decide for himself. After his decision was clear, he refused to change his decision and eventually God made it impossible for him to do so. As we said earlier, God had an important reason for doing this, because it set the stage for a miraculous exodus.

The New Testament gives us another very clear description of God responding to people's choices. In the Book of Romans we read, "The wrath of God is being revealed from heaven against all the godlessness and wickedness of men who suppress the truth by their wickedness, since what may be known about God is plain to them, because God has made it plain to them" (Rom. 1:18-19).

God has revealed knowledge about himself to mankind, but men have chosen to suppress the knowledge, to discredit it, deny it, and remove it from public view. They knew the truth about God, but they chose not to honor him (Rom. 1:21). How did God respond? He "gave them over in the sinful desires of their hearts to sexual impurity for the degrading of their bodies with one another" (Rom. 1:24). He allowed them to fulfill their impure sexual desires.

That was only the beginning, however. Although they knew the truth, they "exchanged the truth of God for a lie, and worshiped and served created things rather than the Creator" (Rom. 1:25). They chose to believe a lie rather than the truth. How did God respond?

He "gave them over to shameful lusts" (Rom. 1:26), and they abandoned the natural heterosexual desires and became inflamed with homosexual lust.

"Furthermore, since they did not think it worthwhile to retain the knowledge of God, he gave them over to a depraved mind, to do what ought not to be done" (Rom. 1:28). There is something ominous about the word "furthermore" in this sequence. Not only did mankind choose to suppress the clear truth about God, they chose to believe a lie and then discarded the truth. How did God respond? He gave them over to depraved minds and they became filled with every kind of wickedness, evil, greed and depravity (vv. 29-31).

Did God turn them over to sexual impurity, homosexuality and depravity? Yes, and He did so in response to their choices. They were free to decide what they would believe and He honored their choices.

The Bible contains many statements about divine election, and people have argued that God is unfair in choosing to bless some and condemn those He did not choose. The Book of Romans also addresses this issue.

In Romans chapter 9, Paul discusses God's sovereign choices and includes examples such as Pharaoh, whom we considered earlier. He writes, "Therefore God has mercy on whom he wants to have mercy, and he hardens whom he wants to harden" (Rom. 9:18). The issue is not one of an arbitrary deity, however, but of God honoring men's choices. On whom does God have mercy? Anyone who will honor Him. Who does God harden? Those who reject Him.

You decide what you will believe and you can choose not to believe what God says. The choice is yours.

Conclusion

You decide what you will believe, so accepting God's truths is a matter of choice. Jesus sternly rebuked His disciples because they refused to believe that He had risen from the dead. God does not treat disbelief lightly. If you do not believe God, you have decided that what He said is not true; therefore, you believe God is a liar.

You not only choose whether to believe, you also choose what you will believe.

Personal Study

Consider the following scripture: "If any of you lacks wisdom, he should ask God, who gives generously to all without finding fault, and it will be given to him. But when he asks, he must believe and not doubt, because he who doubts is like a wave of the sea, blown and tossed by the wind. That man should not think he will receive anything from the Lord; he is a double-minded man, unstable in all he does" (James 1:5-8).

- These verses show the relationship between asking and believing. Recalling that believing is using your faith, what should be the object of your faith when you ask God for wisdom, according to these verses?

- To doubt is to separate or distinguish between, to decide what you will not believe. Based on the verses above, in what ways could you ask God for wisdom, yet doubt?

- Consider the three analogies of a doubting person: a wave blown and tossed by the sea; double-minded (having more than one focus or goal); unstable. What insights do these analogies give about a doubting person?

- Consider the contrasting images of God presented in these verses: 1) giving generously to all without finding fault; 2) not giving anything. To what kinds of people does God respond in these drastically different ways? What does this reveal about how God honors a person's free will?

- What is the significance of the phrase "without finding fault" in the context of God giving wisdom to those who ask and believe?

4

Forgiving When it Hurts

People are capable of committing major offenses against others and even feeling justified in doing so. It is amazing at times to hear people justify their obnoxious or destructive behavior. Yet that is so typical of the world system we live in, which is dominated by self-centeredness (pride).

Even a minor offense leads to another in the form of retaliation or anger. Even unintentional offenses can damage relationships, and the offender may even wonder why the person is angry with them or suddenly cool toward them.

The problem is the desire within every human to protect himself. Some people withdraw to avoid being hurt again. Others use rage as a protective mechanism: "If I make it painful enough for them, they won't hurt me again."

Offenses happen. People get their feelings hurt. Misunderstandings, unfulfilled expectations, careless remarks and other similar experiences in life can cause offenses. So how should you respond when it happens to you?

The world system, which in reality is Satan's kingdom, functions as the exact opposite of God's kingdom. As a result, you can often identify the godly or proper action as the exact opposite of what you feel like doing. What is the natural response in a particular situation? Do the opposite. This obviously is not a principle you can use in every situation because you are renewing your mind to conform to

God's and because you are allowing God to develop His character in you. But it might surprise you how often you can be right by doing the opposite of what comes naturally.

Keep this in mind the next time someone offends you or imposes their will on you. What is the natural response in that situation? Get angry, defend yourself, retaliate. What is the opposite of these responses, simply not doing them? No, the opposite of getting angry, defending yourself or retaliating is responding in gentleness and love, then forgiving the person who offended you. Do not hold them responsible for their action, or try to make sure they "get what's coming to them," or even "turn them over to God" so He can avenge you. Turn loose of the offense and let it go.

You choose to forgive, regardless of the severity of the sin against you. Your willingness to forgive is very important to God, as we see in Matthew 6:14-15. "For if you forgive men when they sin against you, your heavenly Father will also forgive you. But if you do not forgive men their sins, your Father will not forgive your sins." That couldn't be much clearer. There is a direct correlation between God's ability to forgive you and your willingness to forgive others.

Who and what was Jesus talking about when He referred to forgiving men when they sin against you? Earlier in the same teaching He talked about people insulting you, persecuting you and falsely saying all kinds of evil against you because of Him (Matt. 5:11). He referred to someone who strikes you on the face, which is a very offensive place to strike someone (Matt. 5:39). He included those who want to sue you and take your possessions, or force you to serve them, or borrow something from you (Matt. 5:40-42). He said you are to love your enemies and pray for those who persecute you (Matt. 5:44). That list includes just about everyone who might give you opportunity to forgive.

Jesus taught His disciples about forgiveness on several occasions, including the following incident. "Then Peter came to Jesus and asked, 'Lord, how many times shall I forgive my brother when he sins against me? Up to seven times?' Jesus answered, 'I tell you, not seven times, but seventy-seven times'" (Matt. 18:21-22).

Jesus was not specifying a numerical limit of 77, so you have no excuse for telling someone, "Okay, that's 76 times. You only have one more to go, so watch out!" He was using numbers to make a contrast that is easy to remember. Love "keeps no record of wrongs," so a tally of someone's offenses is out of the question (1 Cor. 13:5). In a sense, when you forgive everything someone has done to you, their next offense is the first, so you never have more than one to forgive.

After Jesus stated that we should forgive more than just seven times, that is, virtually an unlimited number of times, He told a relevant parable to demonstrate His point. The story is a familiar one about a servant who was unable to repay an enormous debt to his king, but begged the king to be patient with him. In response, the king was more than patient; he canceled the servant's debt.

The servant immediately found another servant who owed him a meager amount and began choking him, demanding that the man pay him. When the man asked for patience, the first servant refused and had the man thrown in jail. When the king heard about it, he called the servant in and reprimanded him for not extending mercy to the other servant as he had received from the king. The king then had the unforgiving servant thrown in jail. At the end of the parable, Jesus states His main point about forgiveness: "This is how my heavenly Father will treat each of you unless you forgive your brother from your heart" (Matt. 18:35).

Before telling the parable, Jesus essentially said that you must forgive a brother as many times as he sins against you. Then after the parable He states very bluntly that if you refuse to forgive them, your Father will not forgive you.

"Be kind and compassionate to one another, forgiving each other, just as in Christ God forgave you" (Eph. 4:32). "Bear with each other and forgive whatever grievances you may have against one another. Forgive as the Lord forgave you" (Col. 3:13). The phrase, "as the Lord forgave you," suggests He expects you to forgive others to the same degree He forgave you—completely.

Peter had asked Jesus how many times he should forgive his brother, that is, a spiritual brother, another Christian. Ephesians and Colossians refer to forgiving each other, which means other believers. As we saw earlier, you are to forgive those who are not believers, too. So whom do you forgive? Believers and nonbelievers, regardless of what they do to you.

You can forgive others because God forgave you; or stated differently, God's forgiveness of you enables you to forgive others. There are two significant aspects of your relationship with God that enable you to forgive others. One is understanding your need to forgive so you can receive God's forgiveness. Another is your faith in God's care for you, because if God is taking care of you then you do not need to protect yourself from offenses or retaliate for them.

Let us take that second point a little farther and state that God can work every incident to your benefit, including every hurt and offense. "And we know that in all things God works for the good of those who love him, who have been called according to his purpose" (Rom. 8:28). People may deliberately injure you and cause you harm, but God is in control and can cause their efforts to benefit you. Consider, for example, Joseph's evaluation of his brothers' actions: "You intended to harm me, but God intended it for good to accomplish what is now being done, the saving of many lives" (Gen. 50:20).

You can forgive because you know that God is causing everything to work together for your good. If you believe that every harmful thing someone does to you is actually benefiting you, you will forgive them and maybe even be thankful for the opportunity.

Maybe you assume that whoever writes a book has mastered whatever they write about. I can assure you that is definitely not the case with this topic or any other topic in this study. When someone offends me, even unintentionally, any ungodly attitude I have wants me to get even with them. I can even disguise my desire by re-labeling it as a need to help or teach the offender, or whatever. But my self-centeredness is obviously my motivation; they offended *me* and I want to make sure they don't do it again. Even if I see the person offending someone else I may want to intervene simply because they offended me in the past. Do you see how cleverly pride can disguise itself?

One reason you need to forgive others is to enable God to forgive you, as we stated earlier, but that is not the only reason. Should you forgive someone because they did something to you and they need to be forgiven? No, because your forgiveness does very little (maybe nothing) for the offender.

Stop and think for a moment about what part of you gets offended. Your carnal attitude. It is self-centered and responds to certain experiences with hurt, anger, self-pity and other emotions. The emphasis is on yourself, protecting yourself because you don't want to get hurt again, or avenging yourself for what they did to you, or even justifying your feelings of anger and resentment. It feels good when you protect or avenge yourself; it feels natural and right.

Jesus taught that you should have a very different response, however. "You have heard that it was said, 'Eye for eye, and tooth for tooth.' But I tell you, Do not resist an evil person. If someone strikes you on the right cheek, turn to him the other also" (Matt. 5:38-39). The word translated "resist" means to stand against or in opposition to; to oppose or resist. It is a very active and forceful word. The phrase, "evil person," refers to whatever evil causes pain or sorrow; actually, the word "person" is not in the Greek text.

So Jesus' teaching appears to mean that you should not protect yourself from whoever would try to harm you. The idea is not to allow only a second blow, then respond any way you want, any more than Jesus' teaching about forgiving 77 times means to count a person's offenses. The emphasis of Jesus' teaching about turning the other cheek is on not protecting yourself.

Does this mean you should not take reasonable precautions, such as jumping away from a car that is about to hit you? Or getting away from a poisonous snake that is about to strike? Or closing up your house before a hurricane hits? Or getting an inoculation to avoid becoming ill? These address a different issue than forgiveness, so the verses we are considering in this chapter do not apply.

The verse we just examined said not to resist evil, but keep the context in mind: protecting yourself from offense or standing up for your rights. That verse does not mean you should not resist Satan. The Bible very clearly says, "Resist the devil, and he will flee from you" (James 4:7). Also, "Be self-controlled and alert. Your enemy the devil prowls around like a roaring lion looking for someone to devour. Resist him, standing firm in the faith" (1 Pet. 5:8-9). The evil you are not to resist originates with other people, which is why the translators inserted the word "person" in Matthew 5:39, "Do not resist an evil person," but you must resist the devil.

Incidentally, the same Greek word for "resist" appears in Matthew 5:39 (do not resist an evil person), James 4:7 (resist the devil) and 1 Peter 5:9 (resist the devil). Satan is not the one who causes your everyday offenses, rather it is the sinful behavior of the person who offends you.

If you must forgive someone who has hurt you or done you harm, should you simply allow them to do it and never talk to them about it? No, and especially not if they are a Christian. You have an obligation to other believers to help them mature and become more Christ-like, so it is important to give them opportunity to improve. In fact, the Bible gives very clear instruction on how to do it. Earlier in this chapter we referred to Peter asking Jesus if he should forgive another believer as many as seven times. Peter's question was prompted by what Jesus had just said.

> *If your brother sins against you, go and show him his fault, just between the two of you. If he listens to you, you have won your brother over. But if he will not listen, take one or two others along, so that 'every matter may be established by the testimony of two or three witnesses.' If he refuses to listen to them, tell it to the church; and if he refuses to listen even to the church, treat him as you would a pagan or a tax collector* (Matt. 18:15-17).

One purpose for going to a believer who has hurt or harmed you is to give them opportunity to acknowledge their fault and respond appropriately. Another purpose for going to them is to give yourself opportunity to express love and interest for them, denying your own self-centeredness. You should never try to make them feel bad or manipulate them into admitting they were wrong. Those would be selfish motives and therefore sinful. Instead, your goal must be to forgive them, as Peter recognized when he asked Jesus how many times he should forgive.

If the person is not a believer, the circumstances would determine whether you should go to them. Any attempt to manipulate them would be wrong. Your purpose for going would be to express godly character and reject any ungodly motivations.

Maybe you react to this by thinking I have a problem, am an extremist or misunderstand Scripture. Are you sure you are not shifting the blame or protecting yourself by accusing me? My personal biases do not change the truth of Scripture. The Bible says you should not actively oppose those who would cause you pain or sorrow. Instead, trust God to care for you and to work all of your experiences together for your benefit.

This does not mean you should be careless or masochistic. Life will provide enough opportunities for you to practice trusting God without your creating them. These scriptures mean that when someone does something to you, you should not actively resist them. Either God takes care of you as He promises and works it to your benefit as He says, or He is a liar.

A sinful mindset makes you feel so good when you avenge yourself. You feel that person deserves what you do to them and you feel good to be in control. But Jesus said, "You have heard that it was said, 'Love your neighbor and hate your enemy.' But I tell you: Love your enemies and pray for those who persecute you" (Matt. 5:43-44). Paul wrote, "Do not take revenge, my friends, but leave room for God's wrath, for it is written: 'It is mine to avenge; I will repay,' says the Lord" (Rom. 12:19).

God is in covenant with you. He is responsible to protect you and avenge you if it is appropriate and He knows what is appropriate better than you do. God's justice is such that if you punish someone, there is no need for God to punish them also. If someone offends you and you take matters into your own hands by retaliating or seeking revenge, God will not avenge you or punish your offender. And not seeking revenge for yourself so God can get them "better" than you could is missing the point, because you still want revenge. This does not apply to relationships in which you have the responsibility to punish someone, as in a parent/child relationship, as long as you are not motivated by your desire for retaliation.

Wanting revenge is an ungodly desire, the result of living as if you still had a sinful nature. Your pride insists that it is appropriate for you to feel such emotions and it resists admitting you are guilty for being angry. After all, you might think, the Bible refers to being angry without sinning, so doesn't that mean it is okay to be angry?

The scripture in question is Ephesians 4:26-27: "'In your anger do not sin': Do not let the sun go down while you are still angry, and do not give the devil a foot-hold." Notice the quotation marks. This passage quotes a statement in the Old Testament, then explains it or gives an application. If you are using this passage to justify your anger, you are missing the point, because a few verses later we see another reference to anger: "Get rid of all bitterness, rage and anger, brawling and slander, along with every form of malice" (Eph. 4:31). Any anger based on a personal offense is a sin.

I have heard someone protest, "But God gets angry." Yes, but God can be angry and still be sinless. God's anger is always a response to sin, not to a personal offense. There are many things God can and will do that you should not. His word to you and me is always, "Get rid of your anger."

It is your carnal attitude that causes you to get angry or hurt by an offense. Anger originating with worldly thinking is a sin and it causes you to keep thinking about the offense and become bitter about it.

You need to forgive. The only acceptable response to your carnal thinking is to refuse to savor or fulfill such desires, to reject its demands, and starve it to death by refusing to feed it. Let it die! Forgiving someone who has hurt you puts those ungodly desires to death. Anger wants the person held accountable for what they did to you but forgiveness releases them from accountability. Your holding them accountable for an offense really does nothing to them, unless you retaliate or give them a hard time. On the other hand, refusing to forgive them is engaging in worldly behavior and is extremely harmful to you.

The issue in forgiveness is overcoming your sinful motivations. In some cases it may be necessary to keep track of another person's behavior to identify trends. For example, if you are raising a child you need to correct patterns of undesirable behavior, so you cannot treat every incident as if it were the first.

When it comes to forgiveness, however, you need to respond the same way each time by crucifying any sinful desire. Whether your natural response is vengeance or pity, you must put that response to death. You cannot overcome a sinful attitude by appeasing it less than you did in the past. You overcome it by killing it.

If there were a vicious, deadly animal in your house threatening your family, you would not try to appease it, hoping it will be satisfied and leave you alone. No, you would use whatever force is necessary to eliminate it as a threat. That is exactly how you must treat your worldly thinking. And an excellent way to do that is to forgive someone who has hurt you.

When to Forgive

The verses we have examined deal primarily with offenses that others commit against you. We have seen that you are to forgive others when they do something to you. Even the model prayer Jesus gave us, which we call the Lord's Prayer, includes forgiveness of personal offenses: "Forgive us our debts, as we also have forgiven our debtors" (Matt. 6:12).

Are we to forgive everyone for everything they do? I have heard people say that we should, because God forgives and we should be like Him. But God does not forgive everyone. In particular, if someone does not accept God's plan of salvation, God does not forgive his sins. Acts 10:43 states that, "everyone who believes in him receives forgiveness of sins through his name," which clearly means that everyone who does not believe in him will not receive forgiveness of sins. Likewise, if you choose not to forgive someone for what they did to you, God will not forgive your sins either (Matt. 6:14-15). Jesus clearly stated there is a certain category of sin that God will never forgive, as we see in the following verses.

And so I tell you, every sin and blasphemy will be forgiven men, but the blasphemy against the Spirit will not be forgiven. Anyone who speaks a word against the Son of Man will be forgiven, but anyone who speaks against the Holy Spirit will not be forgiven, either in this age or in the age to come (Matt. 12:31-32).

Consider another example. At one point, Jesus quoted a verse from Isaiah to explain why He used parables in His teaching:

When he was alone, the Twelve and the others around him asked him about the parables. He told them, "The secret of the kingdom of God has been given to you. But to those on the outside everything is said in parables so that, "'they may be ever seeing but never perceiving, and ever hearing but never understanding; otherwise they might turn and be forgiven!'" (Mark 4:10-12).

Jesus entrusted the mystery of the kingdom of God to His disciples, but it remained a mystery to the ungodly. His parables revealed important principles to those within the kingdom, but to those outside the kingdom the parables were little more than stories; unbelievers can see and hear the principles but not grasp them. The most intriguing aspect of this statement, however, is that Jesus used parables to prevent the unbelievers from being forgiven: "otherwise they might turn and be forgiven." Rather than trying to formulate a doctrine on whether God wants to prevent people from repenting under certain conditions, keep in mind that the good news of the gospel is available to everyone and that it is not God's desire for anyone to be condemned for sin. We can, however, use this verse to support the concept of God not extending forgiveness under some conditions.

On another occasion, Jesus said to His disciples, "Things that cause people to sin are bound to come, but woe to that person through whom they come" (Luke 17:1). Then He said, "If your brother sins, rebuke him, and if he repents, forgive him. If he sins against you seven times in a day, and seven times comes back to you and says, 'I repent,' forgive him" (Luke 17:3-4).

Notice that your forgiveness of the offending brother is conditional on his repenting, and that this applies when he sins against you. On the surface, this appears to contradict the very clear teaching about universally forgiving sins committed against you, but there is another important principle involved. According to these verses, your first response to a believer who sins against you should be to rebuke him, then forgive him if he repents. This demonstrates the mutual accountability among believers, who are to strengthen each other, build each other up and help each other overcome their carnal tendencies. Just as all Scripture is "useful for teaching, rebuking, correcting and training in righteousness" (2 Tim. 3:16), believers are to provide the same service to each other.

As an example, consider Paul's treatment of the Corinthian believers for the way they treated an immoral believer in the church.

Shouldn't you rather have been filled with grief and have put out of your fellowship the man who did this? . . . I have already passed judgment on the one who did this, just as if I were present . . . hand this man over to Satan, so that the sinful nature may be destroyed . . . . I am writing you that you must not associate with anyone who calls himself a brother but is sexually immoral or greedy, an idolater or a slanderer, a drunkard or a swindler. With such a man do not even eat . . . . Expel the wicked man from among you (1 Cor. 5:2, 3, 5, 11, 13).

The man in question was committing a particular sin and the other believers were tolerating his behavior, possibly out of a desire to forgive his sin. Whatever their motivation, Paul severely rebukes them and directs them to expel the man from their assembly. He says nothing about exercising forgiveness at this stage. In Second Corinthians, Paul addresses the issue again and we can conclude from his statements that the man had repented because Paul instructs the believers to forgive and comfort him (2 Cor. 2:7). Initially, they were to pass judgment on the man and ostracize him, not to forgive him. Only after he had experienced the sorrow of his punishment and repented were they to forgive him.

In this situation, the man was not sinning against members of the congregation, so the believers did not have to forgive a personal offense. The requirement to forgive someone who sins against you does not apply. Instead, the believers needed to hold the man accountable for his actions, and this meant withholding their forgiveness until he responded appropriately.

After Jesus returned from the dead, He imparted the Holy Spirit to His disciples. During that incident, He said, "Peace be with you! As the Father has sent me, I am sending you . . . . Receive the Holy Spirit. If you forgive anyone his sins, they are forgiven; if you do not forgive them, they are not forgiven" (John 20:21-23). This time Jesus is not saying that if you do not forgive someone, God will not forgive your sins; instead He says God will forgive that person if you do. So it is acceptable not to forgive someone's sins in certain cases, and God honors your choice.

Notice the context of Jesus' statement: John's version of the "great commission" as recorded in Matthew 28. Jesus is sending His disciples out as His representatives to perform His work on the earth. He had just breathed on them and given them the Holy Spirit. Now, as Jesus' representatives on earth and with God's Holy Spirit in them, they had the authority to forgive or not forgive sins. But how was that decision to be motivated? In Jesus' behalf and in the power of the Holy Spirit—definitely not by their carnal attitudes.

Many of the verses we have examined require you to forgive, yet others make forgiveness conditional. Based on these Scriptures, we can identify when it is appropriate to forgive.

If you have been offended, you must forgive, always. Your carnal habits make you want revenge or some form of penance from the offender: "They should pay for what they did to me." Forgiving them releases them from guilt and responsibility, but even more important, it denies your carnal desires. When you forgive someone for what they did to you, you arrest your own self-centeredness.

If you become aware of an offense that does not directly affect you, your forgiveness can be conditional. You're not withholding forgiveness for personal reasons—unless you take on the offense, of course—so you do not need to deny any self-centered demands by forgiving. You can be objective about the situation.

What is God's agenda? For nonbelievers, He wants to bring them to the point of salvation and have them released from guilt by accepting Jesus as Savior. They must first repent, then they can receive forgiveness. For believers, He wants to develop godly character in them. As with nonbelievers, they must first repent, then they receive forgiveness. In both cases, forgiveness follows repentance.

Whenever you're directly involved, you must forgive the offense; it is an act of denying any carnal motivation you might have and is for your benefit. Whenever you're not directly involved, your forgiveness is dependent on an acceptable response from the offender.

Life is not simple and you cannot always divide your experiences into neat little categories. What if you have authority over someone who offends you, for example? Maybe the offender is your child or your subordinate at work. What should you do?

You must forgive the personal offense; this is not optional and is for your benefit. You may still punish them appropriately; this is optional and is for their benefit. If you cannot be objective—devoid of revenge and anger—have someone else decide and administer the punishment, if that is appropriate.

Most of us have heard someone say it is easier to die for Jesus than to live for Him and in a sense that is true. It may be possible, for example, to choose to forgive someone who has committed some horrific crime against you because that is the "Christian" thing to do. Yes, even our human nature can rise nobly above a terrible situation and become gracious and forgiving. We have the image embossed on our mind of Jesus hanging on the cross saying, "Father, forgive them," and we can choose to follow His example in extremely difficult situations. In the really hard times we can stir up extraordinary abilities from within ourselves. But your human nature reveals its true self, its normal mode of operation, in the ordinary events of life.

How do you feel when someone cuts you off in traffic or almost causes an accident out of carelessness? Is the horn on your car well-used? What rises up within you when someone continues to interrupt when you are talking? Or when they keep leaving their work materials on your desk and act like it's not a big deal when you speak to them about it? Maybe you try to reconcile with someone who has offended you, but they treat you harshly as if you were totally responsible for the problem. Or maybe you have told your spouse repeatedly that certain thing they do really annoys you, but they just did it for the ten zillionth time this week.

How good are you at forgiving people for the less serious, sometimes minor, things they do? Of course it irritates you, annoys you, disturbs you, or simply displeases you. The issue is how you respond when it happens.

To forgive is to absolve the offender of guilt and responsibility for their actions. Forgiving does not require you to forget the offense. Instead, it means the offense no longer affects your relationship with the person. What they did may even have permanently affected you and the incident may still be vivid in your memory, but you must pardon them and no longer hold them accountable. That is forgiveness.

How to Forgive

The main function of forgiving someone for an offense is pardoning them, which means releasing them from any obligation or penalty. Forgiveness recognizes that an offense has occurred and a penalty is due, but chooses to release the offender.

Forgiveness does not justify a person's behavior with such statements as, "That's okay. I know you're under a lot of pressure." That kind of statement claims they had a good reason to sin, and you can never justify sin. To claim that an act was justified for any reason eliminates the need for forgiveness because no penalty is warranted.

When someone repents or apologizes, do not downgrade the offense. You might hear someone say, "Don't worry about it. It wasn't that bad." But that kind of response bends the standards for good conduct and is not the same as forgiving them. The only effective way for an offender to deal with his guilt is to recognize his sin and repent, not have someone reduce his offense.

When someone apologizes to you, thank them for their apology and tell them you forgive them. Then forgive them, or else you are guilty of lying as well as refusing to forgive. Keep in mind that anyone who has been forgiven is no longer responsible for the offense. To forgive someone is to release them from all responsibility for their action. In that sense it is as though they had never committed the act; their record is clean.

Because we have heard the phrase so often, we can hardly say the word "forgive" without adding the words "and forget." I am not aware of any scripture that says you must forget offenses committed against you. You can remember that an incident occurred and even recall many of the details, yet be confident that God is working in it for your benefit and forgive the offense. If you dwell on the offense and nurture your hurt feelings or anger, however, that is sin and proves you have not forgiven.

If you believe that God works everything together for your benefit, you might even conclude it can be beneficial to remember painful experiences after you have forgiven the person responsible. If the event led to significant personal growth or maturity, helped you develop a godly character trait or overcome an undesirable trait, then you can benefit from remembering it. It becomes a milepost in your life, always reminding you of the progress you have made. It can help you persevere in your current difficult experience. It also helps you become more pliable, willing to change without having to experience tragedy first.

Painful experiences become part of your history and your identity; you cannot deny their existence or their effect on you. Once you have forgiven, you can remember the events and the pain without feeling angry, bitter or frustrated. If you still have self-centered feelings when you think about what happened, you should use the occasion to practice forgiveness. There are benefits to forgiving and remembering, rather than forgiving and forgetting.

Some people want us to believe that we should forgive those who commit crimes against us and not prosecute them. But as it is God's responsibility to protect you and avenge you when appropriate, it is our judicial system's responsibility to protect you and punish those who commit crimes against you. The legal system is to be God's human agency for justice, so let it do its job (see Rom. 13:1-5). If criminal laws were simply a means by which society vents its collective anger against criminals, then imprisonment would be cruel and inhumane punishment, and capital punishment would be nothing short of murder. Those who make such charges against our system of justice apparently assume it is based on the self-centered desire for retaliation, rather than God's principle of accountability for sin.

Some people say you should forgive your offensive children and not punish them. But by not punishing them, you are condoning sinful behavior and that is not an act of love. Love cares enough for the offender to punish them, to teach them the principle of accountability and motivate them to change the way they think. The purpose of punishment is to promote discipline and change behavior, not to seek revenge or relieve frustration. Punishment and discipline are not synonymous, and neither are punishment and abuse.

Conclusion

The issue of forgiveness is about how you respond to your own carnal attitudes. The issue is not the offender's repentance or their punishment, rather it is how you respond. God requires you to forgive those who hurt you, whether they did it intentionally or unintentionally. Your worldly attitudes motivate you to respond with anger, hurt and other emotions. Forgiving others is an excellent way to crucify that kind of thinking.

Personal Study

1.   "If someone strikes you on the right cheek, turn to him the other also. And if someone wants to sue you and take your tunic, let him have your cloak as well. If someone forces you to go one mile, go with him two miles. Give to the one who asks you, and do not turn away from the one who wants to borrow from you" (Matt. 5:39-42).

     • What basic human trait or attitude makes it difficult for you to do what these verses say? Why?

- It is inevitable that someone will strike you, sue you, force you to do something against your will, or even be a nuisance by borrowing incessantly from you. Offenses and injuries are a part of life. What godly character trait must you develop that will enable you to forgive the person who does these things to you? How does it enable you to forgive?

- In what ways does protecting yourself from other people demonstrate a lack of trust in God's promise to care for you?

2. [From the Lord's Prayer] "Forgive us our debts, as we also have forgiven our debtors . . . . For if you forgive men when they sin against you, your heavenly Father will also forgive you. But if you do not forgive men their sins, your Father will not forgive your sins" (Matt. 6:12, 14-15).

    - How would a Christian's eternal state be affected by their unwillingness to forgive?

    - How would a Christian's present spiritual condition be affected by their unwillingness to forgive? Their present mental and emotional state? Their present physical state?

    - What are some of your attitudes and actions that reveal a lack of forgiveness?

5

Thankful for What?

Face it: this is not heaven. You live in a world that is dominated by sin and you can see its putrid effects all around you and even in you. The world is literally bound for hell. Satan and his forces are prowling around looking for ways to devour you and they pose a continuous threat by stealing, killing and destroying.

God is more aware of this than you are and He says that you should devote yourself to prayer, and being watchful and thankful (see Col. 4:2). You may not have any control over what happens around you or to you, but you do have control of your attitude. And God wants you to have a thankful attitude.

"Let the peace of Christ rule in your hearts, since as members of one body you were called to peace. And be thankful" (Col. 3:15). Being thankful is easy if you get what you want, but if you don't like what is happening, you can be thankful only if you believe. When you are experiencing turmoil, danger or loss, your natural (sinful) reaction is to defend yourself and your interests. By believing what God says, on the other hand, you can let the peace of Christ rule within you in spite of your circumstances.

Notice that the verse says to "let" the peace of Christ rule; it is something you choose to do. This verse mentions letting God's peace rule in you and being thankful, and both are related to your faith in God. Being thankful to God is a matter of choice and is possible only if you believe God, regardless of the circumstances.

The Bible encourages you to be "always giving thanks to God the Father for everything" (Eph. 5:20) and to "give thanks in all circumstances, for this is God's will for you in Christ Jesus" (1 Thess. 5:18). How is it possible to be thankful "for everything" and "in all circumstances"? Some would say that every cloud has a silver lining, that you can see good in every situation if you look closely enough. But I don't think the Bible supports an approach to life that simplistically assumes everything is wonderful and somehow everything will turn out okay. The Bible does not promote blissful ignorance.

Biblical thankfulness is based on faith and knowledge. Consider Romans 8:28: "And we know that in all things God works for the good of those who love him, who have been called according to his purpose." If you have responded to God's call to salvation and you love Him, then God works everything together for your benefit—everything.

There is a key Greek word in this verse, *synergeo*, which means "works together." This word is virtually identical to our word "synergy." Synergy is what causes the combined effect of two or more forces to be greater than the sum of their individual effects. This means when two things combine synergistically, a reaction occurs. Consider a scriptural example in Deuteronomy 32:30: "How could one man chase a thousand, or two put ten thousand to flight, unless their Rock had sold them, unless the Lord had given them up?" If each man chases 1,000, then two men would usually chase 2,000. Synergy causes two men to chase 10,000; their combined effect is greater than the sum of their individual effects. Among other things, this demonstrates the importance of believers meeting together (Heb. 10:25) and being united.

That is the way God works in you. He uses your character, experiences and circumstances to produce something of value in you; even those experiences that ordinarily would harm you. He works all events together so they have a compounded benefit for you. He multiplies their effect to multiply your improvement.

Another key word in Romans 8:28 is "good," which in the Greek refers to excellence, significance or usefulness. So God multiplies the benefits of everything you are and everything you experience to produce excellence of character in you. Now notice the first three words, "And we know." Because you know that God works everything together for your benefit, you can honestly be thankful "for everything" and "in all circumstances."

Choose to believe that God does what is best and choose to be thankful. James 1:2-4 reads, "Consider it pure joy, my brothers, whenever you face trials of many kinds, because you know that the testing of your faith develops perseverance. Perseverance must finish its work so that you may be mature and complete, not lacking anything." Again, we see the idea of excellence or perfection: "mature and complete, not lacking anything." You might feel like complaining and demanding happiness when life is unpleasant. During those times, however, recognize that God is compounding the benefits and producing excellence in you. Choose to be joyful and thankful, then persevere and let God continue His work in you.

Just like Romans 8:28, this verse shows the importance of knowing what God is doing: "Consider it pure joy . . . because you know." The only way you can be thankful for everything and in all circumstances is by knowing that God is using them for your benefit to make your character excellent.

What situation have you not been thankful for, or what have you been worried or angry about? Why not choose to believe what God's Word says? How does the Bible apply to you in your situation? How will you respond to what the Bible says?

The proper response is really very simple, though it is not easy: repent and change your attitude about your situation. Choose to be thankful about it. You might feel like you cannot be thankful as long as you are unhappy, but that is based on a carnal attitude. Nowhere does the Bible require you to be happy about your circumstances, but it does require you to be thankful.

Should you be thankful for what Satan does? Or for what his followers and demons do? It would be foolish to think God wants you to be thankful that sin exists and is destroying people. So what can you be thankful for?

1.   God is God. Jesus is the King of kings and Lord of lords. His kingdom exists in heaven, and someday soon He will expand

it to include all of creation once again. Although it appears sin is running rampant, God is in ultimate control of everything. He honors man's free will and allows you to choose whom you will serve. God has set limits on what Satan and man can do, so He is in control. When evil seems to be victorious, can you be thankful God's kingdom is near? Yes.

2.   Sin is a reminder. Learn to recognize sin and identify its destructive power; sin has destroyed man and creation. Develop a hatred for sin and what it has done. This requires a radical change in your thinking, because sin is very enjoyable. Every time you see sin or its effects, let it motivate you to eliminate every sin in your life. You do not belong on this planet; it is not your home. You are an alien to this world and its system. Someday you will leave here and go home to be with your Father, so do not let sin hinder you from graduating successfully from this life. There are no acceptable sins. Can you be thankful that sinful acts around you motivate you to become more righteous? Yes.

3.   Everything can benefit you. God can and will work everything to your benefit, if you allow Him. Can He use a hurtful experience to break the power your sinful attitudes and behavior have over you? Can you be thankful *for* and *in* that? Yes.

That is why Ephesians 5:19-20 says we are to "speak to one another with psalms, hymns and spiritual songs. Sing and make music in your heart to the Lord, always giving thanks to God the Father for everything, in the name of our Lord Jesus Christ." Focus your attention on God by using psalms, hymns and spiritual songs to help you do it. Only by recognizing who God is and what He does, can you always give thanks to Him *for* everything and *in* everything.

If you think like the world, then you feel everything should make sense to you, such as why you should always be thankful. Some people cannot (or more correctly, will not) accept anything they cannot understand. Maybe that includes you. If it does, recognize that as ungodly thinking and reject it, which means you are "denying your flesh" and allowing God to crucify your carnal ways.

Consider an extreme hypothetical example. It is late at night and you are walking to your car alone in a shopping center parking lot. Two men force you into your car and drive to a secluded area. They beat you severely, steal your car and valuables, and leave you abandoned out in the countryside. What can you be thankful for?

Maybe you had the same initial reaction I did: "I can thank God I'm still alive." What does that reveal about your priorities, though? Would you prefer to remain alive in a sinful world than to be set free from all the effects of sin and be with the Lord? But you are still alive after that tragic experience, so what can you be thankful for?

Consider another hypothetical example. Let's say you raise your children in a Christian environment and teach them to live godly lives. When they grow up, however, they turn their backs on God and indulge themselves with pleasure, sex, alcohol or drugs. What can you be thankful for?

You will not find anything worthwhile to be thankful for as long as your attention is on the circumstances. Do not insist on finding something "good" in every experience, or the silver lining in every cloud. Turn to God. Be thankful that He is in control, that every sinful act can motivate you to become more righteous, and that God will use every experience for your benefit if you allow Him.

Such experiences in themselves offer nothing good. Any good comes from the way you respond to them. Do you continue to trust God, in spite of evidence that superficially suggests He is not doing His job of protecting you? Do you choose to intercede for your children continuously in the face of a hopeless situation? Will you stand firmly on God's Word and promises even when your world seems to be falling apart? Does your relationship with God depend on what He's done for you lately?

Let your circumstances push you toward God and motivate you to develop godly character. You really can be thankful in all circumstances and for everything, but only if your attention is riveted on God.

God is in ultimate control of everything, even if sin appears to be out of control. What God says is absolutely guaranteed, and He says that in the end everything will be done according to His will. His kingdom is unshakable; everything else in creation can and will be shaken so the unshakable will remain. "Therefore, since we are receiving a kingdom that cannot be shaken, let us be thankful, and so worship God acceptably with reverence and awe" (Heb. 12:28).

Can you be thankful *in* everything and *for* everything? Yes, but only if you choose to be. Developing a thankful attitude toward God is part of repenting—changing the way you think.

Conclusion

God uses your character, experiences and circumstances to produce something of value in you, even those experiences that ordinarily would harm you. Biblical thankfulness is based on faith and knowledge. When you understand that God works all events together so they have a compounded benefit for you, you can be thankful in everything as well as for everything. You can be thankful that God is God, that Jesus is the King of kings and Lord of lords. You can be thankful that sinful acts around you motivate you to become more righteous. You can also be thankful that God will use even hurtful experiences to crucify your sinful thinking and destroy its power over you.

Personal Study

1.   "Be joyful always; pray continually; give thanks in all circumstances, for this is God's will for you in Christ Jesus" (1 Thess. 5:16-18).

   • What is the relationship between joyfulness and giving thanks?

   • Why would it be God's will for you to be joyful always, pray continually and give thanks in all circumstances?

2.   "Consider it pure joy, my brothers, whenever you face trials of many kinds, because you know that the testing of your faith develops perseverance. Perseverance must finish its work so that you may be mature and complete, not lacking anything" (James 1:2-4).

- "Pure joy" describes a state of complete happiness or satisfaction. How does knowing that a test can produce maturity cause you to have pure joy during trials?

- How can such an attitude cause you to be thankful in severe trials?

3.   "They called the apostles in and had them flogged. Then they ordered them not to speak in the name of Jesus, and let them go. The apostles left the Sanhedrin, rejoicing because they had been counted worthy of suffering disgrace for the Name. Day after day, in the temple courts and from house to house, they never stopped teaching and proclaiming the good news that Jesus is the Christ" (Acts 5:40-42).

- How did rejoicing reflect an attitude of thankfulness?

- How did thankfulness enable the apostles to continue doing the very thing that caused them to be flogged?

6

An Alien in a Human Body

There have been various science-fiction stories and movies about beings from outer space coming to earth. Some of these beings were friendly and some were hostile. Some had bizarre appearances and some looked just like us. Some of these stories were even about people who later proved to be aliens.

I want to describe a true situation that will sound like one of those sci-fi thrillers. There are real people living on earth today who were born and raised here and live normal lives like everyone else but are in reality aliens. On the outside they look like everyone else but there is more to them than meets the eye. They belong to a different world, not this planet. And the exciting part of this true story is that you are one of them. Let me explain.

Jesus made a very clear statement to His disciples as recorded in the Gospel of John: "If you belonged to the world, it would love you as its own. As it is, you do not belong to the world, but I have chosen you out of the world. That is why the world hates you" (John 15:19). You do not belong to this planet or its culture, because God chose you from among its inhabitants to be a citizen of His world. Since you do not belong to this world, its citizens do not love you as one of their own but instead hate you.

Keep in mind that all kinds of people flocked to Jesus and He even became known as a "friend of sinners" (Luke 7:34). Yet He taught that the world hated Him and would hate anyone who loved Him.

Were people attracted to Him because He caroused at their parties or indulged Himself in the things they enjoyed? No, people were drawn to Him because He was the personification of love and excellence of character, because He met their needs and spoke the truth. Once people experienced Him first-hand, however, many of them reacted negatively to Him and rejected Him, maybe even opposed Him. His differences attracted them at first, then they rejected Him because of His differences.

It is human nature to be prejudiced against those who are different. Your normal (that is, sinful) human self-centeredness makes you believe you are totally acceptable as you are and that others should be like you, so anyone who is different from you is not as good as you are. In addition, it causes you to dislike anyone who makes you look bad or feel bad about yourself. Do you see why people controlled by their sinful natures would hate anyone who lives by a higher standard and lives an exemplary life?

If you are comfortable around non-Christians, if they relate to you and enjoy being with you, beware. You certainly should not be obnoxious or self-righteous around non-Christians, but on the other hand, if you fit in well with their crowd, you need to check your attitudes and lifestyle. If you submit to God and humbly live to please Him, "the world hates you."

Sin causes people to hate those who are different. Self-centeredness says, "I am good, and you should be like me." This is the basis of prejudice. If you see a "character fault" in someone, you probably feel the solution is for them to be like you. That is prejudice. Prejudice is a carnal perspective and cannot be legislated out of existence, as decades of civil rights legislation have shown. We must oppose expressions of prejudice, but we also must recognize that prejudice itself will continue until people experience a spiritual conversion. Only God can change a person's nature.

As a Christian, you should not even be content to live in your physical body, because your satisfaction and fulfillment are not related to your physical existence. In fact, you are actually battling your physical body's cravings, and if you stop resisting them, they will win. In this sense, you are even an alien to your own physical body; it tries to trap you and hold you prisoner.

In John's Gospel, we read one of Jesus' prayers to the Father that reinforces the idea of alienation from the world.

I have given them your word and the world has hated them, for they are not of the world any more than I am of the world. My prayer is not that you take them out of the world but that you protect them from the evil one. They are not of the world, even as I am not of it (John 17:14-16).

Many people choose to believe that Jesus was just another man; a very good man, but only human. Those who choose to believe that He is the Son of God know that Jesus came to earth from somewhere else. He did not originate on this planet and therefore is not of the world. The phrase, "of the world," refers to someone who belongs to the world, relates to it, identifies with it, and longs for the experiences it provides. You originally were of the world, but once you accepted Jesus as Savior and Lord, He changed your citizenship and you are no longer a citizen of this world. You still reside *in* the world, but you no longer are a citizen *of* the world. You do not belong here; you are a foreigner, an alien to this culture.

What is the culture of this world? It is a lifestyle based on sinful human nature, which is intensely self-centered. The emphasis of human existence is on what you want, what you think, how you can be in control. The ultimate satisfaction in the human culture is to take matters into your own hands and be accountable to no one other than yourself.

People approve of those who behave like them and they encourage others to practice what they do. The Book of Romans says, "Although they know God's righteous decree that those who do such things deserve death, they not only continue to do these very things but also approve of those who practice them" (Rom. 1:32). Peer pressure is an important tool and people sometimes use it very subtly.

I was an engineer on an installation and test team for a mainframe computer system several years ago. After a new computer was installed, we would spend months checking it out, making the necessary revisions and repairs, before we released it for customer use. Because of the critical nature of the computer, our people would stay on-site to assist the customer and monitor the computer during its initial "burn-in" period. As a result, we would spend days in our offices with virtually nothing to do except wait for a system problem.

Imagine the scene: a crew of about 25 men, many of us fresh out of college, sitting around in temporary offices completely isolated from any supervisors and staff. As you might suspect, practical jokes became a favorite pastime and they often took the form of major pranks or booby traps.

I have forgotten most of the pranks but I still remember people's reactions. Everyone would be quiet and look innocent until the victim sprung the trap, then everyone fixed their attention on him to see how he would respond. The victim usually would simply act irritated until his anger built up and he began to swear. As soon as the obscenities began pouring out of his mouth, the group would erupt into laughter and applause. If the victim just became angry without cursing, the gag did not have the same impact. I began to realize that the goal was to provoke obscene language, and when the victim obliged by offering his choicest vulgarities, the group approved and rewarded him.

Peer pressure can be very subtle at times, but its purpose is always to encourage others to conform. You have seen people do this, and maybe have even done it yourself. Have you ever encouraged someone to eat more after they have had enough, for example, then felt pleased because they overate? In essence, you exerted pressure on them to conform to your desire, then felt pleased when you got them to do what you wanted. People encourage others to wear the same clothes they do, calling it stylish or fashionable. They pressure them to use the same language, to smoke, drink, lie, steal, and so on. They applaud people who conform, who do what they do or wish they could do.

It is very common for people not only to encourage others to behave certain ways, but even abuse those who will not. Peter describes such an attitude: "They think it strange that you do not plunge with them into the same flood of dissipation, and they heap abuse on you" (1 Pet. 4:4). People will pressure others who do not adhere to their standards. If you choose not to indulge in the same behavior someone else does, you can expect them to ridicule you or even become abusive. How often have you contradicted or corrected someone and had them act highly offended and attack your character? People of this world hate those who have different attitudes, think differently or act differently. They will use extreme pressure to make others conform.

Paul writes, however, that you have "died with Christ to the basic principles of this world," so you should not follow the rules and traditions of the world, "as though you still belonged to it" (Col. 2:20). He was referring to "hollow and deceptive philosophy, which depends on human tradition and the basic principles of this world rather than on Christ" (v. 8). This includes human commands and teachings that require certain types of behavior. For example, you certainly should not follow human tradition and standards to be popular or live "the good life." You do not belong to this world. If you do not belong to this world system, then where do you belong? Philippians tells us "our citizenship is in heaven. And we eagerly await a Savior from there, the Lord Jesus Christ" (Phil. 3:20).

The Greek word translated "citizenship" is a variation of a word that refers to the rights of citizenship. The word in this verse, however, emphasizes not the civil rights of a citizen, but the idea that he is a native citizen and he lives in his homeland.

There is a significant difference between a naturalized citizen and a native citizen. As a native citizen, you have the culture in addition to the civil rights. This verse says you are a native citizen of heaven, which means your attitudes and cultural practices are from heaven. Heaven is your homeland.

How is this possible if you were born in sin? Part of this question is a result of using analogies; the Bible's analogies of citizenship, spiritual rebirth, and so on, do not precisely describe what happened when you accepted Jesus as your Lord and Savior. You might not understand even if God told you exactly what He did.

However, the Bible does say that your name was written in the Book of Life before time began, which means God chose you before you were born. Is that what makes you a native citizen of heaven? Maybe. It does give more meaning to being "redeemed," or bought back. He declared you a native citizen of heaven and put your name in the Book of Life. Then you were born in slavery to sin in a foreign world, but He redeemed you (bought you back) and restored your citizenship.

A child who is born to American parents in another country receives an American birth certificate, showing the foreign country as his birthplace. The government considers the child a native American citizen, although he was not born in America. That is what God did by writing your name in the Book of Life, except He did it before time began. You are God's child, born in a foreign world. The Bible says you are a citizen of heaven and explains your mission on earth.

[God] reconciled us to himself through Christ and gave us the ministry of reconciliation: that God was reconciling the world to himself in Christ, not counting men's sins against them. And he has committed to us the message of reconciliation. We are therefore Christ's ambassadors, as though God were making his appeal through us (2 Cor. 5:18-20).

You are Christ's ambassador, representing him in a foreign land. Your mission here includes spreading the message of reconciliation. Hebrews chapter 11 explains faith and how many people in the Old Testament acted in faith. Of them it says, "All these people were still living by faith when they died. They did not receive the things promised; they only saw them and welcomed them from a distance. And they admitted that they were aliens and strangers on earth" (Heb. 11:13).

The words, "alien" and "stranger," are used in this verse and the following ones and are translated from several Greek words. The differences between the words are insightful and give several flavors of meaning but they are not doctrinally significant differences. The various words give different perspectives of the same concept, which we can summarize by the following points:

1. You are strange. You are different from the people of this world.

2. You are a foreigner, an alien to this world.
3. You are a temporary resident. You do not belong here and will eventually leave.
4. You are away from your own people, living temporarily away from home.

Peter uses these words in both of his letters. He even addresses his first letter to "God's elect, strangers in the world" (1 Pet. 1:1). Later in the same chapter he writes, "Since you call on a Father who judges each man's work impartially, live your lives as strangers here in reverent fear" (1 Pet. 1:17). Again, he uses the word, "strangers."

He also makes a very interesting statement: "live your lives as strangers here in reverent fear." You do live here, but you should be a stranger to this world's culture. Why does he say you should live here in reverent fear, though? I think he means you should be afraid of becoming or remaining like this culture, since God will impartially judge everyone's work. God will judge those who belong to this culture, and also judge those who have adopted this culture — believers who live like the world's citizens.

In his second letter he writes, "Dear friends, I urge you, as aliens and strangers in the world, to abstain from sinful desires, which war against your soul" (2 Pet. 2:11). This is similar to the previous verse, which said to live as strangers in reverent fear. How do you do it? By abstaining from sinful desires, as this verse states. Living by your sinful desires is part of this world's culture, but you do not belong to this culture.

Now, back to our original analogy: you are an alien on this planet. If you do what the citizens of this planet do, it will be harmful or fatal to you. If you, as an alien, eat this planet's "food," you will die. The inhabitants of this planet live by indulging their sinful desires. Doing so does not affect their condition because they belong to this world and will perish with it; they are already sinful. As a temporary visitor to this planet, however, you have a different nature and cannot indulge your sinful desires without harming yourself.

Notice that Peter said to abstain from sinful desires, not just sinful acts. If you believe you are okay as long as you don't "do anything wrong," you are in big trouble. The emphasis of the Old Testament was on behavior: it is okay to do this, but thou shalt not do that. Jesus made it very clear that He was raising the standard and placing the emphasis on your attitudes instead of your actions. We understand now that your attitudes determine your actions, that you can perform all the right actions but still have a stinking attitude. Christianity is a relationship with God, not a legalistic set of rules.

How can you abstain from sinful desires? I think you first must realize that it is not a sin to be tempted or to have a sinful thought. Jesus was tempted, but He did not sin. You cannot prevent thoughts from entering your mind, because everything around you triggers thoughts, but you can prevent those thoughts from staying in your mind. Someone said you cannot keep the birds from flying around you, but you can prevent them from building a nest on your head.

The real issue is how you respond to inappropriate thoughts. For instance, you suddenly remember what that person said and how they hurt your feelings. How do you respond to that memory? Do you review the details and refresh the feelings of pain and anger? Do you think about how they had no right to treat you that way, or how you have every right to be angry? Do you hope they get what they deserve, that someone will do something to hurt them, and maybe that someone will be you? Do you think about how cruel or thoughtless they are? If you thought any of these after you remembered the incident, you blew it because you were indulging your self-centeredness, the source of your evil desires. If you really do not know how to respond to such a memory, you should read (or reread) the previous chapters.

Peter says your sinful desires war against your soul, the essence of your character, the real you. Sinful desires do not war against the souls of the citizens of the world, because their souls are sinful and they willingly indulge the desires. But sinful desires do war against your redeemed nature. Some Christians are even voluntary POW's in this war, having surrendered to the enemy and to their carnal desires. We call them carnal Christians, believers who prefer the world's culture to that of their homeland.

Imagine for a moment that your country is at war and you are on the staff of your country's embassy in the enemy nation. If you began sympathizing with the enemy's cause, someone on staff immediately would confront you. If you began associating with the citizens of the country or adopting their customs, your superiors would severely reprimand and maybe even dismiss you. If you condoned the enemy's actions or participated in them, you would be branded a traitor. Yet most Christians are very tolerant of "carnal" behavior. They are so accustomed to living in this world that they are comfortable here and act like its citizens. What a tragedy!

In the Book of Revelation, God addresses the churches and to one of them he makes a very comforting promise. "Since you have kept my command to endure patiently, I will also keep you from the hour of trial that is going to come upon the whole world to test those who live on the earth" (Rev. 3:10). This makes a distinction between Christians and "those who live on the earth." It says an hour of trial is coming on the citizens of this world.

A certain phrase appears several times in Revelation to define those who live on the earth: "the inhabitants of the earth." We find the souls of martyrs in heaven asking how long it will be before the Lord will judge the inhabitants of the earth and avenge their blood (Rev. 6:10). In one of the major prophetic sequences, the seven trumpets, there is a dire warning to the inhabitants of the earth because of the events that are about to occur (Rev. 8:13). All inhabitants of the earth will worship the beast of Revelation chapter 13 and be deceived (Rev. 13:8, 12, 14). The "inhabitants of the earth" clearly does not include true Christians. If you are a believer, you are not an inhabitant of this earth and this is not your home.

A friend once told me she grew up in a slum and, although she now lives in a nice suburb, she still feels comfortable in the slums. She knows she does not belong in a slum anymore, but she feels at home there. Likewise, you may feel at home here on this planet, but you do not belong here. That is why you must reprogram your thinking, to convince yourself that you are no longer "of the world."

The Old Testament contains a story with almost fairy tale qualities, about a young woman who was in slavery with her people in a foreign country. The king of that country banished the queen from the throne because of her disobedience, then authorized a search for a beautiful young woman to replace her. As you probably guessed, the story is about a young woman named Esther.

Esther was removed from her home and taken to the palace. She no longer belonged in the community where she had lived and it would have been unacceptable for her to continue living there. She now belonged to the king.

She had 12 months of beauty treatments to condition and perfume her skin. These were expensive treatments designed for their long-term effects, not just daily makeup to make her look nice that day. Her complexion was no longer left to chance, and every effort was made to guarantee a beautiful complexion. It was now unacceptable for her to have an ordinary complexion.

She had special foods and could no longer eat foods that had undesirable effects — weight problems, body odor or blemishes. She now had to appeal to the king by looking good, feeling good and smelling good.

She was free to choose any clothes or jewelry she wanted to wear when she presented herself to the king. She could no longer dress like a commoner. She could not even lay around the palace in her comfortable home clothes and dress up for dinner. That was no longer acceptable. Esther was no longer a commoner. She belonged to an earthly king.

Now, consider this: one of Jesus' titles is "King of kings," which means He is higher than any other king. You do not belong to yourself anymore; rather, you belong to the greatest king of all. It is not acceptable for you to continue living like a commoner.

I am not suggesting you should live in the biggest house, drive the most prestigious car and wear only high-fashion clothes. These are the priorities of the world system, the system you were redeemed from. These so-called treasures are so unimportant in God's kingdom they are not even worth considering.

My point is that you do not belong in the world system anymore. It is now unacceptable for you to have the same standards, priorities and goals as the world. It is unacceptable for you to continue acting like them and have the same attitudes.

You have been redeemed from the world system and you no longer belong here. You are now an alien to this world.

Conclusion

You are a natural citizen of heaven. Your roots are there and that is your culture. You are living temporarily in this world and you will eventually leave and return home. You are strange by the world's standards and, because your culture is different, the world's citizens are prejudiced against you; you will experience their hatred, harassment and rejection. You are an ambassador here, representing God and bringing His message to the world.

You must retain your heavenly citizenship by abstaining from sinful desires (desires, not just acts). If you adopt this world's culture, you make yourself vulnerable to God's judgment. You need to change the way you think about this world. Keep reminding yourself that you are an alien living temporarily in a human body. You do not belong here and living like a citizen of this world can be fatal. Instead, you should eagerly anticipate the Lord's return, when He will take you to your homeland: heaven.

Personal Study

1. "If you belonged to the world, it would love you as its own" (John 15:19). If unbelievers are comfortable around you because you think and act like they do, not because they are drawn by your godly nature, then you still live as if you "belonged to the world."

   - Which of your attitudes and practices belong to the world system?

   - What specific steps can you take to replace them with attitudes and behavior of God's kingdom?

2. "That is why the world hates you." (John 15:19).

   - Are there any indications that unbelievers oppose you or reject you due to your exemplary lifestyle? Do not include their response to any "holier than thou" attitude you have demonstrated.

3.   "They think it strange that you do not plunge with them into the same flood of dissipation, and they heap abuse on you" (1 Pet. 4:4).

- Identify specific instances of people abusing you verbally or otherwise because you chose not to participate in their ungodly behavior.

- How did you feel when they treated you that way and how should you have felt?

- In what ways have you tried to conform your behavior as much as possible to make yourself acceptable without actually "doing anything wrong" as you see it?

7

An Integrated Guidance System

When I was in high school, my Dad owned an airplane—a single-engine, four-passenger plane. As a family, we did some local pleasure flying as well as cross-country flying on vacations. I never had any interest in getting a pilot's license, but I sometimes navigated for him and even did a little flying, with his help, of course. During that time I learned the importance of having a good guidance system, including instruments and maps, which would help you arrive at your destination.

Airplanes have a variety of instruments the pilot can use to keep the airplane flying at the desired altitude and on the correct heading. There is a compass to show which direction you are flying, an artificial horizon to make sure your wings are level and an altimeter to show your current altitude. Another instrument shows your rate of ascent or descent, so you can fly at a constant altitude, or climb or descend at an appropriate rate. Some small planes have a special receiver that locks on electronic beacons positioned around the country; you can navigate by flying from one beacon to another, and the receiver on your airplane shows whether you are flying directly toward the beacon you have selected. There also is an autopilot that uses the instruments to fly the plane for you. You might say the autopilot comprises an integrated guidance system because it uses many different sources of information to guide the airplane's flight.

People also need guidance systems. Christians in particular often want to know God's will for their lives and might expend a lot of effort to determine what God wants them to do. What am I supposed to do with my life? What should I do about a particular situation? How can I know what God wants me to do?

I suggest that God has given you several sources of information that form an integrated guidance system, and I call it an "integrated" system because all the inputs work together to provide guidance. It is not my intent in this chapter to address the topic of guidance in depth, but rather to help you change your thinking about certain elements of guidance. Before we consider those, however, let us briefly examine the three main elements God uses to provide guidance.

The primary and most important element of guidance is the Bible. In it, God reveals His will for mankind and believers in particular, including basic principles that will help you make everyday decisions. If you are short on money this month and you wonder whether you should rob a bank to pay your bills, your knowledge of the Bible should help you decide against robbing a bank; that is basic guidance. The Bible is the objective standard for all of life's decisions. It is objective because it is based on eternal principles and is not distorted by feelings, prejudices or circumstances. It is the standard by which you must judge everything else.

Scripture sometimes states God's intent very clearly. For example, consider the following scripture: God "has committed to us the message of reconciliation. We are therefore Christ's ambassadors, as though God were making his appeal through us" (2 Cor. 5:19-20). Why did God commit the message to us? So we can serve as Christ's ambassadors to the world, representing Him and appealing to men on His behalf. The purpose is clear.

People would like to believe that God does not exist; or if He does exist, He is not terribly concerned with what happens down here on earth; or if He is concerned, He has to accept what we do because He gave us a free will. The Bible is very clear, however, that God has a purpose, that His will is for everything to support that purpose, and that everything He gives you enables you to do your part in fulfilling His purpose.

Romans 8:28 states that, "in all things God works for the good of those who love him, who have been called *according to his purpose*" (emphasis added). Ephesians 1:11 clearly states that he "works out everything in conformity with the *purpose of his will*" (emphasis added). This means your very salvation is evidence you have a role in fulfilling God's purpose. Well, if you have a significant role, how do you know what it is? How do you know what God wants you to do? The Bible provides critical insight to God's will and if you do not know what the Bible says, you cannot begin to know his will. The Bible is the most important element of guidance and all other elements must conform to it.

The second important element of guidance is the Holy Spirit himself, a subjective witness. He is subjective in the sense that He shows you how to apply God's principles and will in your particular situation. He serves as a witness of God's will because He knows what it is and confirms it to you. Probably the most common way the Holy Spirit provides guidance is by providing you with a sense of peace. If you choose to do God's will, you can expect to have an internal sense that what you are about to do is "right," independent of your state of mind. Conversely, if you choose to do something opposed to God's will, you can expect a lack of internal peace or even a disturbance. As you develop your own spirit, it will also let you know whether you are adhering to proper standards; we usually call this your conscience. The Holy Spirit also directs you by giving you impressions, hunches and spontaneous thoughts, so learn to recognize them as potential elements of guidance, too.

The third important element is circumstances. These are situations God coordinates to confirm His will and assist you in doing it. There are no accidents in life, because God is all-powerful and causes everything to ultimately conform to His will. If what you are doing is God's will, you can expect him to work out the details, often without your involvement.

God may also use angels, dreams, visions, revelation, prophecy and signs to provide guidance, but you should always be certain that the three most important elements confirm it. All elements of guidance from God work together, which is why I refer to an "integrated guidance system."

In addition to these elements, I suggest that God has given you something very fundamental that also reveals His will for you. In fact, this is so basic that you may have difficulty recognizing it at first as an element of guidance.

Your Character

We can often identify God's will simply by considering what He gives us, because He always has a purpose for what He gives. You probably have never considered your character as a source of guidance; a source of aggravation, maybe, but never guidance. But let us consider the fact that God gave you your character, and then the possibility that God intends for your character to guide you.

There are some significant scripture passages that list various character aptitudes; one such passage is in Romans chapter 12. You need to realize that God gave your gifts or aptitudes to you and that you can only use them properly if you change the way you think. Paul writes:

> *Do not conform any longer to the pattern of this world, but be transformed by the renewing of your mind. Then you will be able to test and approve what God's will is—his good, pleasing and perfect will. For by the grace given me I say to every one of you: Do not think of yourself more highly than you ought, but rather think of yourself with sober judgment, in accordance with the measure of faith God has given you. Just as each of us has one body with many members, and these members do not all have the same function, so in Christ we who are many form one body, and each member belongs to all the others. We have different gifts, according to the grace given us* (Rom. 12:2-6).

Paul then lists the operation of several character types, such as prophesying, serving, teaching and encouraging. His statement about renewing your mind is in the context of God's will for your life, the grace and measure of faith He has given you, and the different gifts He has given you to perform your role for the benefit of others, not for personal consumption or enjoyment. This clearly states that what God gave you was grace, a God-given ability that enables you to do God's will. These character types are gifts in the sense that we are to offer our abilities to those who need them. That means the gift is for the person you serve; it is not God's gift *to* you, but rather God's gift *through* you.

In First Corinthians, Paul again speaks of such gifts and provides another list, which includes the message of wisdom, faith, miraculous powers, and others. He again identifies them as different kinds of gifts from God. He states we are to use them for the common good, which means for the benefit of others. And as if to emphasize his point, he states that God gives these gifts "to each man, just as he determines" (1 Cor. 12:11). Later in the same chapter, after using the analogy of a body with many interdependent parts, he provides still another list of character types. In that context he writes, "And in the church God has appointed first of all apostles, second prophets," and so on (v. 28). That is, God has appointed you to your role among believers, in the church, as a part of the "body." He doesn't need to be any clearer about the source and purpose of your character.

In Ephesians, Paul provides a list we often call the "five-fold ministries." Whether you consider this a list of offices or character types is almost irrelevant, because God gives people the character they need to perform His will. Introducing the list, Paul writes, "It was [Christ] who gave some to be apostles," and so on (Eph. 4:11). The Greek phrase translated "gave some" is difficult to translate literally without using a lot of explanation. The Amplified Bible explains that God gave a variety of gifts and that God Himself appointed and gave men to serve us in various roles. As in the previous passages, it is clear that God gave you your basic character type so you can fulfill His plan for your life by using it for the benefit of others. Your character is God's gift to those around you.

Paul recognized this principle and stated that God gave him authority as an apostle to build people up (2 Cor. 10:8). God had a reason for giving Paul such authority, and Paul understood it.

What do you have in mind when you give someone a gift? You want them to like it and find it useful. You are disappointed if they don't like it or haven't learned how to use it. What is your purpose in sending your kids to college; just getting them out of the house? No. You send them to college because you want them to learn something useful that will help them get a job and perform well.

What do you suppose God had in mind when He gave you your character? That you will learn to use it as He intended and become effective as the person He made you.

This really is a matter of functional design; you give your creation what it needs to operate the way you intend. Boats have props and rudders, for example, not tires. Cars are not designed to pull water skiers, so there is nowhere to attach a ski rope. Airplanes are not designed to dive underwater, and you don't put jet engines on a sub because they don't work underwater. You design each vehicle to do the task required of it efficiently.

If human intelligence enables us to design vehicles well, God is smart enough to design you for the task He has for you. Consider the equipment He gave you, and it will tell you a lot about what He expects of you.

I am of average height and am relatively small. I can be certain God does not intend for me to be a basketball player, football line-backer or sumo wrestler. I am analytical, a loner, a thinker, and I enjoy developing and improving things. So it is also clear that I would not be effective as an assembly line worker, sales clerk or receptionist; God didn't give me character traits suitable for those jobs. My point is this: identify the skills and abilities God gave you, because they reveal much about God's intent for your life.

The same reasoning applies to short-term issues as well. If a friend's water pipe broke and water damaged their home and furnishings, what should you do? If they cannot afford the repairs and God has made you financially generous, isn't it reasonable to conclude that God wants you to offer them financial assistance? Or if He made you a skilled workman, shouldn't you consider repairing the damage? As an encourager, you could help them put their trust in God. As an administrator, you could arrange for workmen to perform the repairs. That is, God expects you to use what He gave you to serve others.

What I have described here is a general principle and obviously does not apply to every situation. God occasionally asks us to go beyond ourselves, to do the unnatural, simply because He wants to demonstrate our limitations and His infinite ability. In general, however, you can consider your character as an element of guidance, because it reveals much of God's will for you.

In addition to your own character, godly character also serves as an element of guidance. It is clear from the Bible that God intends for you to be developing your character to become like His. He tells us, "Be completely humble and gentle" (Eph. 4:2), which is totally foreign to your former sinful nature. Later in the same chapter, He says to "put off your old self" and "put on the new self, created to be like God in true righteousness and holiness" (Eph. 4:22-24).

In Philippians chapter 2, God says your attitude "should be the same as that of Christ Jesus: Who. . . made himself nothing, taking the very nature of a servant" (Phil. 2:5-7). This describes an attitude of service based on humility. He also lists some of the character traits that result from developing His nature: "love, joy, peace, patience, kindness, goodness, faithfulness, gentleness and self-control" (Gal. 5:22).

How does this apply to the topic of guidance? God has made it clear that you should be developing His character traits and using them. So when you have a decision to make or have an opportunity to respond to a situation, what should you do? Use the aptitudes God gave you but be motivated by godly character traits.

Go back to our example of a friend's broken water pipe. If you are the financially generous one, do you flaunt your wealth by insisting they accept your money, or in humility make it available to your friend? If you are the skilled worker, do you repair the damage because you enjoy doing that kind of work, or because this is an opportunity to serve your friend? As an encourager, do you emotionally stroke the person only to make them feel better, or do you impart godly joy and peace in a disturbing situation? As an administrator, do you take care of the details just because you want to ensure that things are done "right," or do you serve your friend by having the work done the way they want?

The Book of Philippians challenges us to have the same attitude as Jesus, who was willing to lay aside His status, position, authority and power to become a human. That would be roughly equivalent to you becoming a grain of sand. His purpose was to win your salvation; again, everything God does conforms to His purpose. Then Philippians describes how believers should respond to His example: "continue to work out your salvation with fear and trembling, for it is God who works in you to will and to act according to his good purpose" (Phil. 2:12-13). That statement is very relevant to our topic of guidance and our overall topic of transforming your mind.

He says to continue working out your own salvation. In general, salvation means the same to everyone, but the fine print reveals that it has unique ramifications for each individual. A simple example might be that godliness requires an introvert to become a little more assertive at appropriate times and an extrovert to be a little less assertive at times. Working out the fine print of your salvation is a process that is as unique as you are.

Why should you work out your salvation with "fear and trembling"? Probably because self-centeredness makes you want to be in control everything, including the process of becoming like Jesus. It should be obvious you cannot make yourself like Him, and that becoming like Him requires the death of sinful attitudes and behavior, so you should be greatly concerned that your efforts to work out your salvation might be directed by self-centeredness.

Another very significant part of this verse is, "for it is God who works in you to will and to act according to his good purpose." This means God works in you, developing His character in you, so your will and actions conform to His good purpose. This does not make you a puppet or robot. As your nature becomes more like His as a result of Him working in you, you voluntarily conform to His purpose.

We see this idea reinforced in the following statement: "by his power he may fulfill every good purpose of *yours* and every act prompted by *your* faith (2 Thess. 1:11, emphasis added). As you come to understand God's purpose in a given situation, you apply yourself by using the motivations and skills He gave you. God's purpose has now become your purpose and you begin acting on what your faith tells you God will do. God then will fulfill *your* purpose and respond to *your* faith. In effect, you have accepted ownership of God's purpose, so He cooperates with you and supports you.

Your character aptitudes (those skills and abilities God gave you) and your godly character traits (those traits of God's character you are developing) are useful as elements of guidance. You might say your character aptitudes indicate what you should do, and the godly traits indicate how you should do it. That is the essence of guidance.

The Old Testament primarily emphasized action and specifically obedience to God's Law. The New Testament places much greater emphasis on who we are. We recognize that who we are determines what we do and how we do it. The New Testament instructs us on what we should do, but a significant number of those instructions also relate to who we are and who we should become.

We see examples of God's will being specific, such as it being God's will that Paul go to Rome (Rom. 1:10) and people supporting Paul "in keeping with God's will" (2 Cor. 8:5). In these cases, God's will related to a specific person, place and time. More frequently in the New Testament, we see God's will described in broader terms.

"It is God's will that you should be holy; that you should avoid sexual immorality; that each of you should learn to control his own body in a way that is holy and honorable" (1 Thess. 4:3-4). Also, "Be joyful always; pray continually; give thanks in all circumstances, for this is God's will for you in Christ Jesus" (1 Thess. 5:16-18). It is "God's will that by doing good you should silence the ignorant talk of foolish men" (1 Pet. 2:15). We see that it may be God's will to suffer for doing good and for being a Christian (1 Pet. 3:17; 4:19).

What is God's will for you? He wants you to develop godly character, use the abilities He gave you and live the way He would in your situation. He places great importance on who you are and who you should become.

Other Believers

Another instrument God has given you for guidance is other believers. You may not have any problem asking others for their opinions or advice, but God requires us to be more interdependent than that. And when it comes to receiving guidance, we need to made radical changes in the way we view each other.

There has never been another culture quite like ours. As Americans, we enjoy personal freedoms and liberties very few around the world or throughout history have experienced. We have freedom of choice in most matters, including religion, property ownership, career, housing, entertainment and politics. This is a direct result of the nation's godly heritage, since the Bible is the foundation for such liberties and since God directed many of the early explorers, settlers and founding fathers.

For nearly 400 years people have come to this land to find freedom and opportunity, and for the last 200 years or so our nation has protected their right to do so. Especially since the 1960s, we have placed great emphasis on freedom of expression and personal rights. While these efforts have resulted in a unique culture and major progress in the area of human rights, we must recognize the adverse effects such a culture produces.

Our population has become highly mobile, due in part to the quality of our roads and our ability to use quality communication systems to locate better jobs almost anywhere in the nation. Technology has created vast markets of laborsaving and entertainment devices, and our transportation systems deliver them throughout the nation. We have become a nation of consumers, enjoying the benefits of our culture.

These and other factors have molded us into a nation of rugged individualists. Fiercely jealous of our privileged condition, we have taken it for granted and have become intensely focused on ourselves. Because this is such a major part of our culture, we hardly give it a thought.

Building on a foundation of biblical principles regarding individual liberty, we have become a nation of people who are radical about our right to do whatever we please. If we return to the Bible to discover God's intent for us, however, we discover a principle of interdependence or mutual accountability.

How many red flags go up in your Western cultural mind at the mention of accountability? The concept almost violates our understanding of personal liberties. Does God really expect us to be accountable to each other? If He does, and if we want to please Him, then we need to make some radical changes in our thinking.

Because there is such a wide variety of people and each views the world through their own personality, it is not unusual for people to respond very differently to a given situation. We each have different motivations, different priorities, different interpretations or applications of scripture, and so on. It is a wise person who realizes that he does not see or comprehend all truth, and that he can benefit from the perspectives and opinions of others. I believe God set it up this way so we can work together and serve each other; people in general, and believers in particular, are interdependent. We need each other. That is one reason the Bible addresses such topics as mutual submission.

In the Book of Ephesians, Paul elaborates on how we are to live as children of God. Right in the middle of his remarks, he states, "Submit to one another out of reverence for Christ" (Eph. 5:21). The key Greek word in this verse, *hypotasso*, is a verb that has to do with putting things in order or in their place, and includes the idea of subjection and submission.

The New Testament uses the word in a variety of applications: demons submitting to believers (Luke 10:17), slaves to masters (Titus 2:9; 1 Pet. 2:18), believers to governing authorities (Rom. 13:1, 5; Titus 3:1; 1 Pet. 2:13), wives to husbands (Eph. 5:24; Col. 3:18; Titus 2:5; 1 Pet. 3:1), young men to older men (1 Pet. 5:5), believers to those who serve the saints (1 Cor. 16:16), and everything to Jesus (1 Cor. 15:28; Eph. 1:22; Heb. 2:5; 1 Pet. 3:22). This is the primary word the New Testament uses for submitting, subjecting, or bringing under control; and as you can see, it includes all forms of enforced and voluntary subordination.

Christians are not to submit to the state because it protects them and enables them to live freely, but because God established government and selects governmental leaders. Christian wives are not to submit to their husbands to promote a patriarchal structure, but because doing so provides a living image of the church submitting to Christ, and as such may even win their husbands to the Lord. Slaves are not to submit to their masters because God honors slavery, but because they are in no position to abolish it. Notice that every one of these reasons is independent of the culture; for the believer, submission is a higher law.

Now we come back to the original verse, "Submit to one another out of reverence for Christ." The rule here is that you must be ready to abandon your will for the benefit of other believers, out of reverence for Jesus who died for them.

Submitting is not the same as agreeing or compromising. When you agree with someone, there is no need to change your mind. When you compromise, you retain some power for use later, when it is the other person's turn to compromise. Whether you agree or compromise, you retain some control; submitting, however, is relinquishing control. The real issue is how you respond when you seriously disagree.

You may be struggling about now with the idea of submitting to other believers. Does God mean all believers? In all situations? Even when they are wrong? Isn't that impractical, even foolish?

It might be worth your time to examine the scriptures listed above to identify any conditions for submitting. You won't find any. God calls for us to submit, period. And you can submit only when you disagree.

Telling us to submit to one another is basically the same as telling us to serve one another, to love one another with *agape*, to avoid offending one another, to deny ourselves, to lay down our lives for one another. Submitting to other believers has several benefits. For one, it forces you to confront your self-centeredness and deal with your carnal beliefs. It allows others to develop their aptitudes and become mature as they serve you. It also creates a sense of community and cooperation with other believers.

You may not be ready to submit to other believers out of reverence for Christ. If not, it is better to honestly appraise yourself, than reluctantly agree to submit but have no intention of doing so. As with all of God's commands, you have the freedom to choose obedience. And because some of His commands impose severe spiritual tests, most people are unwilling to obey them. The command to submit to each other probably fits in that category.

It may not always be obvious, but there is always a benefit or solid justification for each of God's commands. Understanding how God works and recognizing His goals for humanity may lead you to conclude that the more difficult commands have greater bene-

fits. Being willing to destroy your sinful mindset is the most difficult commitment that God can demand of you. Yet doing so will
produce the greatest benefits in your present life and your future one.
Therefore, the most difficult commands to obey have the greatest
payoff.

It is significant that the Bible does not say that one believer
should be under another, as in defeat or dominance; being submis-
sive is not the same as being dominated. The Bible uses the Greek
word *hypo* to describe defeat or dominance. A centurion said he was
under authority and had soldiers under him (Matt. 8:9). God will put
His enemies under Jesus' feet (Matt. 22:44), and Jesus will reign
until He does (1 Cor. 15:25). These are examples of people domi-
nating (*hypo*) someone else. The Bible does not advocate that kind
of relationship among believers.

You can even see logically that submitting is not the same as
accepting defeat or domination. Submitting is voluntary. If you feel
like giving in because you have no choice, then you are still struggling for control and not submitting.

The command to submit to other believers will at times violate
your understanding, your will and your ability. That is because it
strikes at the heart of your sinful way of thinking. To relinquish
control is to deny the demands of your self-centeredness, which is
why submitting to other believers is so important.

Before we move to the next topic, maybe you noticed that the
list of those who submit did not include children submitting to their
parents. If you were wondering, the Bible tells children to obey their
parents. The root Greek word means to hear or listen, so to obey
means to do what you hear someone say. The New Testament uses
this word for children obeying their parents (Eph. 6:1; Col. 3:20),
slaves obeying their masters (Eph. 6:5; Col. 3:22), the wind and
waves obeying Jesus (Mark 4:41) and evil spirits obeying Jesus
(Mark 1:27).

What is the difference between submitting and obeying? The
answer may lie in the person's ability to choose. If a person does
what he is told because he has no choice, then he has obeyed. If he
chooses to do what he is told, then he has submitted. If a person has
never learned to obey, it may not be possible for him to submit. In a

related thought, one responsibility of parents is to help their children progress from obedience to submission; if the child never learns to submit, the parents may have to insist on obedience alone.

Paul's statement, "Submit to one another out of reverence for Christ," identifies an important element of your integrated guidance system. You must consider more than one of your guidance "instruments" before making a decision; the more important the decision, the more "instruments" you should use.

Consider an analogy for a moment. You are walking toward the front door of your home just before dark and you see someone standing on your porch. It is too dark to identify them, so your immediate reaction is to protect yourself, possibly by running away. Then the person on your porch speaks to you and by their voice you recognize them as your best friend. Running away would not have been the best response, but with only partial information you might have done it. You need more than one bit of information to make a good decision.

Similarly, if you want to make a decision that honors God, you generally will be more successful if you submit to other believers, rather than relying only on your own perspective. You would be wise to recognize the value of other people's perspectives and knowledge of God.

Let's go back to our broken water pipe example. Maybe you are the financially generous person and you are motivated by true humility to give them the money they need. But another Christian, who is aware of the situation, believes it is God's intent for the person with the financial need to bring their spending habits under control so they can afford to repair the damage. Or maybe you are the one who wants to serve them by arranging for the repairs. But another believer thinks God wants the person to grow up and exercise some initiative of their own.

As Christians, we must learn to submit to one another out of reverence for Christ. Christ gave other believers different motivations and perspectives, which can be invaluable to you when you need to make a decision. Keep in mind that submitting is voluntarily laying your own conclusions and interests aside when you disagree with another.

Having said that, I again need to identify this as a general principle God at times will supersede. From personal experience and observation, I know that God occasionally will ask someone to do something that violates conventional wisdom; but those instances are somewhat rare. If that ever happens to you, make absolutely certain you are operating in humility and be very, very, very certain of your other elements of guidance before you choose not to submit to the counsel of other believers.

God placed you in interdependent relationships with other believers and tells you to submit to them out of reverence for Him. The motivations, perspectives and experience of other believers can be an invaluable element of guidance.

The Bible tells believers to instruct one another, to help one another settle disputes, to serve one another, to rebuke one another with wisdom, to encourage one another and to build one another up. Repeatedly the Bible says for us to love one another. That means you are to consider the other person's needs and interests a higher priority than your own. That will motivate you to do what others need at the time, whether they need a hug or a reprimand, assistance or encouragement to do it on their own.

This also means you must be ready to receive the same expressions of love from others. Accept their instruction, rebuke, advice, encouragement and so on. The relationships you have with other believers are those of an extended family. God has given us each other for assistance and protection. We need each other at all times, including when we are wanting guidance from the Lord.

An Example

Let's put it all together and consider a typical, major question many Christians ask. How can you discover which job God wants you to have?

First, you need to be familiar enough with the Bible to know God's basic standards for His people. That alone eliminates a lot of career choices, such as jewel thief, stripper or drug pusher. Those are definitely out. Realizing that God has given you natural talents, you would be wise to identify those talents and consider which employment opportunities might require them. So far you have two criteria: what is biblically appropriate and what is suitable for your abilities.

Now you are ready to start job hunting. As you consider job possibilities, keep your "spiritual ears" open; that is, be alert to any impressions and such that might be coming from the Holy Spirit, but primarily look for the presence or absence of internal peace. Listen to comments from other believers, as well, because they not only see your situation from a different perspective, they know Scripture and can hear the Holy Spirit, too.

Look for God to make opportunities available, but not just the spectacular ones. God works through innumerable means we would consider typical or mundane, such as employment agencies and classified ads. Rest assured that God can put you where He wants you, but He will guide you only if you are making an effort. You cannot steer a parked car; likewise, God cannot give you peace about what you are about to do if you are doing nothing.

Also, consider your motivation. Are you looking only for a high-paying job because there are so many expensive purchases you want to make? Are you trying to "wow" the job interviewer with your awesome job qualifications? Are you looking for a department full of pagans so you can personally win them all to the Lord? This is a good time for a motivation check. If your primary interest in looking for a job is how it will benefit you, you are clearly being motivated by self-centeredness, which is a sin. If that is the case, you should wonder how much God will work in your behalf to give you the job He wants you to have.

On the other hand, developing godly character traits such as humility, selfless love for others, faithfulness, kindness and goodness will benefit your career in at least three ways. First, you enable God to work more freely on your behalf; God cannot and will not bless efforts directed by ungodly attitudes as much as those motivated by godly character. Second, although people in the world system say you must promote or sell yourself to prospective employers, even nonbelievers admire people with godly character and consider them desirable employees. Third, having the same attitude as Jesus will motivate you to expend yourself for the benefit of others, serving them more effectively, instead of just putting in your time in exchange for a paycheck. This could affect your choice of jobs and cause you to be a superior employee.

This is a brief example of how God uses the various elements of guidance to show you His will. The exact way He leads you will be appropriate to your character, your maturity and His will. God has equipped you with aptitudes and motivations that uniquely qualify you for the role He has for you. That is why you can discover much about God's intent for you simply by examining yourself to identify the character He gave you. As you develop godly character traits and choose to be motivated by them rather than sinful desires, God's will becomes increasingly obvious in each situation.

Conclusion

God has a purpose and His will is that everything support that purpose. He reveals His general will and purpose through the Bible, which we should consider an objective standard for all decisions and actions. His Spirit helps us understand how to apply scriptural principles to our situations and assures us with peace when we make good decisions. He also works out the details of our circumstances to assure and assist us.

Everything God gives you (including your character) enables you to do your part in fulfilling His purpose. Therefore, God's will is for you to develop your character and use it; that is why He gave it to you. You need to change how you view your character and consider it a major revelation of God's will for you.

God places you in interdependent relationships with other believers. As they serve you in love and you submit to them out of respect for God, they will help you understand God's guidance. Because they have different aptitudes and motivations than you do, you can gain a great advantage by carefully considering what they say. This means you need to change how you view their character, as well as your own.

Personal Study

Assume you need to find a new place to live and you want to honor God with your choice.

- How should Bible passages relating to the following topics influence you?
  a. God's basic standards for His people.
  b. Your responsibilities for yourself and family.
  c. Financial principles.
  d. Principles of Christian community.

- How does recognizing your God-given abilities affect the kind of home you choose?

- How should you expect the Holy Spirit to help you find a suitable place?

- How should godly character traits influence you in the following situations?
  a. Identifying the features you look for in a home.
  b. Working with a real estate agent.
  c. Negotiating with the owner or landlord.

- How should each of the following circumstances influence your decision?
  a. The neighborhood or schools may not be a good influence on your children.
  b. The price is just slightly beyond your ability to pay.
  c. You have been looking for a long time. Suddenly you find a house that has everything you wanted and you are the first prospective buyer to look at it, but the schools may not be a good influence on your children and the price is just slightly beyond your ability to pay.

- In what areas might it be beneficial to seek advice from other believers when looking for and selecting a new home?

8

Personal Success

It has been said that the Old Testament is a covenant of prosperity in which God blessed His people materially so they would be successful in the world. On the other hand, the New Testament has been called a covenant of adversity, in which God asks His people to deny themselves worldly success so they will be successful in His kingdom. There are also those who insist that God blesses His people today with material wealth as He did in the Old Testament; after all, the New Testament refers to God lavishing riches on His children.

What should we expect from God today? Does He pour immeasurable wealth on His people, or does He consider poverty a virtue? What does God have in mind when the New Testament refers to riches? What are the blessings of the new covenant? What are the evidences of a successful New Testament believer?

Deuteronomy 8:18 is an important and often-quoted verse: "But remember the Lord your God, for it is he who gives you the ability to produce wealth, and so confirms his covenant, which he swore to your forefathers, as it is today." This verse reminds us that God gives us the ability to produce wealth, which is an important reminder to any believer who would feel proud of his accomplishments. The blessings and curses of the covenant described in Deuteronomy—the Mosaic covenant—related to success by the world's standards:

healthy crops and flocks, protection from enemies, prosperous work and so on.

Many people would extend the material prosperity of the Mosaic covenant into the new covenant that Jesus initiated. They point to such scriptures as 3 John 2: "Beloved, I wish above all things that thou mayest prosper and be in health, even as thy soul prospereth" (KJV). Another significant verse is 1 Corinthians 16:2, "Upon the first day of the week let every one of you lay by him in store, as God hath prospered him, that there be no gatherings when I come" (KJV), which clearly states that God prospers His people materially. And there are many verses that address God's riches, which He gives to His people.

I agree that we are no longer bound by the law of the Old Testament, because Jesus fulfilled that law. And because Jesus took the curse of the law upon Himself, we do not receive the curse if we violate the law. But does that mean that only the blessings of the Mosaic covenant remain for us today? I don't think that is a valid conclusion.

The Mosaic covenant was only one of a series of covenants between God and man recorded in the Old Testament. God also made covenants with Abraham and David, for example. He made another national covenant with the Israelites after the Mosaic covenant before they entered the Promised Land. The Old Testament prophets inform us that He will make still another covenant with Israel in the future (see Jeremiah 31:31-40). Each of these covenants supersedes earlier ones and brings Israel to a closer relationship with God.

In the same way, Jesus' new covenant supersedes all other covenants for those who choose to accept it. The old covenants between God and man provided either blessings or curses, and the man's performance determined which he received. The new covenant, instead, is based on God's grace and our performance is a response to God's grace, rather than a method for earning blessings. Those who would cling to the blessings of the old covenants also overlook the fact that Jesus changed the emphasis from a person's external performance to his internal condition. In essence, Jesus made it more difficult to honor the covenant by escalating the requirements. Refraining from murder is no longer sufficient; now hatred is also forbidden. Not only is adultery taboo, but so is lust. Jesus taught that a man's actions and external condition are not what make him righteous or sinful; this is the result of his internal condition. We recognize that what you are determines what you do, and Jesus shifted the emphasis to who you are.

In fact, the new covenant is entirely new, not just partially, so it has its own blessings and curses. It is reasonable, then, for the new covenant to have different standards for wealth and success than the old covenants. The new covenant even has a different purpose. It transforms people into the image of God, developing His character in them so they can perform His work in heaven and on earth, whereas the old covenants were intended primarily to establish a national presence on earth. Because the purposes, structures and requirements of the old and new covenants are radically different, you should not be surprised if their treatments of material wealth also are very different.

Even if His relationship with man changes with time, God Himself never changes. Neither do His standards. So how does God view material wealth? When He describes the New Jerusalem in Revelation 21, He says the wall is "made of jasper, and the city of pure gold, as pure as glass" (Rev. 21:18). Every kind of precious stone decorates the foundations of the city walls. Each of the 12 gates consists of a single pearl. The street of the city is pure gold, as transparent as glass. God has a very utilitarian view of precious stones and metals such as gold. He apparently considers them the equivalent of concrete, steel and asphalt.

People usually measure their worth by how much they possess, so material wealth is important to humans. But God has worth simply because of who He is. He is God almighty, the supreme being, totally complete in Himself. He needs no possessions to increase His worth, so material wealth has no value to Him. If for some reason He wants more gold or platinum or granite or coal, He can create however much He wants.

Because the new covenant transforms people into the image of God, it also changes their attitudes, standards, perspectives and values. So what should your attitude be toward wealth and success? You obviously should not have the same attitude as non-Christians, so let us examine the New Testament's position on material wealth and success.

There is an interesting list in Hebrews 11 that honors people for their faith. Some of those people voluntarily left what was rightfully theirs and others had it stripped from them. Some experienced mighty deliverance and others perished. Some experienced God's power to overcome and others His power to endure to the awful end. It is significant that everyone God honors in this list lived under one of the various old covenants, which considered worldly success and material wealth as evidence of God's blessing. Many were destitute, persecuted and mistreated, so by the standards of both the world and the covenant under which they lived, they would be considered failures. Yet God holds them up as examples for us.

Is God simply honoring them because they had such hard lives? Is He giving them honor as compensation for what they experienced? No, God honors those people because they had a different perspective than the rest of the world. They knew there was something better, that by comparison the wealth and prestige available in this world are worthless. They considered themselves aliens and strangers on earth, even misfits. Although they lived under a materialistic covenant with God, they laid aside the material blessings to search for something better, which they never found in their lifetime. If God honors them for that attitude under a materialistic covenant, how much more would He honor that attitude under the new covenant?

Defining Success

In our culture success usually wears a dollar sign. We expect real success to produce wealth and a person's wealth is often an indicator of their success. We consider success and wealth synonymous.

That kind of thinking limits the meaning of the word "success," however. I have a rather large dictionary that gives three basic definitions for success, and only one of them relates to material wealth. The other definitions include such themes as accomplishing a goal or fulfilling a standard. Although our culture currently focuses on wealth as an indication of success, it recognizes a much broader definition.

The Bible uses a Greek word group that connotes success, and a little background may help you understand the emphasis of the words. The root word refers to a path, a road, or a journey. Figuratively it describes a procedure or manner in which something is done. You would use the word to describe someone's path of life or manner of life, what they did or how they did it. One derivative is the word from which we get the English word "method." The root word and its derivatives generally relate to how one does something and have no direct bearing on material gain.

The word that interests us in this word group is a rarely used verb, a compound word. One segment of the word belongs to the word group we just described and refers to a way, a road or a manner of life. The other portion of the word means well or well done, as in Matthew 25:21: "Well done, good and faithful servant!" So the compound word means to lead on a good path, to guide well, to bring to a good conclusion, or to succeed. This word occurs in Romans 1:10: "I pray that now at last by God's will the way may be opened for me to come to you," or more literally, "I shall have a happy journey." His success is in achieving his desire to visit them; that would be a good conclusion, a desirable result.

Why should we give this word so much attention? Because it appears in two key verses, which we quoted earlier, that Christians sometimes use to support their belief in material prosperity. The King James Version translates this word "prosper," which causes dollar signs to dance in people's minds. As you can see, however, the word group itself has nothing to do with financial wealth.

Consider the following verse. "On the first day of every week, each one of you should set aside a sum of money in keeping with his income, saving it up, so that when I come no collections will have to be made" (1 Cor. 16:2). The New International Version reads, as quoted here, "in keeping with his income," where the King James Version reads "as God hath prospered him." The Greek text does not say God prospers or increases one's income, although we understand that He does.

The King James translators inserted God into the verse and slightly changed the meaning; as a result, many Christians today use this verse as evidence that God wants us rich. In the context, Paul is explaining how to take up an offering to send to the believers in Jerusalem, so he obviously is dealing with finances or material possessions. Each person was to give according to their ability to give. If their income allowed them to give only the smallest amount, that is what they should give. To use this verse to "prove" that God wants His people to be financially prosperous is to warp the verse's meaning.

The same key word appears in 3 John 2, which we also quoted earlier from the King James Version. This verse contains a variation on a customary wish for good health: "Dear friend, I pray that you may enjoy good health and that all may go well with you, even as your soul is getting along well." Here the key word translates as "go well with you" and "getting along well." Again, there is no direct reference to financial abundance. Paul is certainly not praying that God would financially reward this person because he has been a good man. Instead, he is praying that God would cause everything the man is and everything he does to lead him on a good path, to guide him well, to cause his efforts to succeed. Again, if this verse alludes to financial abundance, it does so very indirectly.

In life and particularly in business, success often leads to monetary gain, but monetary gain is certainly not the only form of success or evidence of it. Success relates to the way you do something. You can be a successful pauper, for example, meaning you get along very well without any money. Success relates to how good you are at what you do. That is the issue. To bring this back to our character study, if you are people-oriented, are you good at relating to people and interacting with them? If so, then you are a successful people-person.

Let us consider Jesus' stance on wealth. To do this, we need to consider another group of words translated "wealth" and "riches." The basic sense of these words is fullness of goods, whether the goods are tangible or intangible.

Jesus contrasts material wealth with spiritual wealth, as if the two were mutually opposing. Consider his statement, "You cannot serve both God and Money," for example (Matt. 6:24). He also asks, "What good will it be for a man if he gains the whole world, yet forfeits his soul?" (Matt. 16:26). At one point He told His disciples, "I tell you the truth, it is hard for a rich man to enter the kingdom of heaven. Again I tell you, it is easier for a camel to go through the eye of a needle than for a rich man to enter the kingdom of God" (Matt. 19:23-24). He clearly was not saying that it is impossible for a wealthy person to enter the kingdom, because when His disciples responded, "Who then can be saved?", He replied, "With man this is impossible, but with God all things are possible" (Matt. 19:26).

So more than wealth is the issue. Wealth is an obstacle to hearing the kingdom message because of the differences of focus. The focus of the rich is return on investment and personal gain. The emphasis of the gospel is giving freely with no expectation or hope of return (see Matt. 5:40-42 and Luke 14:12-13). The rich typically rely on their wealth and possessions, whereas the believer's trust is to be primarily in God (see Matt. 6:33). In this sense, wealth is an obstacle to discipleship.

Jesus told a parable about a dishonest business manager accused of wasting his boss's resources. The boss fired him, so to guarantee that he would find a job elsewhere, he discounted the bills people owed his boss. He was an opportunist and gave away his boss's profits to buy favors for himself. The interesting thing about this parable is Jesus' comments afterward.

"The master commended the dishonest manager because he had acted shrewdly. For the people of this world are more shrewd in dealing with their own kind than are the people of the light. I tell you, use worldly wealth to gain friends for yourselves, so that when it is gone, you will be welcomed into eternal dwellings" (Luke 16:8-9).

The Greek words translated "shrewd" and "shrewdly" suggest the person has a very clear understanding of his situation and uses sound judgment in making preparations. Jesus commends the dishonest manager in the parable for recognizing the seriousness of his situation, knowing that he needed to make preparations, and using the available resources to prepare himself for the future. Both Jesus and the master in His parable acknowledged the man's dishonesty and his embezzlement after he lost his job, yet both commended his shrewdness. This is both interesting and significant. Dealing specifically with worldly wealth, Jesus said to use it to prepare for the future, because it will eventually run out. Then Jesus broadens the context in the following verses.

"Whoever can be trusted with very little can also be trusted with much, and whoever is dishonest with very little will also be dishonest with much. So if you have not been trustworthy in handling worldly wealth, who will trust you with true riches? And if you have not been trustworthy with someone else's property, who will give you property of your own? No servant can serve two masters. Either he will hate the one and love the other, or he will be devoted to the one and despise the other. You cannot serve both God and Money" (Luke 16:10-13).

In a few brief statements, Jesus revealed two extremely important points about worldly wealth: 1) it is not true riches, and 2) it does not belong to you. If you consider money to be true wealth and your own possession, then you are serving money rather than God. To reinforce these points, Jesus then stated, "What is highly valued among men is detestable in God's sight" (Luke 16:15).

So if the world system insists that wealth is a measure of true success, Jesus clearly states that is not the case in God's economy. Demonstrate your honesty and trustworthiness by the way you handle money, and use it shrewdly to secure true wealth in eternity. Paul wrote that you should use the things of the world without letting them engross you—do not become preoccupied with them so that you rely on them—because they are all passing away (1 Cor. 7:31). If anything, success in God's kingdom relates to how you use money, not how much of it you have. Success has very little to do with either financial wealth or poverty.

When God speaks of riches, He clearly is not thinking of money or other worldly possessions. Consider the following, for example:

"For there is no difference between Jew and Gentile — the same Lord is Lord of all and richly blesses all who call on him, for, 'Everyone who calls on the name of the Lord will be saved'" (Rom. 10:12-13). Notice that the Lord richly blesses all who call on Him by saving them; to be saved is to be richly blessed.

The Book of Romans refers to the riches of God's kindness, tolerance and patience (Rom. 2:10) and the riches of His glory (Rom. 9:23). Ephesians speaks of the riches of His grace that He lavished on us with all wisdom and understanding (Eph. 1:8) and the riches of His glorious inheritance in the saints (Eph. 1:18), which means He considers the saints a rich inheritance. He is also rich in mercy (Eph. 2:4). So, the Bible's statements about God's riches have absolutely nothing to do with money or other forms of material wealth.

Paul wrote that he was poor, yet made many rich; he had nothing, yet possessed everything (2 Cor. 6:10). He is making a contrast between the riches of two very different systems. In the world's system, which values material wealth, Paul was poor and had nothing. Yet as an heir in God's kingdom, he possessed everything and made many others rich as well. From the perspective of God's kingdom, the world's wealth has no value at all. That is why Jesus said to prove yourself trustworthy with the world's wealth, so He can then give you true wealth.

We must radically change our view of wealth. If you try to impose the world's standards of wealth on God's kingdom, you have failed to transform your mind and are trying to serve both God and money, which Jesus said you cannot do. Unfortunately, there are many Christians today who believe that godliness is the road to material wealth and comfort. The scriptures we have examined here show these people are seriously mistaken.

True Success

Success has virtually nothing to do with wealth. You can only define it in terms of a goal or purpose; that is, you cannot consider yourself successful unless you have set a goal and achieved it, or fulfilled your purpose. To be a success in the greater sense, your goal or purpose must have value.

What is your purpose in life? Is it a worthy one? In the previous chapter we showed that God has a purpose and He works everything out to conform to it. We also showed that He gave you a specific character so you can do your part in fulfilling His purpose. That means you have a purpose, which we can define as using your God-given abilities to advance God's kingdom.

With that as your purpose, what kind of goals could you set for yourself? One long-term goal could be to develop godly character; that is, to become like your big brother, Jesus. Once you select that as a long-term goal, other shorter-term goals should automatically become clearer to you. I suspect that many of those goals will be as unique to you as your character is, because the character God gave you is exactly what you need to fulfill His plan for your life, and as you mature you begin embracing God's plan as your own.

Personal success relates to how well you have developed your abilities and how effectively you use them. Considering the Bible's emphasis on humility and agape love, it is no surprise that God expects you to use the character and abilities He gave you to serve others. This leads us to conclude that true success involves using your abilities for the benefit of others.

Using your abilities for your own benefit is characteristic of the world system and is a failure in God's kingdom, not a success. Because you currently live in the world system, you would be wise to identify your skills and use them in your work. If you are self-centered, you probably would consider this using your skills for your own benefit, since you get paid for your work. As a believer, you should view yourself as serving your employer, so you use your skills to benefit others. This takes us back to the issue of purpose. Is your purpose to earn income for yourself, or to serve others?

As you transform your mind, making it conform to God's system, you enable Him to cause everything you are and everything you do to be successful, according to His definition of success. Success relates to how good you are at what you are supposed to do.

The ultimate measure of success is hearing the Lord say to you, "Well done, good and faithful servant!" Notice that He says "faithful servant" rather than "productive servant." God calls you to be faithful, recognizing that you cannot be responsible for the results of your efforts when they involve other people or external circumstances.

One day a rich young man approached Jesus, wanting to know how to inherit eternal life. Jesus replied that he should sell everything he owned and give it to the poor, then become His disciple. The man could not accept what Jesus said and went away sad (Matt. 19:16-22). To determine whether Jesus was a success or a failure in this encounter, we must consider His purpose. Was He responsible for making that man His disciple? No, He was responsible for presenting the truth of the Father's kingdom and facilitating the man's decisions regarding the kingdom. If Jesus did that, then His effort was successful even though the man rejected the opportunity He provided. This incident was not a blotch on Jesus' otherwise perfect record because Jesus did exactly what He should have done.

Jesus was perfect in His ministry, though not everyone was willing to receive it. He was entirely successful and is the example we are to follow, yet by many of the world's standards He was a virtual failure. He lived His life financially dependent on others, apparently owned no property of His own, directly influenced relatively few people and died a hideous death as a criminal. Most people would consider that kind of life a failure. But one's purpose is the only measurement of one's success. At the beginning of His ministry, Jesus clearly stated His purpose when he read the Scripture in the synagogue in Nazareth.

"The Spirit of the Lord is on me, because he has anointed me to preach good news to the poor. He has sent me to proclaim freedom for the prisoners and recovery of sight for the blind, to release the oppressed, to proclaim the year of the Lord's favor" (Luke 4:18-19).

Jesus released the oppressed by overcoming the power of Satan, and everything else was a matter of giving people opportunities to respond by preaching and proclaiming the good news. He did all of these and therefore He completed His mission. He was an unqualified success.

The parable of the talents is a good indication of what God expects of you. The two servants in the parable who used what their master entrusted to them were able to increase their holdings. These are the ones to whom the master said, "Well done, good and faithful servant!" They used the resources they had available to benefit someone else; specifically, their master. On the other hand, the master severely punished the third servant because he was more concerned about his own well-being than his master's benefit. He didn't want to risk punishment for losing the master's property and instead brought a much worse punishment on himself for not benefiting his master. There is a clear message here: Using your resources to benefit others leads to success, while being primarily concerned about yourself leads to failure.

How can you measure your success? You must first identify your purpose, which we defined earlier in this section as using your God-given abilities to advance God's kingdom. This includes using the character and abilities He gave you to serve others. That in itself should be another of your long-term goals.

What kind of goals should you set for yourself that you know will please God? The emphasis of the New Testament is on your becoming like God and your vital role in that process is repentance, changing your mind. This does not refer to random changes of opinion but substantial, radical changes such as changing your attitude, your perspective on life, your standards of worth, your desires, your priorities, what you think about. For specific suggestions, read on.

A good place to begin looking for God-pleasing changes is the beginning of Jesus' teaching while He was on earth: the "Sermon on the Mount." Consider the following concepts and see how much you need to change the way you think to conform to them. I am presenting them here because these make good, specific goals for you to set that you can be certain will please God. I suggest you pick a few, maybe just two or three, and begin reprogramming your mind, asking God for His help in the form of guidance, understanding and power. You can rest assured that He will eagerly answer that kind of prayer with love and gentleness, because that is how He works with His children.

130

Consider how the following concepts from the Book of Matthew's account of the Sermon on the Mount (Matt. 5:3-44) require you to change your thinking, and what goals you should set to help yourself make those changes.

- Blessed (happy, enviable and spiritually prosperous) are the poor in spirit (v. 3).
- Blessed are those who mourn (v. 4).
- Blessed are the meek (v. 5).
- Blessed are those who hunger and thirst for righteousness (v. 6).
- Blessed are the merciful (v. 7).
- Blessed are the pure in heart (v. 8).
- Blessed are the peacemakers (v. 9).
- Blessed are those who are persecuted because of righteousness (v. 10).
- Blessed are you when people insult you, persecute you and falsely say all kinds of evil against you because of Jesus (v. 11).
- You are the salt of the earth (v. 13).
- You are the light of the world (v. 14).
- Anger and abusive treatment are equivalent to murder (vv. 21-22).
- Be responsible for settling matters quickly with any adversary (v. 25).
- Looking lustfully at a woman is equivalent to adultery (v. 28).
- Most divorce and remarriage is equivalent to adultery (vv. 31-32).
- Do not resist an evil person; willingly do more than they demand (v. 39).
- Love your enemies (work for the benefit of those who would harm you, v. 44).

Might I suggest these are some of the criteria by which you should be measuring your success? Each of these requires major changes in the way you think, and those changes will be reflected in your behavior. Again, the emphasis is on what you become, rather than what you do, because what you are determines what you do.

I should point out that Jesus did not have to become anything when He came to earth, because He was already perfect. When John baptized Jesus, before Jesus began His ministry, God spoke His approval of Him from heaven. Jesus was already like God and His earthly role was to defeat Satan and give mankind opportunity to enter God's kingdom. Jesus' responsibility was entirely different from yours.

Your responsibility is to become the person God wants you to be, which will enable you to use your personal resources to advance God's kingdom and benefit others. Your role in bringing about that transformation is repenting, radically changing your mind, and God's role is providing the power to make the change happen. Therefore, the most important measure of success for your life is the degree to which you transform your mind, thereby allowing God to do His work through you.

Conclusion

The only way to become successful is to know your purpose, set goals that will help you fulfill your purpose, then work toward those goals. True success is effectively using your skills to do kingdom work, which includes serving God and meeting the needs of other people. Kingdom success has no direct relationship with worldly success; those who are extremely successful in God's kingdom are often failures in the world system. So it is very possible for you to be successful in God's eyes without being a success in the world's view.

God's standard of success for you involves your becoming the person He created you to be and allowing Him to use your unique abilities and personality to do His work through you. That requires a radical transformation in your mind.

Personal Study

1.   Read the parable of the talents (Matt. 25:14-30). The "talent" in Bible days was a unit of money, but for the purposes of this study substitute your personal resources (such as natural skills and abilities) for the money in the parable.

- What are some of your greatest resources?

- In what ways can you use your personal resources to serve God and others?

- What long-term goals can you set to help you develop your resources?

- Setting short-term goals: What immediate steps can you take to change the way you view success?

2.   "So if you have not been trustworthy in handling worldly wealth, who will trust you with true riches? And if you have not been trustworthy with someone else's property, who will give you property of your own?" (Luke 16:11-12).

- If you were to consider your material wealth as belonging to someone else, how would you rate your own trustworthiness?

- What steps can you take to change the way you view material wealth?

9

Being Perfect While Becoming Perfect

"Be perfect . . . as your heavenly Father is perfect" (Matt. 5:48). God's emphasis is on what you are, rather than what you do. For example, the word "repent" means to change the way you think, rather than change your actions. Why? Because who you are determines what you do; your attitude governs your actions. Matthew 5:48 says to *be perfect*, not *do perfectly*.

In Matthew 19:21 Jesus told a rich young man, "If you want to be perfect, go, sell your possessions and give to the poor, and you will have treasure in heaven. Then come, follow me." Although Jesus required the man to perform a specific act, the emphasis was on his condition, rather than his performance. The act of giving away all of his wealth would not make him perfect, because perfection is not a result of your actions. Perfection is one of God's attributes and He is the standard for perfection—"as your heavenly Father is perfect" (Matt. 5:48). The rich young man's problem was his attitude, which focused on the pleasure and security he derived from his great wealth, as we can see by his response. He went away sad, because he had great wealth (Matt. 19:22). His attitude not only made him imperfect, but also prevented him from becoming perfect.

Wealth is irrelevant if you have the correct attitude. Wealth and poverty are material, physical conditions that can affect your attitude if you allow them, but a proper attitude makes wealth and poverty meaningless. As Paul stated,

I have learned to be content whatever the circumstances. I know what it is to be in need, and I know what it is to have plenty. I have learned the secret of being content in any and every situation, whether well fed or hungry, whether living in plenty or in want. I can do everything through him who gives me strength (Phil. 4:11-13).

The key for Paul was an attitude of contentment. The problem for the rich young man was an unwillingness to give up the pleasure of wealth, which prevented him from becoming perfect. The normal human condition is imperfection, obviously, but what does that mean?

Most humans virtually ignore the spiritual realm. Those who acknowledge it frequently want to use it for personal gain through the occult, which promises control, influence, improved personal condition, and so on. The normal human condition is totally self-centered, so that you do things for others because it makes you feel good or promises to benefit you in the future. Carnal thinking motivates you to do everything for selfish reasons. At the least, that is an intensely lop-sided attitude.

From a human perspective, we might say that someone who is totally self-absorbed is undivided or perfect in his attitude, that he is perfectly self-centered. From God's perspective, however, such a person's attitude is divided, incomplete, inferior or blemished. The proper attitude is one of total submission to, and orientation toward, God. That is perfection and anything other than that divides your attention between God's intent and what you want. James uses a similar term, "double-minded" (James 1:8), to describe someone oriented away from God enough to doubt whether God will answer his prayer. Double-minded or divided; both terms describe an imperfect condition.

Let us consider an analogy that might clarify the process of attaining perfection. When you have a partial understanding of a subject, one aspect of the subject may seem to be of supreme importance. As your understanding becomes more complete, you see that it really is not important at all, although it seemed extremely important earlier. Is it primarily a matter of perspective? You probably thought that one aspect was extremely important in this instance because it was one you were more familiar with.

For example, it can seem very important that you have a nice television. Some people even consider it essential to have more than one television, and they can totally justify having them. But let that person spend a week or longer in a typical third world country, where people have no running water, basic sanitation, medicines or a variety of foods. Is that second television really that important anymore? How about the first television? The issue is seeing the "big picture," rather than concentrating on a very small benefit available only to a very small percentage of the world's population.

How might this apply to the biblical concept of perfection? Getting your eyes off of yourself long enough to recognize God and your relative insignificance is an excellent first step. Then being willing to lay aside selfish priorities and accept God's perspective is an excellent second step. God's perspective is perfect; He sees everything exactly as it is and exactly how it affects everything else. He sees the effects of sin—past, present and future. He sees the futility and foolishness of living in sin. He knows that everything associated with or perverted by sin will eventually be totally destroyed. God sees the "big picture." His attitude takes everything into account and in that sense is complete, entire or full. His attitude rejects anything that would detract from the flawless nature of His kingdom, which will ultimately include all of creation. His attitude is therefore undivided, dedicated and unblemished. Complete, entire, full; undivided, dedicated, unblemished—these describe perfection. That is the sense of God's perfection, and it is the perfection He says you are to have, too.

From your extremely limited perspective as a human, being fully committed to God's kingdom appears lop-sided and imbalanced, or at least a restricted perspective. But it seems that way because self-centeredness makes you want to satisfy itself; besides, the sinful world seems normal, because that is all you have ever known. You cannot compare your present condition with the perfection of God's existence, because for now you cannot see God as He is. This means you cannot see the total devastation resulting from sin. Therefore, God's demand for perfection may even strike you as unreasonable, since your perspective is extremely limited—to the point of blindness—and your natural orientation is to do what you want and reject what others demand of you.

Is perfection attainable? Paul clearly taught that it is, because he wrote to one of the churches that his prayer was for their perfection and he encouraged them to aim for perfection (2 Cor. 13:9, 11).

As is so often the case, God asks you to do something that is impossible in your own ability, but is attainable with His help. Perfection is achievable, it is your duty, and it is your hope. You can accept God's command to be perfect and begin to pursue perfection in spite of your lack of understanding. Jesus stated, in relation to His teaching, "If any one chooses to do God's will, he will find out whether my teaching comes from God or whether I speak on my own" (John 7:17). If you do, then you will know; understanding follows obedience, whereas you normally insist on understanding before you commit to doing. Similarly, faith is willing to act with or without knowledge, because its trust is in the one who asks obedience.

Perfection is relevant to your stage of growth. A parent expects one level of maturity from a two-year-old and a much different level from a twenty-year-old. Behavior that might be acceptable from a perfect toddler would be unacceptable from a young adult.

Perfection relates to your spiritual and mental state, not to your action. Action is the result of perfection, not its definition. Perfection is not strict adherence to a list of commandments, but an attitude, a spiritual and mental state constantly focused on God. What you are determines what you do. A person commits sin because he is a sinner; his act of sin does not make him a sinner. Likewise, you are righteous because God declares you so, not because you act a certain way. Your actions are proof of your condition, not the cause.

God's command to be perfect relates to your attitude and therefore applies to everything you do. This is different from other commands, such as those against killing or stealing (Exod. 20:13, 15), which relate to a very small portion of your life. The opportunity and temptation to steal are usually momentary and occasional. Perfection, however, because of the differences between God's nature and yours, requires continuous attention and constant vigilance.

Because we are aware of our imperfect condition, it is interesting how frequently God refers to His people as perfect. "Noah was a righteous man, blameless among the people of his time" (Gen. 6:9). Yet Noah got drunk and became indecent. When he discovered what had happened, however, he spoke the word of the Lord over his sons.

Concerning Job, God said, "There is no one on earth like him; he is blameless and upright" (Job 1:8). Having said that, God knew he had major problems with fear and arrogance. When Job finally realized his folly, he turned to God in true humility.

Think about David and Solomon. "As Solomon grew old, his wives turned his heart after other gods, and his heart was not fully devoted to the Lord his God, as the heart of David his father had been" (1 Kings 11:4). David's heart was perfect; Solomon's was not. David sinned but his perfect attitude caused him to return to God. Solomon sinned by disobeying God, then slid into worse sin and eventually lost everything—his relationship with God and his kingdom.

Each of these men acted imperfectly. God called the three who turned to Him righteous, blameless, upright and devoted to the Lord. The one who did not turn to the Lord became disillusioned ("Everything is meaningless.") and eventually caused the kingdom of Israel to split. What made the difference? The men's attitudes.

Your selfish human nature views salvation primarily as an escape from hell. Its concern is how salvation will benefit you. In contrast, God's plan restores you to man's original state, which was total commitment to God's glory and service. That is real perfection, the essence of Christianity. Godly nature is totally committed to God and has no personal concerns.

God demands perfection of His people, which seems impossible and unreasonable if you think like the world. Human nature's perception is based on human abilities, and its perception is right: godly perfection is humanly impossible. God's plan, however, requires only your willing cooperation; God performs the actual work. As

Jesus said, "With man this is impossible, but with God all things are possible" (Matt. 19:26). Elsewhere, Jesus said, "Everything is possible for him who believes" (Mark 9:23), so perfection is possible as a result of faith. Your responsibility is to accept the work of God and change the way you think.

A young child helping his father does imperfect work. It may even require greater effort for the father to train him, demonstrate correct methods, correct the problems he creates, and clean up his mess. But the father is (or should be) grateful for his child's commitment to him and his desire to help. The child may serve with a perfect heart, but is unable to do perfect work.

In the Old Testament, God saw a man named Abram and chose him to be the father of God's people. God appeared to him and said, "I am God Almighty; walk before me and be blameless [perfect]" (Gen. 17:1). God required a state of perfection, rather than perfect obedience. It is significant that God associated perfection with walking before Him. Only as you remain close to God in your attitude will He release His power in you to accomplish perfection. How can you "walk before God?" By being aware of His presence and His concern for you. Walking before God is living each day with your attention turned to God, eager to please Him, eager to do what He asks. That is a life of perfection.

After God made that statement to Abram, He explained He would make Abram the father of many nations. That required major faith on Abram's part, because he was ninety-nine years old, and his wife was in menopause.

Faith is a vital component of perfection. "Without faith it is impossible to please God" (Heb. 11:6). Faith gives God His place — room for His authority, power and love — and His glory — honor and praise for who He is, appreciation and approval for what He has done. Faith will cause you to provide opportunity for God to work, instead of relying on your own abilities. Let God be God. You will work in cooperation with Him, but He does the needed work.

A primary characteristic of a perfect heart is reliance on God. Your human mind cannot imagine what God can do for you or through you. God tells you in the Bible what He will do, but you normally interpret it from your human perspective and understanding. Your opinion of God is always deficient because you view Him from your human condition of imperfection. How can imperfection comprehend perfection? A child cannot possibly understand why his parents keep emphasizing certain things and encouraging him to do them, but relies on his parents to know and to do what is best for him. In the same way, you cannot possibly understand God's commands, but must accept them in faith and rely on Him to know and do what is best for you.

God's command is for you to be perfect. As you commit yourself to His command and change your attitude about perfection, He will perform the necessary work within you. As stated earlier, this is an example of Him commanding you to be what He alone can make you, or to do what He alone can do through you. Your act of faith and recognition of your dependence on Him will enable Him to do the work. He intends for His command to draw you to Him. He gives *to you* what He asks *from you.*

Your commitment to His plan is only the first step. Next, there is a growth process, in which you put on one trait after another, growing up in Christ, from glory to glory, becoming increasingly like Him. First there is relationship, your commitment to God. Next there is step-by-step obedience, doing what He asks.

You cannot attain perfection through obedience (see Heb. 7:11), because perfection is not the result of right action. Perfection is an inner state that influences actions. It is a motivation, not an action.

Psalm 18:25 states, "To the faithful you show yourself faithful, to the blameless you show yourself blameless." Anyone who lives by their own understanding and relies on their own perspective is not perfect (blameless), and their perspective of God will be erroneous. If you, on the other hand, are perfect before God in your attitude, you will see God increasingly as He is and you will recognize that His nature is perfect. As you live before God with a perfect heart, you will discover how much of His love and blessings flow to you.

"For the eyes of the Lord range throughout the earth to strengthen those whose hearts are fully committed to him" (2 Chron. 16:9). "The eyes of the Lord are on the righteous and his ears are attentive to their cry" (Ps. 34:15 and 1 Pet. 3:12). To the perfect, He will show Himself perfect. As you become fully committed to Him, eager to please Him, and undivided in your attention to Him, you will see that God is fully committed to you, eager to do the best for you, and undivided in His attention to you. In reality, God is this way to all His people, but those who are perfect toward Him will see this more clearly in Him. God will reveal Himself to the person fully devoted to Him.

You might be intent on serving God perfectly, yet not realize how imperfect your knowledge of God's will is. As far as you know, you are doing God's will. God reveals His will by stating that the greatest commandment is to "Love the Lord your God with all your heart and with all your soul and with all your mind" (Matt. 22:37). This describes such an intense desire to see God's will done that all other efforts, programs and attitudes become insignificant by comparison. If this is your desire, every time you recognize a thought or action based on self-centeredness, you will turn to God for forgiveness and the power to overcome your carnal thinking. That is a perfect attitude. The biblical standard is for you to turn from all unrighteousness and hate all evil, especially that within yourself. Commit yourself fully to God's kingdom and oppose everything that is not part of His kingdom.

"Be perfect, therefore, *as* your heavenly Father is perfect" (Matt. 5:48, emphasis added). Your heavenly Father is your only standard of perfection. Your human tendency is to compare yourself with other humans. You can always find someone who is worse than yourself in some way and you can use them to justify your imperfection and feel good about yourself. Biblical perfection, however, is absolute, not relative. The only standard for comparison is the absolute perfection of God Himself. This destroys any hope of achieving perfection by any human effort. On the other hand, it creates a hope of God doing the work.

How is God perfect? What does His perfection cause Him to do? Our primary verse for this chapter reads, "Be perfect, *therefore* . . . ." The word "therefore" shows this command is a conclusion or synopsis of something stated earlier, so let us consider the immediate context, which is part of Jesus' teaching.

"You have heard that it was said, 'Love your neighbor and hate your enemy.' But I tell you: Love your enemies and pray for those who persecute you, that you may be sons of your Father in heaven. He causes his sun to rise on the evil and the good, and sends rain on the righteous and the unrighteous. If you love those who love you, what reward will you get? Are not even the tax collectors doing that? And if you greet only your brothers, what are you doing more than others? Do not even pagans do that? Be perfect, therefore, as your heavenly Father is perfect." (Matt. 5:43-48)

Obviously, this is only a representative listing of acts motivated by perfection, but it is enough to keep most Christians busy to their dying day. Love those who hate you, and cause good to happen to both good and evil people. God's perfection expresses itself in His love and causes Him to deliver His own blessings to everyone around Him. Again, by human effort this is impossible. As God's child, however, you have His Spirit within you, and the Holy Spirit provides what you need to become perfect.

Hebrews 5:8 tells us that Jesus "learned obedience from what he suffered and, once made perfect, he became the source of eternal salvation for all who obey him." Think about it: Jesus, the Son of God who never disobeyed or sinned, learned obedience and became perfect. This same Jesus described Himself as the visible, physical representation of God, and tells us to be perfect as God is perfect. This verse also identifies a relationship between suffering, obedience and perfection. Learning obedience from what you suffer is a vital step in your perfection, as it was for Jesus.

Suffering, itself, does not give birth to perfection, however. If that were the case, we could make each other perfect by inflicting pain on each other. It seems that some people believe that actually works. But Scripture is clear that it is God who does the perfecting. As always, you cooperate with God, and He does the actual work. Your willingness and obedience make it possible for Him to perform His work in you.

The question naturally arises, What kind of suffering makes me perfect? Jesus suffered persecution, so that contributed to His perfection, but He suffered in other ways, too. He became a perfect sacrifice for every conceivable type of sin, which suggests that He had to face and overcome each of them. In fact, Hebrews 4:15 states, "we do not have a high priest who is unable to sympathize with our weaknesses, but we have one who has been tempted in every way, just as we are—yet was without sin."

The ungodly mindset you developed as a sinner insists that you be lord of your life, deciding what you do, when and how you do it. Denying that mindset will result in discomfort and suffering, because its desires are formidable, but enduring that suffering is a key to becoming perfect. Almost all Christians would claim Jesus is their Savior and Lord; most even call Him Lord, but think of Him mostly as Savior. Why? Because of their carnal thinking.

That mindset is inherently self-centered, so it makes you more interested in what you can get out of your relationship with Jesus— let Him be Savior, save you from hell and take care of you—than what you can or must put into your relationship with Him—let Him be Lord, Master, King and Owner. The first step, accepting Jesus as Savior, is an inherently selfish act for most people. The second step, accepting Jesus as Lord, is usually one of obligation and is done grudgingly in the beginning. The third step is one of voluntary abandon, becoming a willing servant.

Some people may accomplish all three steps at the same time, experiencing a radical conversion and immediately selling out completely to Jesus. That kind of conversion may be a result of their personality as much as anything, causing them to embrace the Lord immediately with complete abandon. Most people are not like that, however, and usually go through the three stages: 1) they accept Jesus as Savior for the benefits; 2) they become an obligated servant, serving Him because they know they should; 3) they become a willing servant as they learn to trust Him and rely on Him.

To progress from accepting Jesus as Savior to submitting to Him as Lord is an important transition in your spiritual maturity. To advance from that stage to wanting Him to be Master of every part of your being is another significant step. To have an intense desire to be like Him, to have His nature and motivations, is to reach an even greater level of maturity. In reality, that is what He expects of you, but He honors your free will and allows you to choose the level of maturity you wish to attain. You set the limit on your spiritual growth; God does not want to stop you and Satan cannot. The degree to which you transform your mind determines the extent of your spiritual growth.

The specific commitment required for perfection may be unique to each person, just as their salvation experience is unique to who they are. Jesus challenged a rich young man to give away his wealth to be perfect (Matt. 19:21). If poverty were a universal virtue, however, why did Jesus teach that we should help the poor and provide for their needs? Should we instead try to become impoverished like them and not diminish their piety by meeting their needs? Of course, that is not the case. In fact, the parable of the talents was about great wealth first being entrusted to servants, then given to them. The relevant question is "Whom or what do you worship?" not "What is your net worth?"

While it appears that Jesus lived without material possessions, it may be that was part of His commitment to perfection. As King of kings and Lord of lords, maybe the ultimate way for Him to attain perfection was through voluntary poverty and a lack of earthly authority and acceptance.

Jesus required His closest disciples to give up their former occupations and dedicate themselves full time to ministry. He did not require that of all His followers, however. The issue is renouncing yourself, and that means something different to each of us, although there are some basic similarities since everyone's fallen nature is totally self-centered. God asks total commitment from all of us, but your expression of that commitment will be as unique as you are.

We have seen that perfection relates more to who you are than to what you do. In particular, perfection relates to your mind—changing your attitude and way of thinking. Paul relates perfection to the way he viewed himself and his relationship with God in the following verses.

But whatever was to my profit I now consider loss for the sake of Christ. What is more, I consider everything a loss compared to the surpassing greatness of knowing Christ

Jesus my Lord, for whose sake I have lost all things. I consider them rubbish, that I may gain Christ and be found in him, not having a righteousness of my own that comes from the law, but that which is through faith in Christ—the righteousness that comes from God and is by faith. I want to know Christ and the power of his resurrection and the fellowship of sharing in his sufferings, becoming like him in his death, and so, somehow, to attain to the resurrection from the dead. Not that I have already obtained all this, or have already been made perfect, but I press on to take hold of that for which Christ Jesus took hold of me. Brothers, I do not consider myself yet to have taken hold of it. But one thing I do: Forgetting what is behind and straining toward what is ahead, I press on toward the goal to win the prize for which God has called me heavenward in Christ Jesus. All of us who are mature [perfect] should take such a view of things (Phil. 3:7-15).

For Paul, perfection or maturity is intimately related to the way you think. Changing the way you think leads to a level of perfection; perfection then changes the way you think; changing your thinking produces greater perfection; and so on. So it is possible to have a perfect attitude toward God as you progressively become like Him. However, the only valid standard of perfection is God Himself, as portrayed by Jesus. I think that is why Paul was so intent on sharing Christ's sufferings and becoming like Him.

The verses we just quoted raise several points about perfection.

1. Perfection in humans is relative to their present state. Paul claimed not to have achieved perfection, yet clearly stated that all who are mature, or perfect, should have the same perspective he did. A perfect two-year-old does not behave the same as a perfect forty-year-old. Similarly, a new convert cannot have the same depth of relationship with God as does a mature saint, yet may be considered a perfect new convert.

2.   There is a difference between imputed perfection and attained perfection. On one hand, God declares you perfect as a result of Jesus' sacrifice, yet on the other hand you must develop perfection.

3.   Perfection may not be a continuous state of existence in this life. Each moment brings new opportunity for perfection or imperfection. You may have passed a certain test yesterday, but here it is again. We might consider perfection more of a process than a continuous state.

Jesus was never imperfect, yet He became perfect through suffering. Likewise, you might be perfect for your present level of experience, but the future holds new challenges. With each challenge, you can become perfect in a new area of life, or perfect at a new level of achievement.

Consider a parallel concept. God will not judge you for your evil deeds because Jesus paid the penalty for them and they are no longer an issue. Instead, He will judge your good deeds to determine the extent of your reward. This may also be true of perfection. The record of your imperfection was erased through Jesus' death, so it is no longer a matter of concern. Of course, you are aware of your imperfections, as is God, but let them simply remind you of your humanity and your need to submit continuously to God's plan of redemption. Do not condemn yourself for your repeated failures, but instead focus on attaining greater perfection.

There also seems to be a principle that the more you know of something, the more problems you can identify. For example, candlelight dinners are very romantic because almost anyone looks good in the dark; you cannot see their imperfections. You might even have a terrible food stain on your clothes and still look wonderful in the dark. But as the light increases, you begin to see the imperfections.

My experience in college led me to conclude that the more I learned, the more I realized I didn't know. That has certainly been true since I finished college, as well. As my knowledge and wisdom have both increased over the years, I have become increasingly aware of my inadequacies.

In a similar way, perfection is both progressive and revealing. Each step toward perfection, or the attainment of each level of perfection, reveals additional imperfection. Jesus is the only legitimate standard for comparison. Figuratively speaking, the closer you stand to Him, the more you see your imperfections. The more you examine yourself in light of the Scriptures, the more problems you will see. Don't get discouraged, though, because God is fully aware of your faults and has chosen to temporarily substitute Jesus' perfection for your imperfection while you perfect yourself. It is still a shock to have your imperfections revealed, because as a sinner you learned to cover them up, justify them, ignore them, or even consider them assets.

A perfect mind is pure and has one overriding purpose or goal; it is not divided or sidetracked. Man's overall purpose is to have relationship with God, and anything else is a distraction and an imperfection. Perfection in your relationship with God means that everything else — possessions, achievements, status — is comparatively worthless. Be willing to discard everything mankind considers valuable so you can focus on, or be perfectly minded about, what God considers important.

A young man in love works hard to pay for gifts and a ring for that special lady. He is willing to give up his bachelor freedoms to gain a marital relationship. That is a perfect attitude — total commitment to the goal.

Conclusion

Perfection relates to your spiritual and mental state, not to your action; action is the result of perfection, not its definition. It is a spiritual and mental state constantly focused on God, totally committed to His glory and service.

One key to perfection is renouncing yourself and committing yourself entirely to God's care. Godly nature causes you to be fully committed to God and not have any personal concerns. This allows you to accept what God says in faith, relying on Him to do what is best for you. Perfection in your relationship with God means that everything else is comparatively worthless.

Personal Study

1 "If you want to be perfect, go, sell your possessions and give to the poor, and you will have treasure in heaven. Then come, follow me" (Jesus speaking to a rich young man, Matt. 19:21).

- What possession or area of your life do you secretly hope God does not ask you to give up, and why?

- Identify one attitude you have that would make it very hard for you to give it up.

- How is that attitude preventing you from becoming perfect?

- In what ways does that attitude cause you to be "double-minded," a part of God's kingdom but at odds with kingdom goals and principles?

- List several ways you can change your thinking to overcome that attitude.

2. David was a man after God's own heart; when he sinned, he immediately turned to God for forgiveness and reconciliation.

- What practical steps can you take to develop that kind of attitude?

- What sinful ways of thinking will oppose your efforts to turn to God, and what can you do when that happens?

3. Paul wrote, "whatever was to my profit I now consider loss for the sake of Christ."

- How does maturing change your priorities and attitudes?

- Identify some priorities you used to have as a new Christian that you now realize are not important.

- Which of your current priorities might be based on sinful desires and therefore may need to be changed?

10

A Matter of Integrity

Imagine for a moment that you needed to take a trip out of town for a few days and that you would need a car at your destination. If you were going only a few hours from home, you would automatically plan to drive your own car. Unless you knew your car had a weakness, that is; your brakes occasionally fail and you cannot stop, which could cause a major accident. You might make the trip without any problems, but maybe not, because you never know whether the brakes will fail. Most people would agree your car is unreliable, even unsafe, and would refuse to drive or ride in it.

Stopping is a critically important function you expect a car to perform. Its inability to stop when needed makes its powerful engine, plush interior and pristine paint job virtually irrelevant. We might define your car's purpose as reliably transporting you wherever you want to go in comfort, safety and style. You expect every system in a car to support its overall purpose and a failure by any part can put the entire car's usefulness in jeopardy. Basically, this is a matter of your car's integrity, whether all of its parts do their job without creating problems and work together so it can perform its duty.

Integrity is a concept we normally apply to people, although it is relevant to virtually any system containing more than a single part. The words "integrity" and "integrate" are related and imply a strong sense of wholeness or completeness. A system with integrity has all of its components integrated. It is undivided and unimpaired by its parts, and they all work together to support the whole. All of this implies reliability and trustworthiness.

The same concept applies to people. Someone with integrity has a strict code of behavior and a purpose from which they will not deviate, and this is especially significant when they are experiencing a test or are in danger of being distracted from their purpose.

As they do with other virtues, people exhibit varying degrees of integrity. If you continue to cling to sinful ways of thinking, you will not have absolute integrity but will always have a flaw somewhere that interferes with your performance or commitment. That is the nature of flesh—it perverts, it divides, it opposes. Not only does fleshly desire divide one person from another, it also divides a person internally, causing you to have conflicting desires and motivations. An example that immediately comes to mind is Paul's statements about his own internal conflict.

> *I do not understand what I do. For what I want to do I do not do, but what I hate I do. And if I do what I do not want to do, I agree that the law is good. As it is, it is no longer I myself who do it, but it is sin living in me. I know that nothing good lives in me, that is, in my carnal nature. For I have the desire to do what is good, but I cannot carry it out. For what I do is not the good I want to do; no, the evil I do not want to do—this I keep on doing. Now if I do what I do not want to do, it is no longer I who do it, but it is sin living in me that does it* (Rom. 7:15-20).

Virtually the entire New Testament requires you to get rid of attitudes and behaviors that oppose your godly nature. It encourages you to put off your sinful ways and put on those of a godly nature, to make your attitudes conform to God's, to become like Him, to get rid of anything that interferes with God's purpose and to develop the character traits that enable you to do God's will.

Simply put, the New Testament strongly urges you to develop integrity. It challenges you to integrate all of your being and commit to a single purpose, eliminating everything that interferes with God's purpose for your life.

Like a muscle that cramps and makes you stop whatever you are doing to care for it, self-centeredness will repeatedly insist that you gratify yourself, watch out for your own interests or protect yourself from harm. How many times has someone asked you to help and you declined simply because you didn't feel like doing it and even offered some lame excuse? Your old sinful attitudes are inherently self-centered and opposed to your godly nature, which is humble and serves others. This means you naturally lack integrity, because the sinful ways you learned before you became a Christian always conflict with those of your new nature.

Because we recognize flaws in human nature, we build protective measures into all of our systems. We know that everyone has limitations and we can only rely on them to a certain point. A person may be highly respected and have an excellent reputation, but when they let their guard down momentarily, they fail. It has been said that everyone has a price and that they will eventually compromise if the personal benefit becomes great enough, which is one reason our government has checks and balances. Or why a church usher should never count the offering alone, or why someone with financial problems should never even be an usher. Or why we are alert to compromising situations of all kinds. We know that everyone's integrity is limited and at some point they might compromise. While we might not want to believe this is true of Christians, it is. Which is precisely why the New Testament puts such emphasis on repenting—changing the way you think.

I own a book that is a farcical account of life in corporate America. It gives many examples of how to make the corporate system work to your advantage while doing as little actual work as possible. Most of the examples are both funny and sad. They are funny because they include ingenious ways to make the business environment do things it was never intended to do, and sad because they show the extreme measures people will use to derive all the benefits while avoiding their basic responsibility: earning their pay. Such activities demonstrate a pathetic absence of integrity.

Integrity is an attitude that motivates certain behavior. It will cause you to show up for work on time every day, even when you know no one will notice whether you are late. It will cause you to take care of personal matters on personal time, rather than at work. For example, using your office computer for personal email may be a violation of your integrity as well as company policy. Consider the company time you spend reading and writing personal messages; that time is equivalent to stealing money from your company, payroll money for the company time you spend doing personal business. If your company specifically allows you to do personal business on company time, this does not apply to you. Otherwise, such behavior reveals a lack of integrity.

Maybe this sounds like nothing more than legalism to you. But I suggest that the degree to which you struggle with issues like this is evidence that you have more than one standard of performance, more than one purpose, or more than one person you are serving. If you struggle between what is expected of you and what you want to do, you have conflicting allegiances. And that, by definition, is a lack of integrity.

Proverbs says the "integrity of the upright guides them, but the unfaithful are destroyed by their duplicity" (Prov. 11:3). There are two contrasts in this verse: integrity versus duplicity, and the upright versus the unfaithful. The usual interpretation of the first portion of the verse suggests that a person's high moral standards will cause them to make honorable decisions. While integrity includes high personal standards (moral integrity), that is only part of its meaning. In the broader sense, integrity is a unity of all your resources and efforts, a complete focus, a combined effort to accomplish a goal.

Consider an example of two people who are starting a business together. If they are serious about their business, they will invest their own money in it, and maybe lots of it. Especially in the beginning, they will put in endless hours of work to get the business going. They will seem almost obsessed with the business, and certainly preoccupied. Why? Because starting a business is tough and it requires every effort you can give it, and maybe more.

What if they started their company on borrowed money and then used a sizeable chunk of company funds to buy themselves a luxury "company car"? Then after a month of work, they took a three-week vacation? You would conclude they were not very serious about running their business, that they had divided loyalties. The real problem is a lack of integrity: they claim they want to start a business, but they are focusing on personal benefits rather than business goals. We know that starting a business requires hard work and sacrifices to succeed. It requires total commitment and we expect that of new business owners.

Now imagine that the owners have integrity, apply Proverbs 11:3 and let their integrity guide them. If they must do a lot of business driving and they are fully committed to making their business succeed, how will their commitment influence their transportation choices? They will be more likely to subsidize their company by using their own vehicles and taking a personal tax credit for mileage. Or if they in fact need a company vehicle, they will protect the solvency and profitability of their business when they select one. That is, their commitment to making their company succeed will help them make wise business decisions. It is a matter of integrity.

A person with integrity will focus all their effort and use all their resources to achieve their goal. They will not subvert their goal to do something else and will not violate their personal standards of behavior. Everything about them is focused. Their integrity applies the same standards to every situation, which means their response is predictable. They are consistent in their decisions and behavior, so you can trust them. When faced with a choice, they stick to their standards and goals, and these determine how they will respond. Their integrity will guide them.

In contrast, "the unfaithful are destroyed by their duplicity." Unfaithfulness and duplicity both imply multiple standards or goals. Their action depends on what they believe will benefit them most in a given situation. You may be working with someone like this and they will cooperate with you up to a point. When they see another desirable goal, or their personal interest becomes more important than what you are working on, they abandon you and do something else, even if it means undermining the work they were doing with you.

Duplicity also includes deception. The person in our example may have been making you think they wanted to help you, but all along they had something else in mind. They very likely were using you to get what they wanted.

What we see in Proverbs 11:3 is a contrast between two types of people. One remains focused, adhering to a high standard and consistently applying themselves to a specific end. All of their efforts ultimately are directed toward their goal. The other person has more than one standard or purpose, and they jump from one to the other, depending on circumstances. That person is unreliable because they lack integrity.

In the Old Testament, integrity is synonymous with blamelessness and the same Hebrew word translates both ways. This emphasizes that having integrity means never deviating from your goal or falling short of your standards.

In the dramatic story of Job's afflictions, he at first did not sin in what he said. His wife became fed up with all that had happened and said to him, probably without much gentleness, "Are you still holding on to your integrity? Curse God and die!" (Job 2:9-10). She identified one of Job's strengths: his integrity. God identified the same trait in Job by three times calling him blameless (Job 1:1, 8; 2:3). It was his "regular custom," for example, to sacrifice burnt offerings for his children, just in case they had sinned (Job 1:5). Job was consistent and tenaciously adhered to his convictions. The man had integrity! However, God used Job's experiences to make him face his biggest problem—pride—though God called him "blameless" from the beginning. Job's standards needed some adjustment, but God honored him for his integrity.

Other Old Testament verses reinforce this definition of integrity. "The man of integrity walks securely, but he who takes crooked paths will be found out" (Prov. 10:9). The inference is that integrity means walking straight ahead without turning to the left or right.

Isaiah quotes God as saying, "my mouth has uttered in all integrity a word that will not be revoked" (Isa. 45:23). Here we see the connection between integrity and an irrevocable word. Integrity means there are no exceptions.

The New Testament provides many examples of integrity, although it seldom uses the word. Even the Pharisees admittedly recognized Jesus' integrity. "Teacher, we know you are a man of integrity. You aren't swayed by men, because you pay no attention to who they are; but you teach the way of God in accordance with the truth" (Mark 12:14). They acknowledged that He did not change His message to appease His audience and He was not influenced by who people were because He had integrity.

Paul confronted Peter for his lack of integrity, although he did not use that specific word. Peter had associated with the Gentiles until the Christian leaders arrived from Jerusalem, then he followed the Jewish tradition of separating himself from the Gentiles. Paul identified this as hypocrisy and deviating from the truth (Gal. 2:13-14), which are the opposite of integrity.

Paul gives very clear instruction about acting with integrity in his letter to Titus. "In everything set them an example by doing what is good. In your teaching show integrity, seriousness and soundness of speech that cannot be condemned, so that those who oppose you may be ashamed because they have nothing bad to say about us" (Titus 2:7-8). Do what is good in everything, with no deviation. Teach what cannot be condemned, that which completely conforms to truth. Thus accusers have nothing bad to say, for you are blameless. These are traits of integrity as well as its results.

We have examined several verses that use the word "integrity," but the Bible does not use the word very often. Instead, it uses several words or images that relate to integrity. Let us consider some of them.

Holiness Is Integrity

One of the results of specialization is that each occupation and area of interest has its own lingo. Special words or special uses of common words are necessary for effective communication. That is true of Christianity and the Bible, too, as there are many spiritual concepts that require specialized words. I find that many Christians really do not understand the meaning of the words they use, so they speak the language but do not know what they are talking about. I often feel that way myself.

One group of words in particular has always puzzled me. I look up definitions of the words and I am still not certain what they really mean. This is especially true when the definition of word A uses word B, and the definition of word B uses word A. The group of words I am referring to includes the following: holy, sanctify, conse-crate, hallow, sacred, righteous and pious.

The main word in this group is "holy" and the others relate to the concept of holiness. Let me briefly elaborate on the definition of "holy." I assure you that compared to the various definitions I have found, the following is very brief.

The Old Testament concept of holiness relates to God's divine perfection. Because of our human inability to understand this quality, the Old Testament writers described holiness as the essence of God's nature and then contrasted it with the imperfection of humanity. It was like saying, "God is perfect. If you want to understand what this means, look at yourself and those around you. God is not like that." Holiness at the human level became a separation from Gentiles, from sin, and from licentiousness. Licentiousness is another unusual word that means a person has little regard for standards of any kind and prefers to indulge themselves any way they want, as in "taking license" to indulge in any behavior.

The New Testament concept of holiness rests firmly on that of the Old Testament. Holiness is the essence of God's nature. But what does that mean? We often describe holiness as separation from sin and therefore separation to God; in other words, sacred.

The individual believer and the Christian community are holy as the temple of God's Holy Spirit. The New Testament quotes the Old Testament, "Be holy, because I am holy" (1 Pet. 1:16; Lev. 11:45); we are to be holy in all we do because He who called us is holy (1 Pet. 1:15). We are "a chosen people, a royal priesthood, a holy nation, a people belonging to God" (1 Pet. 2:9). As believers, we are "sanctified [made holy] in Christ Jesus and called to be holy" (1 Cor. 1:2).

I could quote many, many more scriptures about holiness, sanc-tification, consecration and sacredness, but these all relate to the basic meaning of the word "holy." We might even state that holiness is not something we attain through our own efforts—it is a state into which God calls us—yet as believers we are to sanctify ourselves (make ourselves holy). The Bible even calls us saints, which means we are the sanctified or holy ones.

By now you can probably sense or relate to my frustration at not knowing what I mean when I use the word "holy." If God requires me to be holy or sanctify myself (make myself holy), I really need to know what it means.

In my study of scriptures, books and dictionaries, I began to see a common theme that I eventually described with a word not found in my reading: integrity. I believe integrity is the basis of God's holiness and ours. Let me explain.

God's nature is one of absolute virtue and purity, total integrity in which absolutely every characteristic and action is in complete conformity with the whole. You will not find God deviating once from His own standard. Even when He is said to repent, He changes His mind about what He was planning to do, yet He continues to uphold His standard and His nature. God's character and behavior are totally compliant to His moral and ethical standard. He is the epitome of integrity, totally consistent with His own nature.

The standard to which He adheres is so far above that of the rest of creation that it can only be described as "holy." His ways and thoughts are as far above mankind's as the heavens are above the earth (Isa. 55:8-9). Our current understanding of the heavens is one of virtually endless expanse; if there is a limit to our universe, it is so far away we cannot comprehend the distance. So how high are the heavens above the earth? Basically an infinite distance. That is how far God's nature, His holy integrity, is morally and ethically beyond our own. An inconceivably perfect adherence to an incomprehensibly high standard of excellence; that is the essence of God's nature and character. The only word we can use to describe it is "holy."

How does such a concept apply to us mortals? What does holiness mean to our daily existence? How does it influence our attitudes and behavior? Just as godliness means something different to each of us because of our character, holiness will have different expressions in each person. Not only because of different personalities, but because holiness is defined by a standard. The issue is not behavior and external appearance, however, but redeeming your character. We define God's holiness as who He is, rather than what He does. Who God is determines what He does, and so it is with us. Holiness relates to who you are; who you are governs what you do.

Holiness teaching that emphasizes behavior or appearance is overlooking an important point. Improving your behavior without improving your character is legalism. On the other hand, improving your character will change your behavior, and that is progress. Personal holiness is an integrity based on a standard of excellence affecting all areas of human existence. And the only meaningful standard is God's. That is why repentance is essential—you must change your standards. Holiness is impossible without repentance.

A closely related concept is that of righteousness. To be righteous is to be morally upright; without guilt or sin. A state of holiness leads to righteous behavior. If you have integrity, with every aspect of your character adhering to a high standard, then your behavior will be righteous because you will not violate that standard.

The common thread running through all of this is "the standard." Do you live by a respectable human standard? If so, you may have the respect of your peers, but that is totally inadequate for a Christian. So, if being a good person is not enough and it is humanly impossible to become exactly like God, what is a Christian to do? Repent—change your standards, your attitudes, the way you think, what you think about. Change your mind; reprogram yourself. Then live with integrity, conforming yourself and your behavior to what you believe.

My wife and I told our sons as they were growing up, "Do what you know is right." Only now, years later, am I beginning to understand the significance of that instruction. Basically it means to live by your convictions. If you believe something is right, do it. If you believe it is wrong, don't do it. Like so much of our Christian experience, this is more of a process than an event, because God is constantly giving new revelation and understanding. So while you are learning to live with integrity based on your current standard, God is nudging the standard higher. God said, "Be holy because I am holy." In practical terms, that means you should be becoming progressively more holy. You should be looking more and more like your spiritual father, God, and the very image of your big brother, Jesus.

Exclusive Rights

Another aspect of integrity or holiness relates to the dual concepts of availability and responsibility. If you are conforming your attitudes to God's standards, then what does that imply about your responsibility to Him? And as you continue making that transition, integrating your entire nature to support a godly lifestyle, how does that affect your availability to God? What does your relationship with God look like? How will it affect your everyday choices?

It may be helpful to consider these questions using the analogies of contractual and covenantal relationships. A contract is an agreement in which two or more parties agree to exchange equivalent goods or services; usually one party pays for the product or service provided by the other. A contract is a legal agreement and is enforceable by law. It limits the responsibilities and protects the rights and interests of each party. A contract recognizes there can be a conflict of interest between the parties, a disunity, and it imposes penalties for errors or deliberate violations of the contract. Contracts are a vital part of our Western culture, especially in America where we value free enterprise and competition. Even major personal decisions or agreements often involve contracts.

Consider an example. Let's say I develop a new product, but I know only a few potential customers, so I sign an exclusive rights contract with a nationwide distributor. I agree to send all of my products to the distributor, and he agrees to sell my products nationwide in exchange for a percentage of the sales. As long as the distributor and I both honor the contract, it should work to everyone's benefit. Question: If I then begin selling my products on consignment at a local store, what effect does that have on my contract and my relationship with the distributor? Answer: It very clearly violates my contract and very likely will make the distributor my adversary. By violating the contract, I lose its benefits and bring its penalties on myself, because it would include statements that protect the distributor's rights and penalize me for violating those rights. That is the nature of a contract. It protects the interests and rights of both parties and imposes penalties on anyone who violates it.

Since we understand the concept of a contract so well, it is helpful to point out that it does not describe our relationship with God. Knowing what something is not can be as important as knowing what it is. You do not have a contractual relationship with God.

Instead, you have a covenantal relationship. A covenant is also a binding agreement between two or more parties, but with a fundamental difference. It recognizes a shared commitment to ideas, issues, values or goals, whereas a contract assumes there is no such common ground. Words such as love, warmth and personal chemistry are pertinent to a covenant but not a contract. A covenant reflects unity; a contract assumes disunity. A covenant tolerates risk and forgives errors; a contract penalizes them. A covenant binds people together and enables them to meet their common needs by meeting their individual needs, somewhat like a contract but with a very different motivation. Covenants define supportive relationships like those that exist in families.

Marriage is a covenant; in fact, it is an exclusive rights covenant. Two people commit themselves to each other, based on their shared ideas, issues, values and goals. They agree to support each other, work together, serve each other and honor each other. The two become one, developing a shared identity and way of thinking. They reserve their most intimate thoughts and expressions for each other, because each has exclusive rights to the other. If one flirts or becomes intimate with another person, they are violating their relationship with their spouse. Simply fantasizing about someone else is enough to defile their exclusive rights covenant with their spouse. Each person expects exclusive rights to their spouse's love and affection because that is the nature of marriage. The intent of the covenant is for each to support the other and work for the other's advantage. Self-centeredness is in clear opposition to that and will almost always cause problems.

Marriage is an earthly analogy of your relationship with God because you have an exclusive rights covenant with Him. When you became a Christian, you accepted Jesus as both Savior and Lord, and you can have only one Lord. Since Jesus is your Lord, you have an exclusive relationship with Him.

Your covenantal relationship with God is bidirectional, with both of you committing yourselves to each other as in marriage. You are now to have the same ideas, issues, values and goals. You are to support each other, work together, serve each other and honor each other. You are to become one with each other (see John 17:20-21), developing a shared identity and way of thinking. He has given you liberty to call on Him and use His resources, as much as is appropriate for you as a human being to do. In return, He expects you to serve Him alone.

This takes us back to the word "holy," which means separated or devoted to God, for His use alone. We tend to define holiness primarily as a personal condition and try to create it by our own efforts, but that is counterfeit holiness and a poor imitation. Being holy is being reserved for God's exclusive use. That means when you make choices or decisions out of selfish motives, you defile your covenant with God, which requires full devotion to Him. Holiness is an integrity of commitment to the Lord, with all of your attention and energies focused ultimately on serving Him. Integrity: everything about you working together to support your purpose, with nothing interfering. Holiness: being totally available to God, for His exclusive use.

I believe the Bible also uses the term "pure in heart" to describe this level of integrity and holiness. "Blessed are the pure in heart, for they will see God" (Matt. 5:8). Because the word "heart" refers to basic motives and attitudes, purity of heart is a state in which there is no motive or attitude that interferes with complete commitment to God. That is integrity and its result is seeing God as He is.

The apostle Paul refers twice to a pure heart in his letters to Timothy. He describes "love, which comes from a pure heart" (1 Tim. 1:5). He tells Timothy to "pursue righteousness, faith, love and peace, along with those who call on the Lord out of a pure heart" (2 Tim. 2:22). These show us something about a pure heart that makes complete sense. As you purge yourself of anything that interferes with your relationship with God or prevents you from serving Him effectively—that is, as you purify your heart—you will begin to express agape love, that selfless commitment to the benefit of others. You will become like God in that respect. You also will be motivated to pursue righteousness, faith, love and peace, which are character-istics of God's nature and His kingdom.

"Pursue righteousness, faith, love and peace." Self-centeredness prevents you from becoming righteous or even being interested in it, because righteousness is having nothing separate you from God or interfere with your relationship, and self-centeredness does both. It also inhibits your faith in God, because it motivates you to trust in yourself and be primarily concerned for your own well-being, which are the opposite of trusting God regardless of what happens to you. Almost by definition, self-centeredness is the opposite of agape, a selfless concern for the well-being of others. Peace is more than the absence of turmoil; it is a unity of purpose and effort. Self-centeredness, however, will always oppose God's purpose and refuse to cooperate with Him, so it destroys peace. Righteousness, faith, love and peace can only become part of your relationship with God as you reject self-centeredness and fully commit yourself to Him, developing a pure heart. Purity of heart is an integrity of motives and attitudes, in which nothing distracts you from focusing on God. Holiness requires purity of heart.

Another term for purity of heart is single-mindedness. While this term does not appear in Scripture, its opposite does: double-minded. This describes someone who is divided in their thinking, loyalties or attitudes. James says such a person is "unstable in all he does" (James 1:8), and rightfully so, because you don't know which position he will take or how he will act in a given situation. James instructs the double-minded person to purify his heart (James 4:8), which shows that purity of heart is the antithesis of double-mindedness as well as its cure. David also took a strong stand against double-minded-ness. In one of the Psalms, he wrote at great length about his love for God's law and his commitment to it. In that demonstration of single-mindedness he wrote, "I hate double-minded men, but I love your law" (Ps. 119:113).

In the context of New Testament Christianity, we can identify a carnal believer as double-minded. They have made a commitment to the Lord but continue to act as their own lord. They want the benefits of the kingdom—primarily eternal safety from punishment for sin—but they want to continue indulging their sinful desires. They have an exclusive rights covenant with God but want to maintain their right to do whatever they want. They want the benefits of righteousness but none of the responsibilities. How tolerant do you suppose God is of double-mindedness? Considering how many times and how many different ways He tells us to get our act together, I conclude that God is very intolerant of double-mindedness. Yet, some degree of double-mindedness is typical for Christians. That is exactly why God urges us to change the way we think.

How do you purify your heart and overcome double-mindedness? By repenting, by transforming your mind, by changing the way you think. It is essential for you to reject every thought that opposes God's intent and make every thought a captive to His standard. You need to become increasingly focused and avoid anything that would distract you from your purpose.

It is imperative that you develop personal integrity and become holy, fully dedicated to serving the Lord. That is God's intent for you. "For he chose [you] . . . before the creation of the world to be *holy* and blameless in his sight" (Eph. 1:4, emphasis added). Jesus loved you and gave Himself up for you to make you holy, cleansing you through the Word to make you holy and blameless (see Eph. 5:25-27). "Therefore, I urge you, brothers, in view of God's mercy, to offer your bodies as living sacrifices, *holy* and pleasing to God—which is your spiritual worship" (Rom. 12:1, emphasis added). "As obedient children, do not conform to the evil desires you had when you lived in ignorance. But just as he who called you is holy, so be *holy in all you do*" (1 Pet. 1:14-15, emphasis added). Whatever you do for your own motive is a violation of your holiness, your complete dedication to God.

You are for God's exclusive use and benefit. He bought you with His Son's blood. He redeemed you from the destruction of sin. He placed His own Spirit in you to teach you and guide you. He is molding you into the image of His Son. He placed himself in covenantal relationship with you, pledging to care for you and protect you. He transferred your citizenship to Heaven. In exchange, you are for His exclusive use and benefit, holy, sacred, the temple of His Holy Spirit.

Like me, maybe you respond, "This is a free country. I'm free to be my own person and do what I want." While that is true of American citizenship, you are now a citizen of heaven and governed by its principles (Phil. 3:20). God paid a great price to buy you from sin and you no longer belong to yourself (1 Cor. 6:19-20, 7:23). The Greek word used in this context describes the buying of merchandise and involves a legal transfer of ownership, so you now belong to God.

How do you use your spare time? Most of us constantly preoccupy our minds with some form of entertainment. This is like the military tactic of jamming enemy radar and communications by filling them with garbage, except we are doing it to ourselves in this case. It is easy to flood your mind continuously, keeping it busy with inconsequential things. Even without such stimulation, your mind automatically locks on to whatever interests you, or whatever worries you, or angers you, and so on. Think about it. You belong exclusively to God and you are using the resources He gave you primarily for your own pleasure and benefit. That violates your covenantal relationship with God, just as your spouse would violate your relationship by longingly daydreaming about someone else.

This does not mean you can never watch television again— unless, of course, God specifically asks you to give it up for a while. Nor does it mean you should never rest or enjoy your hobbies or have fun with your friends. God created you in His image and that means you have the godlike ability to enjoy yourself. And as a human being, you need occasional diversion and recreation. A problem begins to develop, however, when these become your focus. Sin will always pervert God's design and cause the fringe benefit to become the goal. God gave you the ability to enjoy life, but enjoying life is not to be your focus.

"Therefore, holy brothers, who share in the heavenly calling, fix your thoughts on Jesus, the apostle and high priest whom we confess. He was faithful to the one who appointed him" (Heb. 3:1-2). You are holy, set aside for God's exclusive use. You share in the heavenly calling, which means God has summoned or urged you to stand with Him and promote His kingdom. You are to fix your thoughts on Jesus, because He is the example you are to follow, and His example is one of faithfulness to God.

Keep in mind that you have an exclusive rights covenant with God, not an exclusive rights contract. In a contract, the parties easily become antagonists. Each protects his own rights, each fulfills his obligation only if the other does, and it is appropriate to force compliance and punish noncompliance. In a covenant, however, the parties remain protagonists. Each disregards his own rights and well-being, so no protection is necessary. And there is unconditional commitment to the well-being and benefit of the other.

It should be very evident by now how important it is to transform your thinking. God's desire is for you to develop integrity, to be so unified in your attitudes and motives that you no longer oppose what He is doing. That requires some effort on your part to reject any state of mind that does not comply with His standard.

Conclusion

Integrity motivates you to focus all your effort and use all your resources to adhere to a standard or achieve a goal. As a Christian, you will find your standards continuously changing to become more like God's and your goals becoming increasingly like His. This is a natural result of becoming more like Him, but can only occur as you transform your mind (repent). Once you have begun that process, you will immediately experience a conflict between those standards and your previous sinful ones. Then you will see the need for integrity—commitment to serving God rather than yourself, and the ability to stick to God's standards.

Holiness is complete commitment to God's purposes and service, and every deviation reveals a lack of integrity. Because God realizes you are still human, He graciously offers you the benefits of holiness while allowing you to develop greater integrity. As a result, integrity will be more of a process than an event, like every other aspect of becoming like God.

This demonstrates the need for continued repentance. As God reveals more of His nature to you, it is your responsibility to transform your thinking, attitudes, standards and priorities so they conform with His. Conforming yourself to your current under-standing of God's nature reveals great personal integrity.

Personal Study

1.   What impact do the concepts of integrity, holiness and exclu-sive rights have on the following?

    • What you do with your time.

    • What you think about in your spare time.

    • How you make decisions.

    • Your choice of entertainment.

    • How you view your occupation.

    • Your attitudes regarding your marriage and family.

    • Your attitudes about proper diet, rest and exercise.

    • Choosing alluring clothing.

2.   How can you identify attitudes, thoughts or motivations that violate your integrity?

3.   What specific steps can you use to develop greater integrity?

4.   How can you measure your level of integrity?

11

How Do You Feel About That?

The emphasis of this study has been on repentance—how you think and what you think about. To repent is to change your mind. We have considered how this will affect your standards, priorities, perception, attitudes, and so on. But there is one other area that we have not addressed specifically that falls within this domain, and that is how repentance will affect your feelings.

Maybe all of this discussion of "mind" subjects and the rational way we have treated repentance—reprogramming yourself, controlling your thoughts, and so on—has led to you to conclude it is irrelevant to the way you feel. It is, however, extremely relevant. Maybe you view people as either left- or right-brain, rational or emotional, objective or subjective. The principles we have examined actually apply to all people, regardless of how they think or whether their feelings are more important to them than rational thought. All believers need to repent, regardless of their orientation.

Where do your feelings and emotions come from? Even if you are strongly intuitive, emotional or subjective, your feelings and emotions still coincide with what you think and believe. And your approach to repentance is the same as a rational person's.

A wide variety of factors can influence your feelings. You are a highly integrated being, in which your spirit, mind and body interact with each other. Consider some ways in which your spirit and body affect your mental state.

Spiritual factors. Your spirit has a major role in determining your character and many personality elements are actually spiritual in nature. Examples include whether you are an extrovert or introvert, an optimist or pessimist, what aptitudes you have, and so on. If this is true, then your spiritual nature will strongly influence your mental state. That is, your natural disposition and the extent to which you have redeemed your character will strongly influence your feelings.

Physiological factors. The condition and general health of your physical body also affects your mental state. If you are ill or have chemical imbalances, hormonal imbalances, injury or discomfort, your attitude is likely to be affected.

External factors. The environments you spend time in, your responsibilities and the demands others place on you can affect your mental state directly. They also can affect you indirectly because you may have to do tasks that do not come naturally to you, therefore your performance will not reflect your true nature.

Our culture has swung from a strongly rational, analytical posture during its scientific age to one that places great emphasis on feelings. We may have swung from one extreme to the other. We now are very concerned about how we feel and whether we are enjoying ourselves. There are many indicators of this: the booming entertainment industry, extreme sports and in-your-face behavior, to name a few. Some people would even warn us not to invalidate another person's feelings, and suggest that it is acceptable for them to feel the way they do.

Are your feelings sacred or beyond evaluation? No more than your thoughts are sacred. Are all feelings acceptable? No more than all thoughts are acceptable. Let me offer some examples, which you may feel are rather extreme but demonstrate my point.

What if someone broke into your home and stole your television, stereo and computer? And when the police caught him, the thief complained that he only had a 13-inch black and white television for entertainment. He said he really wanted better equipment and even dreamed about having the latest home entertainment center. When he saw your equipment, he really wanted it badly, so he took it. How would you respond? "Well, if you really wanted it that badly, it's yours. I won't press charges"? Not likely!

What if your spouse committed adultery and when you confronted them they explained they had an insatiable desire for the other person. They were sure you would not object since they wanted the other person so badly and had such strong feelings for them. What would you do? Try to be sympathetic and understanding? I don't think so!

What if someone did not like what you said and slugged you in the face? They explained that you made them really angry and they just felt like breaking your nose. Would you respond, "Oh well, since you felt so strongly about it, it's okay"? Never!

Or imagine offering this explanation to the Lord: "I know you wanted me to change my attitude. But being the way I am makes me feel good. Besides, changing seems like a lot of effort and I just didn't feel like working that hard."

Granted, these are extreme examples, but they help us see the principle. Feelings are not sufficient justification for action, and not all feelings are acceptable. Consider the following statements: "That's just the way I feel. I can't help it;" "I don't care. I really want it;" and "I can't get over what you did. You made me really angry."

These statements are pretty common and are widely accepted by most people. They express feelings, desires and emotions, and most of the time we use them to close discussion on the topic at hand. They communicate an attitude that honors feelings above all else. Is it possible they also reveal that the person is unwilling to accept responsibility for themselves by passing the buck and claiming victim status?

Consider the third statement, "You made me really angry." That statement simply cannot be true, because no one can make you angry against your will. What they do may cause you to have initial feelings of anger, but whether those develop into full-blown anger is up to you. You generally are not responsible for the initial thoughts and feelings that pop up; that is, unless they spring from an attitude you have been nurturing. Otherwise, you need not feel guilty for thoughts of anger, self-centeredness, lust or any other sin that suddenly pops into your mind or affects your emotions. You still have thoughts and feelings from your previous life as a sinner, and Satan is eager to exploit them. The question is what you do with the original temptation. If you nurture that feeling or entertain that thought, then you accept ownership of it and you become responsible for it.

No one can make you angry against your will. When someone hurts you, your old sinful thoughts and emotions pop up, and these are what motivate you to feel sorry for yourself, get angry, retaliate or whatever. As soon as that happens, you must consciously overcome that initial response by replacing it with appropriate thoughts and attitudes. You cannot simply erase those thoughts and stop feeling that way; you must replace them with legitimate ones. Transforming your mind is a continuing process, because your old way of thinking will continue to produce temptations for you to overcome.

What if I hypothetically told you, "I don't believe God loves me, because He doesn't do for me what the Bible says He will do, and because He doesn't answer my prayers. I feel like God either doesn't exist or care about me." How would you respond? Would you assure me it is okay to feel that way or would you try to convince me otherwise? And if you did try to persuade me that God loved me, would you not be invalidating my feelings? No, you might demonstrate that my feelings are not valid, but that is not the same as invalidating them because you did not make them invalid. If my feelings are based on incorrect assumptions, unreasonable expectations or bias, they need to be changed and I am responsible for changing them.

At this point, anyone who knows me might be thinking, "Come on, Larry. You're a rational, logical, analytical kind of guy. What do you know about feelings?" Actually, I know quite a bit about feelings, emotions and desires. I am an intense person but not very demonstrative, so a lot can be going on inside with very little showing on the outside. I have a wide range of emotions and many of them are intense. Certain human situations make me cry, whether I see them in pictures and videos or in person. I can feel elated about a success or discovery. I can be ecstatic or furious; I know emotions and the feelings that accompany them. I understand desires and have a lot of them, some acceptable and some not. I am not a machine; I am human.

You cannot know how many times I have said to myself, "I really, really do not want to do this. But I will do it because I need to do it." Quite frankly, I sometimes felt that way about working on this book. Even today, I had blocked out some time to work on this chapter but kept thinking of other things I would prefer doing. I had to force myself to open this document in my computer and begin reading it. Sure, I believed I knew God's will on this matter and even knew some ideas I should include in the text, but I had to battle my feelings before I could get started. As I read what I had drafted earlier and saw the reality of it, my feelings began changing radically.

The point is this: you are responsible for your thoughts, your feelings, your desires, your perspective and your priorities. Repentance includes everything related to your attitude, including your feelings, emotions and desires.

Any concern I have about someone invalidating me or my feelings comes directly from my self-centered mindset, which basically believes anything I want or do or think or feel should be acceptable. None of us likes to be corrected because it implies we are not completely acceptable the way we are. And self-centeredness typically motivates us to shift the blame to the person who pointed out our problem, claiming they are intolerant, or whatever. People usually will get angry with you, for example, if you call them a sinner; the fact that they get angry is evidence that you were right.

I should point out, however, that God was the first to state that man's relationship with Him was not right, that man's behavior was unacceptable, that man needed to repent. God was the first to reject man's sinfulness and He will continue to do so. In fact, He even tells Christians to overcome each other's sinful ways through teaching, correction and encouragement. So instead of whining and feeling sorry for yourself when someone corrects you, accept responsibility for your fault and make the necessary changes.

When God talks about you becoming spiritually mature and like Him, He doesn't say you don't have to do it if you don't want to: "Be holy, for I am holy, unless of course you prefer not to be holy." No, God's solution is for you to change the way you think and what you think about. You must "take captive every thought to make it obedient to Christ" (2 Cor. 10:5), and that includes emotional and intuitive thought as much as rational thought.

An emotion is a mental state that develops subjectively rather than through conscious effort. You might define a feeling as a state of mind that results from emotions, sentiments or desires. You would be subjective if your mental state is governed more by your perception and feelings than by facts and standards.

Everyone has feelings, just as everyone has thoughts. What kind of feelings and thoughts you have and how you express them are determined by your character, which is predominantly spiritual in origin. Because your spirit's development is dependent on what it receives from God's Spirit and your mind (through Bible reading, teaching, meditation, and so on), transforming your mind is a crucial factor in your spiritual development.

Your basic character will probably remain the same as you transform your mind, though you can expect your thoughts and feelings to change. If you are by nature an emotional person, for example, the nature of your emotions and the way you express them may change significantly, though you remain emotional.

The more subjective you are, the more your attitudes and actions will be based on your state of mind, your perception or opinion. As your basic motivation changes from self-centeredness to humility and agape, you will remain subjective, but your perceptions, opinion and state of mind will change, as well as the way you respond to them.

Think about the gasoline engine in your car. If you run it on the cheapest gas you can find, it becomes harder to start, idles roughly and may hesitate or buck when you accelerate. If you consistently use high quality gas, however, your car's performance will be exceptional. The engine is still an internal combustion gasoline engine, but the way it performs is entirely different. That is how your performance will change as you purify what you feed your mind.

How can you change your feelings? The same way you change any other attitude or state of mind. "[W]hatever is true, whatever is noble, whatever is right, whatever is pure, whatever is lovely, whatever is admirable—if anything is excellent or praiseworthy—think about such things" (Phil. 4:8). Do this, and your mind will change.

You will develop new priorities and standards. Your feelings, emotions and desires will change. Your outlook on life will change. This really is not an option; God expects you to do it.

The Bible actually has a lot to say about feelings, emotions and desires. Let us consider just a few verses, beginning with the Book of Ephesians. "All of us also lived among [those who are dead in their transgressions and sins] at one time, gratifying the cravings of our carnal nature and following its desires and thoughts" (Eph. 2:3). Did God suddenly remove all of your sinful cravings and desires when you became a Christian? Of course not. Does this verse imply that all desires are evil? Not any more than it suggests that all thoughts are evil. It refers to those that originated with your former sinful nature.

> *So I tell you this, and insist on it in the Lord, that you must no longer live as the Gentiles do, in the futility of their thinking. They are darkened in their understanding and separated from the life of God because of the ignorance that is in them due to the hardening of their hearts. Having lost all sensitivity, they have given themselves over to sensuality so as to indulge in every kind of impurity, with a continual lust for more* (Eph. 4:17-19).

The author, Paul, insists that you no longer live a certain way, which means you can choose to do so. He speaks of darkened understanding and ignorance resulting from hardening of the heart. The heart usually refers to your inner nature, including your feelings, desires and emotions. When the Bible speaks of someone with a hardened heart, it means a person who is callous toward God, who is self-centered, who considers their own desires more important than God's. Focusing on what you want and how you feel is an indication of hardness toward God. Paul also states this can cause you to lose all sensitivity, which is synonymous with having a hardened heart. He shows this leads to sensuality, which is a preoccupation with the feelings your senses produce. And because such feelings are momentary, you can easily develop a continual lust for more.

A few verses later, Paul wrote that you should "put off your old self, which is being corrupted by its deceitful desires" (v. 22). Sinful desires are deceitful because they lead you to believe you can find true happiness by indulging them, but that is not true. You may feel good for a while, having gratified your sinful desires, but that is not true happiness.

"Do not let the sun go down while you are still angry" (v. 26) addresses the emotion of anger. Since you obviously cannot stop the sun from going down, this verse clearly means you should overcome your anger. You may be thinking, "But, I'm so angry!" So, what's your point? God expects you to deal with your feelings if they are inappropriate.

"Do not let any unwholesome talk come out of your mouths, but only what is helpful for building others up according to their needs, that it may benefit those who listen" (v. 29). I know, sometimes you just want to tell that certain person off, but that is no longer acceptable. Speak only what builds them up, not what tears them down.

Notice this is not just talking about how you interact with Christians. Look at the context and you will see this is about how you are to be, not about whom you are with. This rules out all derogatory or belittling remarks, or in-your-face statements. You are to speak only what is wholesome and builds the person up.

"Get rid of all bitterness, rage and anger, brawling and slander, along with every form of malice" (v. 31). Bitterness is clearly an attitude or emotional state, as is anger. Malice is a desire to do someone harm, a spiteful attitude. What are you supposed to do with such feelings? Get rid of them.

Maybe you feel rather helpless at this point, because you have tried to suppress those inappropriate feelings, but without success. You feel like you are a captive of your feelings, that you can't help the way you feel.

On the contrary, the situation is not hopeless because God has already done everything you need Him to do. Before salvation, you could do nothing but sin, because you were enslaved by sin (Rom. 6:17). Among other things, that means you were unable to control inappropriate feelings or desires. Now you are free from sin's bondage (Rom. 6:18), which means you can choose not to sin. Jesus ransomed you from sin, so you are no longer its hostage. You chose to accept His gift of salvation and apply it to yourself, so you now are free to choose whether to apply God's plan of redemption to the rest of your nature.

Not only did God give you the ability to choose, He empowered you to make your decisions effective by placing His own Spirit within you. The Holy Spirit will teach you the ways of God, remind you of Jesus' teaching, and provide the power you need to do God's will. You have the freedom to choose to become like God and His power is available to implement your choice. You need nothing else.

God has done everything He needs to do and given you everything you need to be successful and mature. Now it is up to you. You are responsible for bringing your attitudes, feelings, standards, priorities and everything else into line with God's.

Maybe you are still telling yourself, "I can't help myself. This is just who I am." That is not true for a Christian. It certainly is true for a sinner, who is a slave to their own carnal nature. They cannot help themselves; they have no option other than sin. As a believer, however, you are set free from sin and have a choice. That means you also have responsibility for the choices you make.

As Christians, we often think we are okay as long as we don't actually do anything on the "Thou shalt not" list. That suggests that we can control our behavior and not worry about our stinking attitudes. If so, we are missing an important point, because God's emphasis is on who we are. Who we are determines what we do. This was Jesus' point when He told the Pharisees a person is made unclean by what is in his heart, not by failing to ceremonially wash his hands (Matt. 15:10-20).

So far we have focused on the inappropriate feelings and emotions from your old (sinful) nature. The Book of Ephesians provides examples of godly feelings, such as a husband's love for his wife (Eph. 5:25). The kind of love the Bible advocates is a combination of attitude and action. It is a personal humility and regard for another person that motivates you to perform acts that benefit them. Such love is more than an attitude, but it clearly involves feelings, emotions and desires. Paul tells husbands three times in one paragraph that they should love their wives (Eph. 5:25, 28, 33).

It is interesting that Paul does not tell wives to love their husbands. Some people say it is natural for a wife to love her husband, so she does not need to be told. While most women are subjective and therefore are more likely to have feelings about their husbands, those will not necessarily be feelings of love. Biblical love is foreign to human nature, regardless of gender. Instead, Paul says that wives should respect their husbands (Eph. 5:33). Like love, respect is an attitude that motivates action and produces certain feelings and emotions.

How can you as a husband begin to love your wife, or as a wife begin to respect your husband? By changing your mind where necessary. Think about whatever is true, noble, right, pure, lovely, admirable, excellent or praiseworthy in your spouse (Phil. 4:8). As you change your thinking, your attitude will begin changing and begin motivating the right actions and producing the right feelings.

After addressing husband and wife attitudes, Paul moves on to the children. He quotes one of the Ten Commandments: "Honor your father and mother" (Eph. 6:2; Deut. 5:16). Again, honor is an attitude that produces certain feelings and motivates specific actions.

He then instructs slaves to obey their earthly masters; in today's context he would say, "employees obey your bosses." But obedient actions are not the main point, because he says to obey "with respect and fear, and with sincerity of heart" (Eph. 6:5). Respect, fear and sincerity are definitely attitudes that produce certain feelings and motivate specific actions.

It should be clear by now that God holds you accountable for your attitudes and their resultant feelings, emotions and desires. You are no longer a slave to them, but instead have the ability and power to bring them under God's control. And doing so is part of growing up to be like your Father. How do you feel about that? You should feel wonderfully relieved, because there is hope that every part of your being can be pleasing to God, including your feelings.

Speaking of being like your Father, does God have feelings, emotions and desires? Yes, He does. The Bible describes several of them directly and we see others reflected in Jesus and His parables. Let us briefly consider some of them.

Most people will agree that God can be angry. In fact, some people seem to think that anger is God's dominant characteristic. The parable about an unmerciful servant portrays God as the master, who "in anger . . . turned him over to the jailers until he should pay back all he owed" (Matt. 18:34). Jesus became angry when the religious leaders watched Him carefully to see whether He would heal someone on the Sabbath (Mark 3:1-5). Paul wrote that God "will give to each person according to what he has done . . . for those who are self-seeking and who reject the truth and follow evil, there will be wrath and anger" (Rom. 2:6, 8). And God was angry with the Israelites for testing and trying Him in the wilderness (Heb. 3:7-11). Yes, God can be angry, but He has many other emotions as well.

He experiences delight. The Old and New Testaments both show God expressing His delight with His Son, Jesus (Matt. 12:17-18, Isa. 42:1). The Greek word translated "delighted" is also translated "pleased" in other verses, although "delight" more accurately describes the emotion. When John baptized Jesus, "a voice from heaven said, 'This is my Son, whom I love; with him I am well pleased [delighted]'" (Matt. 3:17). God uses the same word to describe His feelings toward you: "Do not be afraid, little flock, for your Father has been pleased [delighted] to give you the kingdom" (Luke 12:32).

God laughs, but not necessarily in response to humor. "The kings of the earth take their stand and the rulers gather together against the Lord and against his Anointed One. . . . The One enthroned in heaven laughs; the Lord scoffs at them" (Ps. 2:2, 4). And "the Lord laughs at the wicked, for he knows their day is coming" (Pss. 37:12, 59:8). These verses describe a scornful laughter, coming from contempt or derision. God's righteous people will laugh in the same way at an evil person (Ps. 53:6-7). Jesus' "Sermon on the Mount" introduced God's kingdom and the effects it will have on those who enter it. In that context, Jesus said, "Blessed are you who weep now, for you will laugh" (Luke 6:21). There are two similar words in the Greek, one meaning "to laugh" and the other meaning "to laugh at" someone. When Jesus said those who weep will laugh, he spoke of joyous laughter, rather than scornful.

Another emotion or feeling related to joyous laughter is that of rejoicing. One of Jesus' parables portrays God as rejoicing over a sinner who repents (Luke 15:5-6). The Lord rejoices in His works (Ps. 104:31). Usually when the Bible describes God as rejoicing, it is over Israel. For example, "as a bridegroom rejoices over his bride, so will your God rejoice over you [Zion]" (Isa. 62:5). Also, "I will rejoice in doing them [Israel] good and will assuredly plant them in this land with all my heart and soul" (Jer. 32:41). And, "The Lord your God is with you [Israel], he is mighty to save. He will take great delight in you, he will quiet you with his love, he will rejoice over you with singing" (Zeph. 3:17).

Compassion is another of God's feelings revealed in Jesus. "Filled with compassion, Jesus reached out his hand and touched the man" (Mark 1:41). God Himself is "the Father of compassion" (2 Cor. 1:3). And the Lord, the Son of God, "is full of compassion and mercy" (James 5:11).

Because of His compassion, God has longings and desires for His people. "O Jerusalem, Jerusalem . . . how often I have longed to gather your children together" (Luke 13:34). The night before Jesus died, He told His disciples, "I have eagerly desired to eat this Passover with you before I suffer" (Luke 22:15). And James refers to the "righteous life that God desires" (James 1:20). Have you ever thought about God having longings and desires? He does. But He is God, so why would He ever have to desire anything? Because He gave you a free will and He longs for you to choose Him and His kingdom voluntarily.

God also experiences the contrasting emotions of happiness and sorrow. He is happy about each sinner who repents (Matt. 18:13). Happiness apparently is one of God's frequent emotions, based on Jesus' parable of the talents; He tells the faithful servants, "Come and share your master's happiness!" (Matt. 25:21, 23). When faced with the results of sin, however, God experiences sorrow. The Old Testament describes Jesus, the Messiah, as "a man of sorrows" (Isa. 53:3). The night He was arrested, Jesus began to be sorrowful and troubled, then told His disciples, "My soul is overwhelmed with sorrow to the point of death" (Matt. 26:37-38). Believers should experience "godly sorrow" when confronted about their sin (2 Cor. 7:10-11).

So, does God have emotions? Definitely! He has anger and delight; He laughs with derision at His enemies and rejoices over His people; He has compassion for those who need His help; He desires for people to experience the benefits of His kingdom; and He experiences both happiness and sorrow. These are obviously legitimate emotions for God to have. Since He created you in His image and encourages you to become like Him, these are legitimate emotions for you, too.

The issue is not whether emotions or feelings themselves are appropriate, but whether they are motivated by godliness or sinfulness. How do you handle inappropriate feelings, those that originate with your sinful ways of thinking? And how do you foster appropriate feelings, those that originate with your godly nature? By repenting. This not only shows the importance of transforming your mind, it also shows that your emotions, feelings and desires will change as you become more like God.

Conclusion

Your feelings and emotions coincide with what you think and believe. Therefore, you can expect the way you feel to change as you repent. God calls on you to repent—whether you are objective or subjective, intuitive or rational—knowing that your attitudes, standards and priorities affect what you do and how you feel.

God has a broad range of feelings and, because He created you in His image, you have emotions, too. Feelings can originate with your ungodly attitudes or your godly nature. You are not a slave to your feelings, any more than you are a slave to sin, but you are accountable for your feelings just as you are for your thoughts. As you continue the repentance process, you can expect your emotions, feelings and desires to change as you become more like God.

Personal Study

Clinical research continues to show a direct relationship between a person's state of mind (their feelings) and their physical health. In general, stress produces hormones that over the long term are detrimental to the body's cells, making them vulnerable to viruses, diseases and a wide assortment of ailments. Emotional stress occurs in many forms, such as anger, fear, irritability, anxiety and tension.

1.   What forms of emotional stress do you frequently experience?

2.   In what ways might obedience to the first group of scriptures below lead to the benefits of the second group?

   a. The following scriptures address bringing your feelings under control.

   • "If it is possible, as far as it depends on you, live at peace with everyone" (Rom. 12:18).

   • "Do not be anxious about anything" (Phil. 4:6).

   • "Get rid of all bitterness, rage and anger, brawling and slander, along with every form of malice" (Eph. 4:31).

   b. These scriptures are about health and healing.

   • "Do not be wise in your own eyes; fear the Lord and shun evil. This will bring health to your body and nourishment to your bones" (Prov. 3:7-8).

   • "By his wounds you have been healed" (1 Pet. 2:24).

3.   What practical steps can you take to redeem your feelings?

12

Proper Judgment

From time to time you will hear one Christian tell another they should not judge others. "Judge not" is a pretty common quotation among believers, but universally prohibiting all forms of judgment and evaluation leads to confusion, in the least, and anarchy, in the extreme.

Among the spiritual manifestations listed in First Corinthians, we find "the ability to distinguish between spirits." This describes an ability to judge between subjects, to distinguish between persons, to discern. This is an essential role of the church and there are those who are especially gifted with this ability. Can we consider judging between spirits an essential role in the church, yet consider the more common form of judging earthly matters to be unimportant or even undesirable?

Let us consider some Scriptures frequently used to prohibit any form of judging.

"Do not judge, or you too will be judged. For in the same way you judge others, you will be judged, and with the measure you use, it will be measured to you" (Matt. 7:1-2). This is part of Jesus' teaching and, by itself, it clearly says not to judge others, or you will receive the same kind of judgment. However, consider the rest of the teaching.

"Why do you look at the speck of sawdust in your brother's eye and pay no attention to the plank in your own eye? How can you say to your brother, 'Let me take the speck out of your eye,' when all the time there is a plank in your own eye? You hypocrite, first take the plank out of your own eye, and then you will see clearly to remove the speck from your brother's eye" (vv. 3-5).

Did Jesus say you should not acknowledge that the other person has a speck in his eye? Or that you should not remove it? No, He said to clean up your own act before you help others clean up theirs. Self-centeredness motivates us to tolerate our own massive problems while expecting virtual perfection in others. Jesus places the emphasis on personal responsibility, but He does not rule out seeing imperfection in others, which is a form of judging.

He also said, "I pass judgment on no one" (John 8:15), so some believers contend that we should not judge, either. If only they would read Jesus' next statement. "But if I do judge, my decisions are right, because I am not alone. I stand with the Father who sent me" (v. 16). He made a similar statement earlier. "By myself I can do nothing; I judge only as I hear, and my judgment is just, for I seek not to please myself but him who sent me" (John 5:30). So when Jesus said, "I pass judgment on no one," He was not saying He never used judgment. Rather, He never relied solely on His own judgment, but instead judged as His Father would.

Jesus judged people and their actions, especially the religious leaders, and He sometimes condemned their actions. He said they made mistakes because they didn't know the Scriptures, and they created unnecessary religious burdens for people. He drove their businesses out of the temple, which was a pretty strong judgment of their practices. He called them painted burial vaults and snakes, which was an extremely strong judgment of their motives. He told His followers not to emulate them by praying to attract attention to themselves or by taking the seat of honor at the table. By His teaching, Jesus showed the importance of judging others. If you do not judge a person's actions, how can you know whether to follow their example?

Another frequent quotation is Romans 14:13, "Therefore let us stop passing judgment on one another." If you look at the context, you see that Paul is addressing disputable matters, such as what different people consider sacred or acceptable. His point is that we are not to judge others as sinful because they have different religious standards.

By focusing on a few Scriptures and ignoring their contexts, Christians have come to a conclusion that is the opposite of what the Bible actually teaches. Consider the following verses that show the importance of exercising good judgment.

Jesus answered one of many accusations from unbelievers by telling them, "Stop judging by mere appearances, and make a right judgment" (John 7:24). If they should not have judged at all, He would have said so.

Paul told the church at Corinth to judge what he said for themselves (1 Cor. 10:15, 11:13). He had opened the letter by discussing the wisdom the believer receives from the spirit. In that context he wrote the following.

The man without the Spirit does not accept the things that come from the Spirit of God, for they are foolishness to him, and he cannot understand them, because they are spiritually discerned. The spiritual man makes judgments about all things, but he himself is not subject to any man's judgment. 'For who has known the mind of the Lord that he may instruct him?' But we have the mind of Christ (1 Cor. 2:14-16).

Paul is explaining that human intellect cannot grasp spiritual truths. Therefore, if you receive spiritually derived understanding on some matter, you should not accept someone's intellectual judgment of it; their spiritual judgment, yes, but not their intellectual judgment. Paul wrote that the spiritual man judges all things, which includes someone else's spiritual understanding. The issue in this passage of Scripture is not whether to judge, but how to judge. The intellect cannot properly evaluate the spiritual. Your spirit evaluates or judges all things, then reveals the truth to your intellect. You have the mind of Christ, which is God's spiritual perspective guiding your human spirit, which in turn guides your intellect.

At some point, everyone recognizes the limit of their own judgment and asks someone for their opinion. We initially wait to ask because we want to work it out ourselves. Some of us wait a long time, but eventually we all ask.

Your old selfish, proud attitude wants you to succeed on your own, not to rely on others for help; you want to be adequate and autonomous. You want to come to your own conclusions and you value them more than the conclusions of others. You resent those who come to different conclusions and you resist their efforts to impose their opinions on you. The driving force behind such an attitude is self-centeredness, and that is one reason God says we should judge each other. Accepting a different judgment than your own forces you to humble yourself.

When you make a judgment, you compare the facts as you see them with what you believe to be right or good. Judgment can be very subjective. So what happens when someone else views the same facts and makes a different judgment? Each of you believes his judgment is better and may try to persuade the other person. This happens all the time, and for a legitimate reason.

Consider, for a moment, the "body" analogy the New Testament uses to describe the community of believers. How do the members of the body serve each other? One way is to offer their special abilities in service to the others. Each is to offer himself to the others for the common good.

Your character influences your perspective, and therefore how you see the facts, as well as which facts you consider more important. Your character also determines how you think, and therefore how you judge. So if you have a community of believers with a wide variety of personalities and therefore differing judgments, how can they serve each other? By judging each other. Just as each brings a unique ability to the community, each also brings a unique perspective and judgment.

Offering your opinion or judgment to others is the easy part. Your self-centered attitude wants others to know and accept what you think, so it is very natural to tell them. The hard part, however, is accepting the opinions or judgments of others. Obviously, it would do no good for everyone to express their opinion if no one listened, so God also tells us to submit to each other; that is, accept their judgment.

Consider an example. Let's say you have to make a decision, so you consider the facts, come to a decision and act on it. Then another believer, perhaps your spouse or friend, comes to you and explains why you should not have done it. Whose judgment do you accept, yours or theirs?

The natural (self-centered) reaction is to defend your decision. The supernatural reaction is to humble yourself, then remind yourself that God gave us different character types so we could serve each other. This will enable you to listen to them and try to see the situation from their perspective. You may or may not need to change your decision, but you certainly need to consider their judgment.

This does not mean you should automatically discard your opinion because another believer has a different one. It means you should recognize the validity of opinions other than your own. Of course, the more godly each believer becomes, the better this system works, but it works even with immature Christians.

Evaluating, judging and forming opinions are an important part of Christian living. The character God gave you affects how you do it and the conclusions you come to. It is possible to abuse this responsibility and become judgmental or condemning, but that does not mean you should avoid using your judgment. You eat, though the potential for gluttony exists, so do not let the fear of extremes or abuses deter you from doing what you should.

If we as believers are to evaluate or judge each other and submit to each other's judgment, then it would be easy to conclude that we are somehow accountable to each other. But are we? Accountability has to do with authority; when under someone's authority, you are accountable to them. Accountability requires you to explain how you fulfilled the responsibility given to you. It indicates that your actions are subject to the review of a higher authority.

Does the Bible state that one believer has authority over another? No, it describes us as brothers or peers. Some have oversight of others, but the emphasis is on protection, provision and development, not on control. Jesus specifically said believers were not to be lords over each other; His emphasis was on service. Does the Bible state that a believer can be morally or legally responsible to another, having to explain or justify his actions? No, not to another believer.

So among believers, judgment has nothing to do with one having authority over another. We are to discern what is good and what is evil. We are to use godly judgment to evaluate people's attitudes and actions, including our own. Never should we judge such matters using only our opinion, however. Feel free to offer your opinion when appropriate, but never use it to judge. Jesus is "the righteous Judge" (2 Tim. 4:8) and we are to become like Him.

Paul reprimanded the believers at Corinth because they failed to judge wickedness among them. He specifically stated they should identify any believer among them who is "sexually immoral or greedy, an idolater or a slanderer, a drunkard or a swindler" and not even associate with them (1 Cor. 5:11). Because they had allowed such a person to continue in his sin, Paul explained the importance of using righteous judgment. He wrote, "Are you not to judge those inside [the church]?" (v. 12). He then advocated judging disputes among believers in the church.

> *If any of you has a dispute with another, dare he take it before the ungodly for judgment instead of before the saints? Do you not know that the saints will judge the world? And if you are to judge the world, are you not competent to judge trivial cases? Do you not know that we will judge angels? How much more the things of this life! Therefore, if you have disputes about such matters, appoint as judges even men of little account in the church! I say this to shame you. Is it possible that there is nobody among you wise enough to judge a dispute between believers? But instead, one brother goes to law against another—and this in front of unbelievers!* (1 Cor. 6:1-6).

Paul states very clearly that it would be better for believers "of little account in the church" to judge disputes between believers than to take the matter before professional secular judges. It clearly is important for Christians to judge and to do so righteously as God would do.

Jesus told the crowd, "Stop judging by mere appearances, and make a right judgment" (John 7:24). The issue is not whether we judge, but how we judge. It is essential that we rely on God's judgment and principles when we must judge. Jesus said it best: "By myself I can do nothing; I judge only as I hear, and my judgment is just, for I seek not to please myself but him who sent me" (John 5:30). Do not judge to please yourself, using only your opinion. Rather, decide the matter as God would, on the basis of Scripture and His perspective.

Conclusion

Evaluating, judging and forming opinions are important parts of Christian living. The character God gave you affects how you do it and the conclusions you come to, so you can expect your judgment to be different from others'. It is equally important to consider other believers' opinions, because their character allows them to see the same situation from a different perspective. This helps you see past your limited perspective. The key is to see and decide the matter on the basis of Scripture and spiritual insight as Jesus did.

Personal Study

1. "Stop judging by mere appearances, and make a right judgment" (John 7:24).

   - Describe an incident in which someone criticized you because they thought you had an improper motive, but in fact they misjudged your motive. Consider how differences in personalities cause people to have different motives. What insight does this give about judging other people?

   - How can you make a "right judgment," according to God's standard, and what does that require you to do?

2.   "Therefore, if you have disputes about such matters, appoint as judges even men of little account in the church! I say this to shame you. Is it possible that there is nobody among you wise enough to judge a dispute between believers?" (1 Cor. 6:4-5).

   •   If you become involved in a dispute with another believer, what are some ways you can apply these verses?

   •   Consider Matthew 18:15-20 as a related passage. What is the spiritual significance of asking other believers to judge the dispute?

Part 2

Changing the Way
You Think
About God's Kingdom

13

Kingdom Values

Your thoughts naturally focus on the so-called important issues in the world—family, work, possessions, getting ahead in life, experiencing life, and so on. It is easy to relate to this way of thinking, because it is so predominant and such a natural result of living on earth. There is a strong reality about it because you continuously experience it both physically and mentally. How could you possibly deny the value of thinking this way?

The issue is not whether the world system is real or whether you should think about it. Rather, it is a matter of realizing the greater reality of another system and reshaping your thinking so you can live effectively in it.

You are a spiritual being who happens to be temporarily living in a physical body. Your mind is a liaison between your spirit and body, and is strongly oriented toward your physical existence and life on earth. But your spiritual strengths and capabilities greatly surpass those of your mind and body.

Because your mind focuses almost exclusively on your earthly existence, and because it has been programmed all your life to accept the world's ways, you very naturally accept the world's values and standards. Because you are a Christian, however, your spirit has new life—it is born again—and you are a member of God's kingdom. You still live on earth, but you no longer belong here and you no longer owe allegiance to the world system. That means you no longer have to think the way people in the world system think and you can have different values. In fact, not only is it possible for you to think differently, you really must.

The predominant theme of this book is repentance, or changing the way you think. Because you no longer belong to the world system or Satan's kingdom, it is reasonable to conclude that your values and standards must change to conform to God's kingdom. "What is highly valued among men is detestable in God's sight" (Luke 16:15), so moving from Satan's kingdom to God's requires a major shift in your values. The question now becomes whether God has clearly stated the values of His kingdom.

It is very significant that the Gospels record an in-depth teaching Jesus presented in the early stages of His ministry on earth. Put yourself in Jesus' place. His role on earth was to introduce people to His Father and His Father's kingdom, then make it possible for people to become part of that kingdom. If He wanted to teach about the kingdom, what it is and how it works, He should begin with basic principles and show some practical ways the kingdom differs from their current system. That actually is what He did, and His introductory teaching about the kingdom is what we call the Sermon on the Mount.

Permit me to list phrases from that teaching to show that it is about God's kingdom. He spoke of the kingdom of heaven (Matt. 5:3, 10, 20; 7:21), sons of God (Matt. 5:9), reward in heaven (Matt. 5:12), the least or greatest in the kingdom of heaven (Matt. 5:19), your Father in heaven (Matt. 5:45, 48; 6:1, 9, 14, 32; 7:11), God's kingdom (Matt. 6:10), and treasures in heaven (Matt. 6:20). We could call the Sermon on the Mount "An Introduction to God's Kingdom."

Sinful man cannot relate to God, comprehend His nature or understand His kingdom. Much as a toddler cannot comprehend social graces and must be taught laboriously with rules, such as "Don't do this" or "Behave this way." Because God still loved His creation and had a plan to redeem it from sin, He had to develop a concept of His kingdom that man could understand: the do's and don'ts of the law. So we wound up with a list of rules: Don't murder, don't steal, observe the Sabbath, and so on. The law of Moses was the only legitimate concept mankind had of God and His kingdom for thousands of years. That is, until Jesus came.

Jesus' purpose on earth included introducing people to a more accurate image of God and His kingdom. Jesus frequently made such statements as, "If you have seen me, you have seen the Father." He also used analogies to present images of the kingdom: "the kingdom of God is like . . . ." He was explaining what the kingdom is, how it works and what its principles are.

In His Sermon on the Mount, Jesus used the list of rules they understood, and explained the motivation and process behind the law. Sinful man, separated from God and having a terribly inaccurate concept of God, could only understand and accept specific laws, such as "You shall not murder." Jesus explained there is much more to it, however. Whereas the law prohibited specific actions, Jesus identified the motivating attitudes. He moved the focus from the external to the internal.

To understand the motivations behind God's law is to have a clearer understanding of God Himself. It is God's nature, rather than His laws, that governs His kingdom. Jesus' role was to shift the emphasis from God's edicts to His character. A child has little comprehension of a gracious demeanor until he learns he cannot slug somebody for doing something he does not like. The law must precede character development.

The law brought man to a point of impossibility: "How can I possibly observe all these rules? I can't do it!" At the right time, Jesus introduced God's nature: "If you change your character to be like God's, you can easily honor these rules. Better yet, the rules will no longer be necessary." That is the purpose of the Sermon on the Mount: to shift the emphasis from obedience to character, from a list of rules to attitudes. God knows that attitudes determine actions. If someone were to control their behavior without changing their attitude, the results would be both temporary and frustrating. If instead they corrected their attitude, then correct behavior would immediately follow. We can see this emphasis on attitudes in Jesus' teaching.

In the very first remarks of His introduction to the kingdom, Jesus presents an overview of kingdom values. What we call the

Beatitudes are actually kingdom values, concise statements of attitudes that God values very highly. If we want our attitudes to be compatible with God's, we should consider His statement of values.

At first reading of the Beatitudes, they seem to be almost arbitrary statements, as if God were choosing to bless random groups of people: the poor in spirit, those who mourn, the meek, those who desire righteousness, the merciful, the pure-hearted, peacemakers and the persecuted. These are all admirable qualities for God to select, but the list is somewhat puzzling. To begin with, some of these categories appear beyond an individual's control: poorness of spirit, meekness, pure-hearted and persecuted. Second, only a few are clearly the result of personal effort: peacemaking, for example. As humans, we prefer lists of tasks we can do to qualify for rewards, and this seems an unusual list.

If we consider that one of the primary themes of the New Testament is repentance, or changing the way we think, we begin to see the relevance of the beatitudes. With that in mind, let us consider some of them.

Poor in Spirit

Jesus was going throughout Galilee, the northern region of Israel, teaching in the synagogues, preaching the Good News of the kingdom and healing every disease and sickness among the people. As word spread about Him, people came from all over the region to receive healing and to hear His teaching.

One day, a large crowd was gathering around Jesus and His disciples, so He went up a mountainside and sat down so the people could see and hear His teaching. His disciples gathered around Him and He began to teach them.

The first recorded statement of His teaching is "Blessed are the poor in spirit, for theirs is the kingdom of heaven" (Matt. 5:3). The phrase "poor in spirit" does not recur in the New Testament, therefore its obvious interpretation is probably the best.

The word translated "poor" is the standard word for a poor person, someone who is destitute. When we say someone has no spirit, what do we mean? Only that they have no will to do anything on their own. If we say someone is a spirited person, we mean they are full of vigor and courage, that they assert themselves and do things their own way with great energy or confidence. So the phrase "poor in spirit" describes someone who is spiritually destitute. Such a person lacks a domineering character or attitude, considers himself unequipped to care for himself or do what he desires, or even lacks the personal desire to do so.

We must recognize, however, that this is not a universal principle. We are not to envy everyone with a poor self-image, for example. To understand Jesus' statements, we must keep them in the context of His teaching, which is the kingdom of God. Taking these statements out of context would grossly distort their meaning, because they are meaningful only within the context of God's kingdom.

Poorness in spirit has to do with humility, a poverty of self-interest, the most honored attribute in God's kingdom and the basis of all the others. It causes a person to perceive himself as nothing compared to something greater than himself. It is the exact opposite of self-centeredness, the fundamental characteristic of sinful human nature.

Ordinarily, the world system considers someone lacking in spirit as worthless or pitiful. People normally respect someone who considers himself self-sufficient or is "full of himself." Such people see little need for God. Jesus said that someone who is poor in spirit is blessed, which means they are enviable or better off than others. Why would Jesus consider them enviable? In part, because they recognize their need for help and are willing to rely on God. That is an excellent attitude for someone in God's kingdom to have. People with such an attitude have met the primary kingdom entrance requirement: humility or selflessness.

Jesus told His disciples repeatedly that the absolute greatest person in the entire kingdom of God is one who is like an inadequate, helpless, dependent little child. Humility, or poorness of spirit, is the first and most important attitude for kingdom citizens to develop.

Jesus demonstrated His poorness in spirit by laying aside His glory and becoming a man. He did not become poor by doing so. His personal glory is less important to Him than the glory of the Father and His kingdom, so He laid aside His personal glory to advance or promote that of the kingdom. Jesus has always been poor in spirit.

Jesus said we are to envy such people, "for theirs is the kingdom of heaven." The literal translation of that phrase is, "for the kingdom of heaven is of such people." I think this has two equally valid meanings. It means the kingdom belongs to such people, and such people belong to the kingdom. We might rephrase Jesus' statement as follows: The kingdom of heaven consists of people who recognize their personal inadequacies.

Notice the verb is in the present tense: "for theirs is the kingdom" or "the kingdom of heaven is of such people." Most of the other Beatitudes will be fulfilled in the future, but this one is at least partly fulfilled in the present.

What was your real reason for becoming a Christian? Did you want to escape hell, or to enjoy heaven? These are the initial reasons for most Christians, but they are self-centered motives and violate the "poor in spirit" clause. People normally accept Jesus as Savior out of selfish motives, because they do what they believe will benefit them the most. They want to protect themselves from harm and secure a pleasant future for themselves; they want to avoid hell and enjoy heaven. As believers mature spiritually and learn to overcome their self-centeredness, they begin to understand their real purpose is to serve. Even if a new believer has an immediate grasp of this, it takes spiritual maturity to comprehend the extent of this service and to overcome old sinful habits so they can serve with power and effectiveness.

God has several reasons for you to become a Christian: 1) You become a child of God, and God wants children (see Romans 8:29, for example); 2) You represent Him before men, demonstrating His nature and performing His business; and 3) You use your God-given skills and strengths to promote God's kingdom.

Those who are poor in spirit belong to the kingdom. Self-centeredness or self-interest of any kind will greatly reduce your kingdom effectiveness. Radically reprogramming your mind will allow you to see yourself and the world from God's perspective. Then you will see that you are totally inadequate for the task and will gladly let God work through you to do kingdom business. That is when you will realize the greatest fulfillment and effectiveness possible for a human being.

Being poor in spirit means forfeiting aspirations for personal glory to become a citizen of God's kingdom. This requires a radical change in attitude. Humility, a complete lack of self-centeredness, is the first kingdom value Jesus identified, probably because it is the most basic and most essential.

Those Who Mourn

The second kingdom value Jesus presents is also puzzling at first: "Blessed are those who mourn, for they will be comforted" (Matt. 5:4). Again, we must realize this is not a universal truth, but is relevant only to God's kingdom. Who in their right mind would envy someone grieving for a lost loved one, for example? We also realize that not everyone on earth who mourns will be comforted, or even should be comforted. Are you prepared, for example, to comfort someone who has committed a terrible crime and is mourning because they got caught? No, this beatitude is relevant only to God's kingdom.

The Greek word for "mourn" also means "grieve." And the Greek word for "comfort" also means to exhort, or urge someone with strong argument or advice. What typically causes people to mourn or grieve? Personal loss, such as the death of a loved one, the loss of an important possession or the loss of an important opportunity. In the world system, people mourn over personal loss.

Keep in mind, however, that the preceding Beatitude addressed the poor in spirit. Such people consider their personal desires or needs relatively unimportant. Would someone "poor in spirit" be likely to mourn a personal loss? No. So Jesus' statement about people who mourn being comforted is valid only in the context of God's kingdom.

God's kingdom has had several earthly phases since Adam and Eve sinned: 1) at first it was not evident at all; 2) then it was evident only through Judaism; 3) now it is evident through Christianity; and 4) in its final phase it will be evident as a literal earthly kingdom. What would cause someone to mourn during the kingdom's current phase? The existence of Satan's kingdom would cause them to mourn, because of the awful effects of sin on mankind and all of creation. Anyone with an intense longing for the completion of God's kingdom and the fulfillment of His will would mourn. Also, anyone who recognizes the depravity of mankind, the great distance man has fallen, and his personal responsibility for God's sacrifice would have cause to mourn.

The grammatical form of the phrase "for they will be comforted" indicates the ultimate comfort is in the future, when God's kingdom is fulfilled here on earth as it is in heaven. Anyone who mourns for the fulfillment of God's kingdom on earth will receive comfort when the kingdom is complete. There is also a more immediate fulfillment. Those who grieve for God's kingdom will receive strong encouragement from the Holy Spirit and God's people that He has ultimate control and that His plan will be accomplished.

It is not possible to mourn for God's kingdom unless you are poor in spirit. Mourning for the kingdom requires a high degree of identification with the kingdom, its values and its king. This is the opposite of normal human nature, which is primarily concerned with itself.

Your worldly thinking justifies an "acceptable" level of ungodly behavior. You might even tell yourself, "I'm only human. God knows I am not perfect and He makes allowances for my imperfection. He won't send me to hell over a minor infraction. To demand perfection of an imperfect being, such as myself, is legalistic, unrealistic and harsh."

Without humility, you can easily rationalize that your sin is not so bad, or is even acceptable. Mourning over sin, including your own, requires a poorness of spirit.

Yes, there are degrees of sinfulness, because God speaks of certain sins receiving greater punishment. But He also says that if you violate only one aspect of His law, you are guilty of it all. That is, under the law and without the blood of Jesus, the "smallest" sin is enough to send you to hell.

Likewise, there are degrees of righteousness, since God refers to "the greatest" in His kingdom, and those who receive the greater reward and honor. But He also says that everyone who accepts His plan of salvation is His child, receives His Holy Spirit and is righteous. That is, every believer is destined for heaven on the basis of God declaring him righteous.

What about the issue of sin? Sin is completely appropriate in a sinner's life, and inappropriate in the believer's life. Do sinners occasionally do noble, honorable, good acts? Yes, but because they are sinners, those acts are not sufficient to send them to heaven. Do Christians occasionally sin? Yes, but because God has declared the believer righteous, his sinful acts alone will not send him to hell. Sin is completely unacceptable in the believer's life and will limit his effectiveness in God's kingdom, but will not keep him out of the kingdom until he chooses to live for himself and ignore God.

There are no acceptable or tolerable sins for the believer. Like manure on a banquet table, sin is repulsive to God. And since you are made in His image, your sin must be repulsive to you, too. The real issue here is not sin, but perspective. As long as you look at sin from a human perspective, some of it is not all that bad. If you look at it from God's perspective, however, sin in your life becomes repulsive, disgusting, sickening and heartbreaking. Is changing your perspective of sin important? It is of critical importance. The New Testament discussion of repentance is directed almost entirely to Christians.

Those grieved by evidences of sin are enviable. They see sin from God's perspective and will be comforted when God sets up His kingdom on earth. You will not purify yourself unless you first grieve over your sin; love for God and a desire to please Him are not enough. You must view sin as God does and grieve over its effects. That alone will motivate you to change.

The Meek

"Blessed are the meek, for they will inherit the earth" (Matt. 5:5). To the Greeks, a meek person had a mild temperament, was friendly, gentle and pleasant. Our English concept of meekness includes showing patience and humility. Meekness comes from humility, the first of the kingdom values. On the other hand, self-centeredness is the opposite of humility and leads to roughness, hardness, violence and anger.

In the world system, does the mild, friendly, gentle, pleasant person gain all the earth has to offer? Not at all. These are gained by aggressive, competitive behavior. So Jesus' statement about those who are meek is not a universal statement; it applies only within the context of God's kingdom.

Those within the kingdom who are gentle, humble, considerate and patient are to be envied, because they will inherit the earth. It is significant that they will inherit the earth, rather than gain it by their own efforts. We must focus our efforts on entering the kingdom, and inheriting the earth is one of the kingdom benefits. Later in Jesus' teaching, He talked about those preoccupied with what they will eat and drink, or what they will wear. He said, "your heavenly Father knows that you need them. But seek first his kingdom and his righteousness, and all these things will be given to you as well" (Matt. 6:32-33). This is consistent with Jesus' statement about inheriting the earth.

Desire for Righteousness

"Blessed are those who hunger and thirst for righteousness, for they will be filled" (Matt. 5:6). The key word here is "righteousness." It means having a status or position acceptable to God, with nothing hindering your relationship with Him. It implies there are no issues separating you, no offenses and no blemishes on your record. It also implies acceptance and approval, that you are meeting God's expectations. Righteousness is a gift from God (Rom. 5:17), which you receive at salvation through faith in Jesus (Rom. 3:33). You cannot achieve it by human efforts (Gal. 2:21).

To hunger and thirst for righteousness is to have an intense desire for it—even an insatiable desire. The ungodly obviously do not have an intense desire for righteousness. If the ungodly do not want it and God declares a person righteous at salvation, then Jesus could only be referring to believers who have an intense desire for righteousness. Only believers would have such a desire for an open relationship with God that they want nothing to stand between them.

In fact, God's kingdom and His righteousness are to be top priorities for believers (Matt. 6:33).

This is not a casual interest, such as "Oh, yeah. It would be nice to have some if possible." Instead, you must have a complete dissatisfaction with the status quo and basically be desperate for righteousness.

Because God gave you a free will, you must choose to pursue spiritual matters. God will not force righteousness on you any more than He forces maturity or relationship. Being hungry and thirsty for righteousness is the result of choices. You must decide for yourself that righteousness has great value and you want it.

If you have had children, you know you loved them even when they had messy diapers. The repulsive aroma might temporarily separate you from your darling toddler, but you don't love them any less. Your relationship is simply less pleasant until they are clean again. In the same way, self-centeredness is repulsive to God but does not cause Him to stop loving you.

The dominant characteristic of sinful human nature is self-centeredness or pride. It is a concern for your own well-being, interests, preferences and thoughts. All acts of sin and all other forms of sin are motivated by self-centeredness. Because it is the original sin and is the basis for all other sin, self-centeredness is not a small matter.

What effect does your self-centeredness have on God's love for you? You need to recognize every expression of self-centeredness as offensive to God. That includes choosing what you want without considering God's intent. Or having hurt feelings when someone speaks against you. Or wanting to justify yourself when someone believes you were wrong. Or making sure people know your opinion. Or feeling disappointed when you don't get what you want. Or resenting someone for what they did to you. You probably will object, "But that is just human nature!" I agree, it is self-centered human nature. And it stinks in God's presence.

Jesus will cleanse you of all unrighteousness; not just most of it, or what is widely recognized in Christian culture as sin, but all of it. It is true that God declared you righteous when you accepted Jesus as your Savior, because He paid the penalty for your sin. It is also true, however, that you still have a carnal attitudes that continue to be unrighteous. The first step in becoming righteous is recognizing the problem. Then you can change your perspective until you see all expressions of self-centeredness as repulsive.

We have a problem as Christians. We are the children of God—the recipients of His Holy Spirit and God's representatives on earth—yet we are lax about sin. We tolerate our own self-centered attitudes, we accept them as perfectly normal and remain unconcerned about them. Instead, we must realize the value of righteousness and develop an insatiable desire for it.

Let me offer an analogy. It is physically impossible for more than one person to drive a car at any given moment. If I am driving, the only way for someone else to drive is for me to get out of the driver's seat. Similarly, it is not possible for you to serve God and others effectively in agape, which is based on humility, as long as you remain self-centered. You cannot be driven by humility and self-centeredness at the same time. The only way for Jesus to cleanse you of all unrighteousness is for you to address your own self-centeredness.

The Book of Hebrews records the following statement by God about Jesus: "You have loved righteousness and hated wickedness; therefore God, your God, has set you above your companions by anointing you with the oil of joy" (Heb. 1:9). It is fairly easy for us as Christians to love righteousness, but as humans it is more difficult for us to hate wickedness. Notice that God anointed Jesus because He loved righteousness and also hated wickedness. I suspect we cannot expect God's anointing to be on us in a significant way until we hate sin as He does.

If you live for yourself and reject Jesus as Savior and Lord, you are a sinner destined for hell. If, on the other hand, you accept Jesus as Savior and Lord and live to please Him, you are righteous and destined for heaven. There is no middle ground. Even the most admirable and noble sinner is going to hell and even the most carnal Christian is going to heaven.

Your personal righteousness does not determine your eternal destiny. There is no way you can become righteous enough by your own efforts to deserve going to heaven. The believer's desire for

righteousness springs from a desire for intimate relationship with
God; nothing, absolutely nothing, must interfere with that relationship. That is what Jesus was talking about when He said, "Blessed
are those who hunger and thirst for righteousness, for they will be
filled."

The Persecuted

Of the remaining Beatitudes, the ones about the merciful and the
peacemakers are virtually self-explanatory. We considered purity of
heart, the subject of another beatitude, in a previous chapter.

The final two Beatitudes relate to those who are persecuted and
both describe an immediacy of reward: "theirs *is* the kingdom of
heaven" and "great *is* your reward in heaven" (vv. 10, 12, emphasis
added). The first group of persecuted consists of those who have
such a state of personal righteousness that unbelievers deliberately
annoy or harass them. The second group is mistreated because they
associate with Jesus; "people insult you, persecute you and falsely
say all kinds of evil against you because of me" (v. 11).

Based on the context, Jesus clearly is not suggesting that His
followers persecute the unrighteous and, in so doing, provoke the
unrighteous to persecute them in return. Yet that evidently is what
some Christians believe, because they denounce sinners for sinning
or treat them with contempt. Of course sinners will sin; they are
enslaved by their sinful nature and can do nothing other than sin. But
God does not condemn sinners now. "God did not send his Son into
the world to condemn the world, but to save the world through him"
(John 3:17). As long as God withholds judgment on the world and
sinners are still alive, they have opportunity to accept God's redemption. As a believer, you are to live an exemplary life, modeling godly
nature and giving yourself for the benefit of others. That lifestyle is
the antithesis of harassing sinners for their sinful behavior.

The Holy Spirit convicts "the world of guilt in regard to sin and
righteousness and judgment" (John 16:8). To convict someone is
to prove them guilty of an offense, or to make them aware of their
guilt. This is the Holy Spirit's role and He may occasionally do it
through you, but infrequently. A look at the New Testament shows

that believers are to rebuke each other in love to encourage growth and discipline (see Luke 17:3; 1 Tim. 5:1, 20; 2 Tim. 3:16-17; 4:2; Titus 1:13; 2:15). God rebukes His children because He loves them (Heb. 12:5-6; Rev. 3:19). Jesus rebuked a storm (Matt. 8:26), a fever (Luke 4:39) and demons (Matt. 17:18; Mark 1:25; 9:25; Luke 4:35, 41). In each case His rebuke was part of delivering people from oppressive or life-threatening situations. Jesus also rebuked His disciples (Mark 8:33; 16:14; Luke 9:55).

The Greek words translated "rebuke" in the previous verses also mean to expose, convict, correct, refute, warn and show fault. There are verses using these Greek words that allow you to confront sin in non-believers' lives as an agent of the Holy Spirit: John 16:8 (convict), Ephesians 5:11 (expose) and Titus 1:9 (refute). Out of these three, only one verse clearly allows you to expose, warn or rebuke sinful deeds by sinners: Ephesians 5:11. Compare that with the many times God says you should rebuke fellow Christians in love, and it becomes clear whom you should rebuke and what your motive should be.

There is very little precedent in the New Testament for rebuking a sinner about his sin, probably because sinners usually are not receptive to it. If you rebuke a sinner, he is almost certain to resent it and persecute you in return; that would be consistent with his self-centered nature. John rebuked Herod and went to prison, eventually losing his life as a result (Matt. 14:3-12). Human nature resists unsolicited input, especially criticism. So you cannot expect a sinner to be happy you disapprove of his sin. Instead you should expect him to reject your position and even justify himself. But he cannot get away from "something inside" that persistently makes him uneasy about what he does. And that "something" is the Holy Spirit. Once the Holy Spirit convicts, rebukes or warns someone of their sin, you need to offer a solution rather than more conviction.

Occasionally, you may need to rebuke a sinner. How is it possible to know whether you should? Let me suggest several "green lights." First, humility should cause you to have no personal motive or agenda. You should also have a strong desire to do what is best for them regardless of personal risk, which really is the definition of agape. Finally, you should have a confidence or certainty, in spite of any uneasiness; you could describe this as spiritual peace in spite of emotional feelings. "I need to do this for their benefit and I'm willing to do it regardless of the risk."

You are to emulate Jesus, who responded to sin by giving Himself, doing what was within His power to do to help sinners. "While we were still sinners, Christ died for us" (Rom. 5:8). You cannot die for someone's sin and it is unnecessary to do so because Jesus died once for all. So, what can you do? Your duty is to spread the Good News, the gospel. The Holy Spirit is convicting people of their sin, setting them up for your arrival with the Good News. If someone rejects your Good News, you are to respond the way Jesus taught His disciples to respond: go on to someone else (Matt. 10:14). Jesus said, "I am sending you out like sheep among wolves. Therefore be as shrewd as snakes and as innocent as doves" (Matt. 10:16). He didn't say be as threatening as snakes; rather, be shrewd and use practical wisdom. As to how you are to treat sinners, be as harmless and innocent as a dove.

If you live a godly life and present the gospel, maybe even rebuke a sinner when appropriate, those who prefer sinfulness may persecute you. If so, you should consider yourself blessed, and even rejoice and be glad, according to the Beatitudes.

If you bring persecution on yourself by your obnoxious behavior, however, what good is that? Peter addresses the subject of suffering for doing good versus bad. "For it is commendable if a man bears up under the pain of unjust suffering because he is conscious of God. But how is it to your credit if you receive a beating for doing wrong and endure it?" (1 Pet. 2:19-20). The only persecution that God places any value on is sin's persecution of righteousness. Any Christian who treats others without humility and love is not acting righteously, and therefore any persecution they bring on themselves has no kingdom value.

You can be confident that simply minding your own business and becoming like God will bring persecution on you. People persecute those who are different from them or who make them look bad, which is why people persecuted Jesus.

"If the world hates you, keep in mind that it hated me first. If you belonged to the world, it would love you as its own. As it is, you do not belong to the world, but I have chosen you out of the world. That is why the world hates you. Remember the words I spoke to you: 'No servant is greater than his master.' If they persecuted me, they will persecute you also. If they obeyed my teaching, they will obey yours also. They will treat you this way because of my name, for they do not know the One who sent me" (John 15:18-21).

So do not be afraid of rejection, harassment or persecution. If people treat you that way due to your godly nature and behavior, then consider yourself blessed. If they treat you like that because you are obnoxious or have an attitude of spiritual superiority, then you need to make radical changes in your thinking.

Conclusion

Based on the kingdom values God presents in the Beatitudes, we can identify some worthwhile changes for you to make in your thinking. These changes will help you make the transition from slavery in the world system to effective partnership in God's kingdom.

It would be extremely beneficial for you to become poor in spirit; this speaks of humility, which is the most basic and most essential trait of godly character. Learning to grieve over evidences of sin in yourself and the world around you is one of the results of seeing sin from God's perspective. Meekness will make you gentle, considerate and patient; and it will cause you to inherit the earth's benefits, rather than have to earn them by your efforts. Developing an intense hatred for sin can lead to an insatiable desire for righteousness, which enables you to have intimate relationship with God. Be aware that living an exemplary, godly life will cause unbelievers to hate you and persecute you for making them look bad; but also be aware this gives you an immediate identity with the kingdom and immediate reward in heaven.

Personal Study

1. "Blessed are those who mourn" suggests it is beneficial and desirable for you to mourn for God's kingdom.

    *   What changes in your priorities, attitudes and perspective would enable you to mourn for God's kingdom?

    *   How can you begin to hate your own sin and mourn for the effects it has had on God's kingdom?

2. Compare "Blessed are the meek, for they will inherit the earth" (Matt. 5:5) with Matthew 6:25-33.

    *   What qualities of a meek person would permit God to give them material blessings?

    *   What worldly attitudes would prevent God from doing so?

3. Consider the analogy of hungering and thirsting for righteousness.

    *   In what ways is having an intense desire for righteousness similar to hating sin? In what ways are they different?

    *   What choices or changes can you make that will enable you to develop an intense hatred for sin?

    *   What choices or changes can you make that will enable you to develop an intense desire for righteousness?

4. Consider the concept of being persecuted because of righteousness.

    *   If righteousness is having no issues separating you from God, no offenses and no blemishes on your record; and

if it means you have God's acceptance and approval, that you are meeting His expectations; then how might your righteousness cause unbelievers to hate you and persecute you?

- How might godly character initially attract unbelievers then cause them to hate and persecute you?

- How can you avoid taking such hatred and persecution personally?

14

Legal Matters

For us to understand the significance of our legal position in God's kingdom, we must go all the way back to Adam. Before God created man, He said, "Let us make man in our image, in our likeness, and let them rule over the fish of the sea and the birds of the air, over the livestock, over all the earth, and over all the creatures that move along the ground" (Gen. 1:26). Then after creating Adam and Eve, He said to them, "Be fruitful and increase in number; fill the earth and subdue it" (Gen. 1:28).

Adam ruled the earth and everything in it. God told him to subdue the earth, which literally meant he was to walk on it and use it as he saw fit. Adam had authority over all the earth. For the creatures in heaven, all activity surrounded God's throne because He was the ruler. On earth, however, Adam was the ruler. This caused God and Adam to have a unique relationship because they had so much in common.

Psalm 8:4-5 gives us some interesting insight about Adam's responsibility and his relationship with God: "What is man that you are mindful of him, the son of man that you care for him? You made him a little lower than the heavenly beings and crowned him with glory and honor." The word translated "care" literally means "go to," as in to visit or attend to someone. Also, the phrase "heavenly beings" is the Hebrew word *elohim*, the plural form of "god." This cannot mean God made man a little lower than the angels, as some would suggest, because it clearly states God crowned man with glory and honor, which He has not given to the angels. These verses tell us that God, who is worthy to receive all glory and honor, made man a little lower than Himself and crowned man with glory and honor. God, the ruler of all creation, visited Adam, ruler of the earth. They had much in common, so they could visit and "talk shop," virtually as peers.

When Adam sinned, Satan received Adam's authority. After that, Satan legally was the prince of the world. When Satan offered Jesus the world in exchange for His worship, he made a legitimate offer because the world was his to give. Adam not only lost his authority over the earth, he lost his glory and honor. Losing his glory may have been what caused him to be naked or notice that he was naked, as described in Genesis 3:10.

But there continues to be something in man's nature that causes him to know he should have authority on earth. Sin has perverted that knowledge and causes him to want authority for his own benefit. In our present state, if we have power and authority, it is natural for us to use them for ourselves. We often become domineering or demanding and abuse our authority.

God's concept of authority is service, rather than dominance. Humility and agape, the primary traits of godly character, cause us to consider the other person's needs and be unconcerned about our own. Godly character causes us to use power and authority to serve others, not ourselves.

As we have seen, Adam had power and authority over the earth. The earth was his to use as he thought appropriate, because he was its ruler. Adam's sin had profound significance for him and for his domain; all of creation has been subjected to frustration and decay as a result of Adam's sin (see Rom. 8:20-22).

There is hope, however. "For if, by the trespass of the one man, death reigned through that one man, how much more will those who receive God's abundant provision of grace and of the gift of righteousness reign in life through the one man, Jesus Christ" (Rom. 5:17). One consequence of your salvation is the restoration of authority, which enables you to reign in life.

There has been a lot of teaching on the authority of the believer, and it is based on scriptural truth. But I think there is an important fact missing in the application of that teaching: that the purpose of the believer's authority is to serve. Everything you do as a believer must be motivated by humility and agape, and that includes exercising your authority.

Spiritual authority in the hands of a carnal Christian is generally ineffective and sometimes even harmful. The carnal believer still focuses on himself and tries to use his authority for his own advantage, which renders his authority largely ineffective (see James 4:3). His attempted misuse of his authority produces only limited results, which can cause confusion and doubt. This may be harmful if it makes people wonder whether God's Word is really true.

It is essential that you change the way you think if you are to use your authority effectively. To begin with, you will not even use your spiritual abilities until you are convinced you have them and can use them. Repenting, or changing the way you think, does not impart spiritual abilities; it releases them.

All authority other than God's is delegated. Jesus gave His disciples authority to drive out demons and to cure every kind of disease and sickness; that is, He delegated His authority to them. When the centurion approached Jesus about his sick servant, he understood that authority is delegated, and Jesus commended him for his understanding (see Matt. 8:5-10). God gave you some of His authority by delegating it to you. You are to use it in His behalf, that is, in His name. You are to use it as He would: to do kingdom business.

Consider for a moment the keys you use to open the door to your home or to start your car. Keys are pretty ordinary and in today's culture they are essential. Keys have specific purposes. For one, they permit access to something of value; if something were not of value, you probably would not lock it up. Second, access to something of value implies a certain amount of responsibility for the way you use it. Giving someone a key is a sign of trust, privilege and responsibility.

In Matthew 16:19, Jesus tells Peter, "I will give you the keys of the kingdom of heaven." Based on the universal significance of keys, we can conclude that Jesus was giving Peter access to the treasures of heaven. As mentioned earlier, giving someone a key clearly implies a certain amount of trust and responsibility.

In other Scriptures, Jesus said we were to store up treasures in heaven rather than on earth. To store up something means to save it up, store it away, to reserve it or even hoard it. I think this has two implications. First, it suggests we will receive rewards in heaven and should not expect them on earth. This is typically called delayed gratification because it means you are willing to wait for the benefits of your current efforts. If you were to go to college, for example, you might be willing to submit to several years of hard work with no pay, expecting your efforts to pay off in the future with a good job. That is a form of delayed gratification.

The Book of Revelation describes some of our future rewards as Christians. We will have the right to eat from the Tree of Life. The second death will not hurt us. We will receive some of the hidden manna. We will receive a white stone with a new name on it. We will receive the morning star. We will be dressed in white and made a pillar in God's temple. And we will have the right to sit with Jesus on his throne. One of Jesus' parables suggested one reward might be to rule cities. These are obviously future rewards and we could easily consider them treasures in heaven.

When Jesus spoke of storing up treasures in heaven, He may have been suggesting something else as well. He could have meant we can receive treasures now, but kingdom treasures rather than earthly ones. Let us pursue this concept a bit.

There are New Testament verses that refer to treasures or riches that do not fit the world's definition of valuables. Paul said his purpose was "that they may have the full riches of complete understanding, in order that they may know the mystery of God, namely, Christ, in whom are hidden all the treasures of wisdom and knowledge" (Col. 2:2-3). He refers to full riches of complete understanding, plus treasures of wisdom and knowledge hidden in Jesus. That is, he considered certain knowledge, wisdom and understanding to be riches and treasure.

In another place, Paul wrote of the knowledge of the glory of God in the face of Christ, then described that knowledge as "treasure in jars of clay" (2 Cor. 4:6-7). The treasure he spoke of is the knowledge of God's glory as perceived in Jesus.

What is the purpose of all this understanding, knowledge and wisdom? These are like the treasures of a skilled craftsman, the understanding, knowledge and wisdom that enable him to perform superior work. In the same way, the understanding, knowledge and wisdom we receive through Jesus and about Jesus enable us to be effective members of His kingdom, doing God's work with great effectiveness and skill. We have this understanding because Jesus gave us the keys of the kingdom. The kingdom keys give us access to what is reserved for kingdom use.

Jesus made an interesting statement in John chapter 16. He said the Holy Spirit "will bring glory to me by taking from what is mine and making it known to you. All that belongs to the Father is mine. That is why I said the Spirit will take from what is mine and make it known to you" (John 16:14-15).

Why would the Holy Spirit show us what belongs to Jesus? So we would know what is available for our use and benefit. Everything that belongs to the Father also belongs to the Son. Everything that belongs to Jesus is available for us to use.

Based on what the Scriptures declare about treasures and riches, you need to change your perception of what is valuable. The valuables of the earthly system have no value in the kingdom. God's streets are of such pure gold they are transparent, yet they have the same value we place on asphalt. The foundations of the New Jerusalem's city walls are of what we call precious stones; they have the same value we place on concrete. The city gates each consist of a single, gigantic pearl; they have the same value we place on ordinary metal. One perspective is that these are used for common purposes because there is such material wealth in heaven. Another perspective, however, is that kingdom values are entirely different.

In God's kingdom, the real treasures are knowledge of who Jesus is, understanding of all the ramifications that has for our position in God's kingdom, and the wisdom to use that knowledge and understanding to glorify God by doing His work. He has given us the kingdom keys and authorized us to use His power to perform His work in His behalf. He can do this because He has legally brought us into His kingdom and delegated His authority to us. Let us consider those two points.

In an earlier chapter, we showed that you are now a citizen of heaven (Phil. 3:20). You are now an alien to this world and its system, so you are no longer obligated to serve it. Jesus has redeemed you, buying you back from your slavery to sin. He has purchased your freedom with His own blood, so you no longer belong to yourself. The very fact that you consider Jesus Lord is evidence of your citizenship in His kingdom. He has transferred you to His kingdom and made you a child of God. Therefore, it is legitimate for Him to delegate authority to you and make you responsible for kingdom business.

After Jesus' resurrection, He told His disciples, "All authority in heaven and on earth has been given to me. Therefore go . . ." (Matt. 28:18). When He received all authority in heaven and on earth, He immediately delegated authority to His disciples. To whom did God originally give authority over the earth? Adam. Who received authority over the earth when Adam sinned? Satan. When did Jesus win back authority over the earth? When He defeated Satan and rose from the dead. When will Jesus exercise full authority over the earth? When He sets up His kingdom on earth. Where does that leave us in the meantime? We are to use His authority on earth, though the earth is in enemy hands.

Jesus is quoted in Revelation 1:8: "I am the Living One; I was dead, and behold I am alive for ever and ever! And I hold the keys of death and Hades." All the power of sin has been broken! It is an accomplished fact. Yet God has allowed Satan to continue to rule the earth temporarily and has placed His believers here with authority to use His power. Why?

I think there are several reasons. This is a demonstration to all of creation of how believers are to work in His behalf, even in a hostile environment. It also demonstrates God's redemptive power to transform people back into His original intent, even in a hostile environment. And it is front-line, hands-on training for believers to learn how to use God's resources under the absolute worst conditions. All of creation saw Adam fail. All of creation has either seen or experienced the effects of Adam's sin. Now God is demonstrating

His redemptive power by bringing man back to his position, a little lower than God Himself. Eventually, we will be higher than Adam was originally. That is how God works. What Satan intended for evil, God causes to work for good. Satan meant to pull Adam down from his position of authority, but God will use the opportunity to raise man to even higher authority.

So why do we not see believers exercising God's authority? Partly because we do not perceive Satan as defeated and relatively powerless compared to God's power in us. This causes our thinking to center around how we should respond to various problems and ailments. This is reactionary, defensive and backward. The key is our state of mind, our perception.

You currently have everything you need to be effective for God's kingdom. If you are not effective, it is because you do not realize your situation or have not learned to use what God has given you. The spiritual victory has been won! The real battle is now in your mind.

It is up to you to conform your mind to spiritual reality. You must mentally believe before you can spiritually perform. You choose what you will believe, and you can always find evidence to support your beliefs. The issue is not what you observe, but what you decide to think. You must recognize, admit and accept responsibility for what you believe. Repenting—changing the way you think—is crucial to your being effective in God's kingdom, fulfilling God's expectations of you, and becoming all that God created you to be.

Even sinners are successful when they choose to believe they have within themselves what it takes to succeed. That is why motivational seminars work. Your situation is infinitely better.

As a child of God, you recognize your inadequacies in the big issues of life—which is an attitude of humility—and that God in you is more than adequate for anything. That understanding leads to real success! Relying on the absolute, unlimited power and authority of God who lives within you, rather than your personal abilities, not only defines true kingdom success but also produces consistently successful results. This includes redefining success and recognizing the source of success. These require changing the way you think.

As recorded in the beginning of Luke chapter 17, Jesus told His disciples they must rebuke a brother who sins, then forgive him if he repents, even if he does it several times each day. This rocked the disciples back on their heels and they responded, "Increase our faith!"

> *[Jesus] replied, "If you have faith as small as a mustard seed, you can say to this mulberry tree, 'Be uprooted and planted in the sea,' and it will obey you.*
>
> *Suppose one of you had a servant plowing or looking after the sheep. Would he say to the servant when he comes in from the field, 'Come along now and sit down to eat'? Would he not rather say, 'Prepare my supper, get yourself ready and wait on me while I eat and drink; after that you may eat and drink'? Would he thank the servant because he did what he was told to do? So you also, when you have done everything you were told to do, should say, 'We are unworthy servants; we have only done our duty'"* (Luke 17:6-10).

After doing what the Master tells you, your attitude should be, "I have only done what I was told." But this response takes on real significance when you consider its context: using your faith to uproot a tree and throw it into the ocean. "So what's the big deal? I am a servant of God and I only did what He told me. He did the work." This means you cannot feel responsible for the results, whatever they are.

Consider the incident in which Peter and John healed the crippled beggar at the temple gate. You know how it happened: "Silver or gold I do not have, but what I have I give you. In the name of Jesus Christ of Nazareth, walk" (Acts 3:6). It was a miracle and it immediately drew an excited crowd.

Peter's response to the miracle was very revealing. "Men of Israel, why does this surprise you? Why do you stare at us as if by our own power or godliness we had made this man walk?" Peter then made it very clear that he was not responsible for the miracle; the results came from his acting in Jesus' name, in His behalf, and using the faith He supplied. In essence he said, "I didn't do it."

Paul and Barnabas had a very similar experience, also involving a crippled man. Paul was telling a crowd the Good News of the kingdom, and the crippled man listened intently. Paul looked at him and saw that he had faith to be healed, so he called out to the man, "Stand up on your feet!" The man jumped up and immediately began to walk. The crowd went wild! People began shouting that Paul and Barnabas were gods come down in human form and the priests of the city brought bulls and wreaths to offer as sacrifices to them.

Paul and Barnabas rushed into the crowd, shouting: "Men, why are you doing this? We too are only men, human like you" (Acts 14:15). Then they immediately directed the people's attention to God. They refused to accept any glory or credit for the miracle.

Consider one more example. The church at Corinth was split by factions loyal to Paul and Apollos. Paul reprimanded them for their jealousy, quarreling and worldly attitudes. Notice how he puts the issue into perspective.

What, after all, is Apollos? And what is Paul? Only servants, through whom you came to believe—as the Lord has assigned to each his task. I planted the seed, Apollos watered it, but God made it grow. So neither he who plants nor he who waters is anything, but only God, who makes things grow. The man who plants and the man who waters have one purpose, and each will be rewarded according to his own labor. For we are God's fellow workers; you are God's field, God's building (1 Cor. 3:5-9).

Paul and Apollos were nothing more than servants; only God is important. As men, they were God's fellow workers, unimportant in themselves. By human standards, Paul and Apollos were mighty men of God, but they considered themselves insignificant, unworthy of attention.

As Paul stated about himself, you are God's fellow worker. Whatever task God has assigned you, it is He who produces the results; therefore you are not responsible for them, because you are a servant of almighty God. While the Bible uses the terms "servant" and "fellow worker" to describe certain aspects of your relationship with God, you are much more than that. He has actually adopted you into His family, making you a legal heir of His kingdom and giving you legal authority to conduct family or kingdom business. You represent God and His kingdom here on earth and you conduct His business in His behalf. Considering the various analogies the Bible uses, you should consider yourself merely a kingdom representative.

Just as God originally gave Adam authority over the earth, He has given you slightly different authority. He began by legally redeeming you from your bondage to sin, liberating you from sin's effects, and adopting you into His family. He planted His Holy Spirit within you to tutor you in the ways of His kingdom and empower you to do kingdom business. He authorized you to conduct business in His behalf as a legal member of His family. He is progressively developing you into His image so you can have increasingly intimate fellowship with Him and grooming you so you can become increasingly effective in kingdom work.

Having received this incredible ability, authority and responsibility, however, you must constantly remind yourself that you are acting in God's behalf. You are not responsible for the results because you did not make them happen. You were merely the person God chose to work through. What matters is being in God's kingdom so He can work through you.

Jesus sent His disciples out to minister in the surrounding towns and they returned with exciting stories to tell, but Jesus' response quickly put the matter in perspective. "I have given you authority to trample on snakes and scorpions, and to overcome all the power of the enemy; nothing will harm you. However, do not rejoice that the spirits submit to you, but rejoice that your names are written in heaven" (Luke 10:19-20). The demons do not flee from your power; Jesus is King of kings and Lord of lords, not you. You are simply the agent through whom Jesus did the work.

The New Testament uses a specific phrase, "in His name," that reveals the legal nature of your work here on earth. To act in the name of someone is to use their authority and resources in their behalf to do what they would do in a given situation. This is a legal phrase, not a magical one; simply reciting the words does not produce the desired result. Rather, it reveals the power and authority behind your action, much like a police uniform or badge.

To act in Jesus' name is to act as if you were Jesus by doing what He would do. As we have seen, He has given you the keys to the kingdom, meaning that you have access to God's resources and treasures. His treasures include God's wisdom, knowledge and understanding. His resources include His Holy Spirit within you. With this in mind, let us examine some verses that refer to people acting in God's name and Jesus' name.

Jesus said, "whoever welcomes a little child like this in my name welcomes me" (Matt. 18:5). The New Testament frequently describes Jesus as having little children around Him or using them in His teaching as examples of desirable attributes. To welcome a little child in His name is to do it as He would, with the same motivation and honoring the same childlike nature.

He also said, "where two or three come together in my name, there am I with them" (Matt. 18:20). For believers to gather in His name suggests they have the same purpose He did: to advance the Father's kingdom and give Him honor. Even false messiahs will come in His name (Matt. 24:5). This means they will claim to be acting in His behalf, but in reality will not.

"I tell you the truth, anyone who gives you a cup of water in my name because you belong to Christ will certainly not lose his reward" (Mark 9:41). Jesus will honor even the simplest act performed in His behalf. This shows how meaningful every seemingly insignificant act becomes when you do it as His representative. You figuratively become His body, acting as if you were Jesus Himself. And doing so allows you to earn rewards. What could be better?

"You did not choose me, but I chose you to go and bear fruit— fruit that will last. Then the Father will give you whatever you ask in my name" (John 15:16). Notice the sequence in this verse: bear fruit, *then* the Father will give you whatever you ask in Jesus' name. By now it should be obvious this verse does not mean God will indulge your every whim as long as you tack the words, "in Jesus' name," on the end of your request. If you are not asking what Jesus would ask in your situation, you are not asking in His name. Also notice the relationship between producing fruit that will last and asking in Jesus' name. It is possible the analogy of bearing fruit includes winning souls, although the analogy most frequently used for that is a grain harvest.

Bearing fruit represents being productive in other ways as well, including developing godly character or fruit of the spirit (Gal. 5:22-23); speaking good things (Matt. 12:33-37); loving other believers (John 15:9-17); giving financially (Rom. 15:26-28); goodness, righteousness and truth (Eph. 5:9); and every good work (Col. 1:10). The kind of fruit you should produce is largely determined by who you are.

If you have the gift of teaching, for example, you would be most fruitful whenever you teach others. You would also be fruitful when you lead someone to the Lord or drive out a demon or heal a sick person, but you can expect to produce that kind of fruit less frequently or less effectively. You do not need to feel guilty for not producing as much evangelistic fruit as an evangelist, bringing souls into the kingdom. Always be ready to explain your faith and to help someone commit their life to the Lord and pray that God would give you that privilege as you look for opportunities to do so. But even then you are more likely to use your teaching skills to save someone—explaining, convincing, informing and presenting evidence.

God chose you to go and produce results that will last forever, which means those that are compatible with and promote His kingdom. The kind of results you produce will generally be a result of your character.

Chapters 14, 15 and 16 of the Gospel of John record an in-depth explanation Jesus gave His disciples of the relationship they would have with the Trinity after He returned to heaven. He stated that anyone who had seen Him had seen the Father, indicating how close and how much alike they are. He uses the analogy of the vine and the branches to show how close we must be to Him and how we must rely on Him. He explained how the Holy Spirit will reside in us, and what His role is. In the first half of John chapter 14, Jesus describes the intimate relationship He and the Father have. He even states that the words He spoke and the work He did were actually the Father's (v. 10). That is, He spoke and acted in the Father's behalf.

Then He included His followers in the circle and explained that we will do even greater things than He did. Afterward, He made the statement we so often quote: "And I will do whatever you ask in my name, so that the Son may bring glory to the Father. You may ask me for anything in my name, and I will do it" (John 14:13-14).

Notice that He promises to respond to anything we ask in His name, in His behalf. Also notice that your ability to ask in His name and His response to your requests are the result of intimate relationship and cooperation. In that context, He makes a very powerful statement and reiterates it for emphasis: "I will do whatever you ask in my name . . . . You may ask me for anything in my name."

Because of your position in God's family and kingdom, He has legally authorized you to ask for anything in Jesus' behalf. You have authority to act on your own discretion to do God's work in His behalf, unlimited access to His resources, and the complete support and cooperation of the Trinity. You have everything you could possibly need to do God's work, not to indulge your whims or promote your own agenda, but to do God's work in His behalf. That is the force of Jesus' statement, "I will do whatever you ask in my name." This also reveals the source of the work that is done; Jesus said *He* will do whatever you ask. Your role is merely to ask.

Later in the same chapter, Jesus reinforced the importance of intimacy in this working arrangement. And He stated again that He was speaking on the Father's behalf.

> *"If anyone loves me, he will obey my teaching. My Father will love him, and we will come to him and make our home with him. He who does not love me will not obey my teaching. These words you hear are not my own; they belong to the Father who sent me. "All this I have spoken while still with you. But the Counselor, the Holy Spirit, whom the Father will send in my name, will teach you all things and will remind you of everything I have said to you"* (John 14:23-26).

Let me point out this is another instance of the "in my name" clause. When Jesus returned to heaven, the Father sent the Holy Spirit in Jesus' name. That means the Holy Spirit is continuing the work Jesus began, acting in His behalf. That is the essence of acting "in His name."

In this chapter we are examining your legal authority to conduct kingdom business, and in a later chapter we will discover what that business really is. One definitive statement Jesus made about such business, which we will now examine, includes the "in my name" phrase.

At the beginning of His ministry, Jesus quoted the Book of Isaiah to declare His mission on earth, which included releasing the oppressed (Luke 4:18-19). Immediately after stating His mission, He went to another town and drove an evil spirit out of a man, releasing the man from demonic oppression. Driving demons out was characteristic of Jesus' ministry. It was one of the primary reasons He came to earth and He did it frequently. When He left the disciples to return to heaven, He told them, "these signs will accompany those who believe: In my name they will drive out demons" (Mark 16:17). By now, the meaning of that last statement should need very little explanation. In Jesus' name you will drive out demons; you have the legal authority, the heavenly resources and the Trinity's support to do it in Jesus' behalf.

A clear example of this occurred when a slave girl followed Paul and Silas around, shouting and disrupting their ministry. "She kept this up for many days. Finally Paul became so troubled that he turned around and said to the spirit, 'In the name of Jesus Christ I command you to come out of her!'" (Acts 16:18). Paul drove the demon out in Jesus' name.

In closing, let us look briefly at a few other verses related to acting in Jesus' name. The Book of Acts records that Barnabas took Saul to the apostles in Jerusalem. "He told them how Saul on his journey had seen the Lord and that the Lord had spoken to him, and how in Damascus he had preached fearlessly in the name of Jesus" (Acts 9:27). Saul preached in the name of Jesus, in His behalf.

Paul encourages believers to "always [give] thanks to God the Father for everything, in the name of our Lord Jesus Christ" (Eph. 5:20). He makes an even more encompassing statement in Colossians: "And whatever you do, whether in word or deed, do it all in the name of the Lord Jesus" (Col. 3:17).

It is important that you see yourself as a child of God, a representative of Jesus and His kingdom. As you change your perception of yourself, you will understand why you must always be aware of your attitudes and actions. Jesus said that if anyone had seen Him, he had seen the Father. Similarly, you are the only representation of God most people will ever see.

In the next chapter we will consider the logistics involved in this arrangement.

Conclusion

The legal matters are complete. God has legally transferred you to His kingdom and adopted you as His child. He has authorized you to operate under the laws of His kingdom and use His resources to conduct His business in His behalf. You are His child and legal representative on earth.

As God's representative, you are authorized and empowered to conduct His business in His behalf. To act in Jesus' name is to act as if you were Jesus by doing what He would do. God has given you access to His resources—His Holy Spirit within you, and treasures—His wisdom, knowledge and understanding. He has given you everything you need to be effective in His kingdom.

Personal Study

1.   "What is man that you are mindful of him, the son of man that you care for him? You made him a little lower than the heavenly beings and crowned him with glory and honor" (Ps. 8:4-5).

   - In what ways does having the Holy Spirit within you parallel the relationship God had with Adam in the Garden of Eden?

   - How is your relationship already better than Adam's?

2.   Paul wrote about "the full riches of complete understanding, in order that they may know the mystery of God, namely, Christ, in whom are hidden all the treasures of wisdom and knowledge" (Col. 2:2-3).

 •   How can the knowledge and wisdom hidden in Christ enable you to be an effective member of His kingdom, doing God's work with great effectiveness and skill?

 •   Why is knowing Jesus' role invaluable to understanding your position and responsibility in God's kingdom?

 •   How might you study the New Testament to discover who Jesus is? The Old Testament?

3.   Consider the concept of being a kingdom representative.

 •   How should this affect your opinion of your purpose in life?

 •   How should this affect your priorities and goals?

 •   Explain why being a kingdom representative makes it essential to have "the full riches of complete understanding" and "the treasures of wisdom and knowledge" (Col. 2:2-3).

15

Logistics

We saw in the previous chapter that you legally are God's representative to this foreign world you live in. His plan of redemption has bought you back from the world system, paid the penalty for your sins and adopted you into His family. As your heavenly Father, God authorized you to use the resources of His kingdom to conduct His business in His behalf.

When it comes to knowing and adhering to the law, God literally wrote the book. Everything He does is perfectly legal and legitimate. The god of this age, Satan, is the one who tries to skirt the law and even blatantly violate it, but not so with God. When He directs you to conduct His business, you can be confident everything is legitimate and appropriate.

Okay, now that you have your job description and authorization to conduct kingdom business, do you have what it takes? In this chapter we will examine your capacity to do God's work and see whether you are properly equipped and supplied.

God's Dwelling

The first point we must affirm is that God has not sent you out on your own; you are not alone and left to your own devices. The moment you accepted Jesus as your Lord and Savior, God implanted

His own Spirit within you, so from that moment on He has been with you continuously.

God "anointed us, set his seal of ownership on us, and put his Spirit in our hearts as a deposit, guaranteeing what is to come" (2 Cor. 1:21-22). To be anointed is to be set apart for a specific purpose, so anything else you do is either of no significance or even wasteful. And because he purchased you—redeemed you, bought you back from slavery to sin—He can legitimately put His seal of ownership on you. You are no longer your own; God secured the rights to your life at the price of His Son.

If you were to stop at this point in the verse, you could easily develop a sense of drudgery. You would be like an obligated servant who must serve because of what his master has done for him; he has no choice, only an obligation. This is not how God sees you, however. Having anointed you for a specific purpose and put His seal of ownership on you, He put His Spirit in your heart or spirit.

God Himself actually lives within you the same way your own spirit does. I suppose if you were cynical, you could view this much like an ex-convict who has a radio transmitter attached to him so the parole officer could track him. God is not watching you like a parole officer. He put His Spirit within you to fulfill part of His desire for you: a continuous, intimate relationship between you and Him. God is the only source of life in all of creation and that life flows from Him, through your spirit into the rest of your being. His presence in you literally sustains you.

As significant as this is, His Spirit in you is mostly a deposit that guarantees more to come in the future. As an engagement ring is a down payment, a promise of much more to come, the Holy Spirit in you and all that He brings and makes available to you are a guarantee of what is to come. Paul restates this point later in his letter to Corinth with a little more explanation.

For while we are in this tent [temporary earthly body], we groan and are burdened, because we do not wish to be unclothed but to be clothed with our heavenly dwelling, so that what is mortal may be swallowed up by life. Now it is God who has made us for this very purpose and has given us the Spirit as a deposit, guaranteeing what is to come (2 Cor. 5:4-5).

His Spirit in your earthly body now is a guarantee of a heavenly body for you later. Paul even said God made you for the purpose of replacing your earthly body with a heavenly one. To me this demonstrates what a victorious celebration it will be for God to "upgrade" you to your heavenly body, as the final phase of your redemption.

Your spiritual salvation occurred when you were born again. The current phase of your redemption is the renewing of your mind. And the last phase will occur in a moment, when you are changed in a flash, in the twinkling of an eye at the last trumpet. He will change you from mortal and perishable to immortal and imperishable. All the saints throughout history will experience the transformation and cut loose with a celebration, the likes of which has never been seen. Free at last! No more carnality, no more trauma from the effects of sin. Fully redeemed at last!

As totally incomprehensible as that experience is to us, God's main purpose is to demonstrate His power and glory to every creature. He is God, and there is no one like Him. That statement has been the motivation behind His plan of redemption throughout history. Sin perverted His creation and brought death upon His highest creature, man. By redeeming man from the effects of sin, God demonstrates to all those creatures who rebelled against Him that He alone is God and that His kingdom is supreme.

You and I have been on the front lines of the battle since the moment we were conceived, but the battle is not about us. The battle is between God and Satan and their respective kingdoms. And each phase of your redemption has been a victorious demonstration of God's power. So by placing His Spirit within you, He is guaranteeing to you and all of creation that He is already victorious, His kingdom has come and His will must be done. And you and I enjoy the benefits.

This is such an important concept that Paul states it a third time in another epistle. "Having believed, you were marked in him with a seal, the promised Holy Spirit, who is a deposit guaranteeing our inheritance until the redemption of those who are God's possession—to the praise of his glory" (Eph. 1:13-14). There it is again: the ultimate purpose is the praise of His glory. God's Spirit in you is part of His plan to display His glory.

"Do you not know that your body is a temple of the Holy Spirit, who is in you, whom you have received from God? You are not your own; you were bought at a price. Therefore honor God with your body" (1 Cor. 6:19-20). A temple is a structure set apart for God's use, and your body is a temple of God, the Holy Spirit. Your body is God's house. The context of the verses we just quoted is sexual immorality, but the principle is much broader. Christians say they are dedicated to God, then entertain impure thoughts, self-centered attitudes, and so on. How would you like the county using your house as a garbage dump? Is God any more at home in a believer still ruled by his sinful attitudes?

You know how personal your home is. When you are in the market for a home, you might look for weeks or months to find the house that is right for you. You would not feel at home in a house lacking those certain features you wanted, or in a place having features you definitely do not want. Your home must be compatible with your lifestyle and interests.

God feels the same about living in you. He is righteous and holy, meaning He is completely separated from sin and the world system, and completely dedicated to His purposes. As His dwelling, He expects you to become compatible with His lifestyle and interests. To be a suitable dwelling for God, you need to be striving for holiness and purity.

If you had a long-term guest in your home, you would accommodate their needs and interests as much as possible, not only to make them comfortable, but also to assist them. As God's dwelling, how does your condition affect God's freedom to perform His business? Through the Holy Spirit in you, Jesus is working to make you an appropriate temple or dwelling.

Christ loved the church and gave himself up for her to make her holy, cleansing her by the washing with water through the word, and to present her to himself as a radiant church, without stain or wrinkle or any other blemish, but holy and blameless (Eph. 5:25-27).

God is righteous and holy, and He is working to make you holy and blameless, without any blemish at all. Much of what God does in your life is to develop holiness and righteousness in you, to make you like Himself. As His child, He wants you to be like your Father. As His temple, He wants you to be a suitable dwelling. Your home is where you are comfortable and free to be yourself. If God is at home in you, He is free to be Himself, the King of all creation, God almighty.

As God's dwelling, you are responsible for what you do to yourself. "Don't you know that you yourselves are God's temple and that God's Spirit lives in you? If anyone destroys God's temple, God will destroy him; for God's temple is sacred, and you are that temple" (1 Cor. 3:16-17).

The key Greek word in these verses occurs twice and is translated "destroy." The word primarily means "destroy" or "corrupt." From the Bible's perspective, anything corrupted is destroyed, because integrity, single-mindedness and purity are important biblical themes. The emphasis in these verses is your physical body serving as God's temple, so everything you do to your body affects God's dwelling. Whether you abuse your body by exposing it to corruption (sexual immorality, drunkenness, and so on) or by neglecting it's needs (such as nutrition, rest and exercise), there are many ways for you to destroy God's temple.

All this talk about destruction can be confusing—you destroy yourself, so God destroys you—unless you examine these verses from the perspective of your covenant relationship with God. Remember, we are considering your physical body as God's temple.

Part of God's covenant with you includes supernatural health, which supersedes the normal human cycles of sickness and disease. For example, consider the following verse. "And if the Spirit of him who raised Jesus from the dead is living in you, he who raised Christ from the dead will also give life to your mortal bodies through his Spirit, who lives in you" (Rom. 8:11). God's Spirit in you gives your mortal, physical body life; the Greek word translated "give life" refers to natural or physical life. So the Holy Spirit in you imparts life through your spirit to your entire being, resulting in natural health and life. But covenant terms and promises are conditional; God will deliver as long as you are faithful to His instructions.

If you persist in behavior that would corrupt your physical body, thereby violating the terms of your covenant with God, He is no longer bound to His promise of divine health. He would then be justified if He withheld divine health and allowed you to experience the consequences of your actions.

A similar statement relates to celebrating the Lord's Supper. "For anyone who eats and drinks without recognizing the body of the Lord eats and drinks judgment on himself. That is why many among you are weak and sick, and a number of you have fallen asleep" [in death] (1 Cor. 11:29-30). This is another example of your actions or attitude nullifying God's promise of divine health, resulting in weakness, sickness and even death.

This passage about recognizing the Lord's body likely has several applications. For one, it includes recognizing that Jesus' body received all sickness and disease on your behalf, so you can be healthy and not die prematurely. It also means recognizing other believers as the body of Christ and serving them with love; serving in love is one of the terms of the covenant and physical health and vitality are covenant blessings. And, the passage means you should recognize yourself as the Lord's physical body on earth and the temple of His Holy Spirit; the power of His Spirit within you radiates life to your spirit, mind and body. By overlooking Jesus' physical suffering on your behalf, failing to serve other believers in love or ignoring the presence of God within you, you leave yourself vulnerable to physical weakness and sickness.

If you abuse or neglect your physical body, you are corrupting God's temple, and all He has to do to bring destruction on you is to withhold the divine health that flows from His Spirit within you. "If anyone destroys God's temple, God will destroy him; for God's temple is sacred, and you are that temple."

It is interesting that your physical body is only a temporary shell and a vital part of your existence in this sinful world, yet God declares it to be His temple. Scripture repeats each of these points clearly and repeatedly, yet they seem incompatible. More than anything else, your physical body represents the putrefied results of sin. God, on the other hand, represents total sinlessness. This leads me to conclude that God has a very significant reason for making your temporary shell and the center of your worldly existence His dwelling.

This should lead us to several conclusions. For one, it should counter the belief of some Christians that the physical body has no value at all, so we should not even dress it attractively. This is somewhat like asking the King of the universe to stay in a bare, run-down, unpainted shack. The purpose of caring for your body is to glorify your Father, not to feel better about yourself.

It also demonstrates God's sovereignty over all, including His victory and power over sin. Think about a military analogy: What would you communicate to your enemy by setting up your headquarters on his most strategic location? Think about it.

Third, the Holy Spirit in you is a guarantee of more to come, so declaring your physical body as His dwelling is a strong assurance of a new body in the future. Not even those believers who have died and are living in paradise have received their new bodies yet. According to First Corinthians, "We will all be changed—in a flash, in the twinkling of an eye, at the last trumpet" (1 Cor. 15:51-52), and the last trumpet has not sounded yet.

Because God does not use words carelessly, I wonder about His choice of words in that passage. In particular, the word "flash" intrigues me. In this context it might only describe the speed at which He will change us—as quickly as a flash or the twinkling of an eye. I suspect, however, that it also describes the appearance of our conversion from our temporal bodies to our eternal ones. The Greek word translated "flash" is *atomos*, which might suggest an image of an atomic bomb blast, the brilliant light generated when atomic structure changes or disintegrates. This relates to Jesus glowing like the sun when He transfigured before His disciples. You will receive your new body in a brilliant momentary flash. And the fact that God uses your disposable physical body as His temple now can only assure you of that exciting moment in the future when He will relieve you of it forever.

As a hammer cannot drive a nail by itself, you cannot perform God's work by yourself; you are His instrument. God gave an Old Testament prophet a word for his king: "Not by might nor by power, but by my Spirit" (Zech. 4:6), meaning that God's Spirit rather than human effort will perform God's work. God works through humans, using their skills and abilities, but kingdom business requires the King's Spirit. God requires you to perform the necessary actions, but His Spirit within you produces the results.

Your entire spiritual experience has been a cooperative venture involving you and the Holy Spirit. The Spirit attracted you to the Father and you responded. The Holy Spirit assured you of the validity of God's salvation package and helped you use your faith to accept it. Upon your spiritual conversion, He took up residence and began His in-house program of teaching, guiding, assuring and developing. You and He have worked together all this time, possibly without you even realizing it.

When you speak the Word of God, it is the Holy Spirit within you who causes it to produce results. When you lay hands on the sick, the Holy Spirit flows through you to deliver healing. When you command demons, the Holy Spirit within you is the force behind the words. His actions are so closely related to yours it is almost impossible to distinguish between them.

God does not work through you by remote control from His throne room way up in heaven. His Spirit is within you, right on the scene. It is He who empowers you to do kingdom business. Believe me, you do not have what it takes to produce worthwhile results. Your enemy is too much for you alone and you are not personally adequate for doing God's work. God knows that, so He placed His Spirit within you to provide the muscle. The Holy Spirit within you is not just a convenience or nicety. His presence is essential to your well-being and effectiveness.

Godliness

Many of the problems you experience as a Christian are the result of trying to do spiritual business in your natural state. You try to act godly without being God-like, or do godly work without developing godly character. To become effective in God's kingdom, you must become a suitable residence for the king, and that requires you to become like Him.

The ultimate goal of redemption is to transform the believer into the Christian, the God-like one; for you to be like God in character, attitude and action. Not a son of God on a lower level, but a son of God like Jesus. The Book of Ephesians describes one way God transforms you into the image of Jesus.

It was he who gave some to be apostles, some to be prophets, some to be evangelists, and some to be pastors and teachers, to prepare God's people for works of service, so that the body of Christ may be built up until we all reach unity in the faith and in the knowledge of the Son of God and become mature, attaining to the whole measure of the fullness of Christ. Then we will no longer be infants, tossed back and forth by the waves, and blown here and there by every wind of teaching and by the cunning and craftiness of men in their deceitful scheming. Instead, speaking the truth in love, we will in all things grow up into him who is the head, that is, Christ (Eph. 4:11-15).

Maturity, attaining to the whole measure of the fullness of Christ, and growing up into Christ, are all descriptions of God's intent: He wants you to be like Jesus. God wants to fill His kingdom with His peers; not immature, underdeveloped, inferior beings. He wants meaningful two-way relationships, which He can only have with peers. He wants to entrust His business to qualified people, and only Jesus or someone like Him is qualified. The power of God transforms you into an exact representation of Himself—an icon, an accurate image. That enables you to be an associate of God, a laborer who works alongside Him in His kingdom.

In the previous chapter we considered your responsibility for doing God's business. Now we see that you need God's character to conduct His business. Your sinful attitudes and behavior would prevent you from doing God's business because they are inade-quate for the job and opposed to God's work. In addition, your self-centeredness would cause you to misappropriate God's power and try to take credit for the results. But God will not share His glory and His work cannot be done by human effort. Only godly character working in cooperation with God's Spirit can accomplish anything worthwhile.

A Natural Ruler

When God created Adam and Eve, He created them in His own image and told them to fill the earth and subdue it. The earth was their possession and they were to have full authority over it. God also told them, "Rule over the fish of the sea and the birds of the air and over every living creature that moves on the ground" (Gen. 1:28).

In his original state, man was the image of God and he was over everything on earth except God Himself. He was fully qualified to rule because God created him to do so. In eternity, you will rule with Christ. God's plan of redemption eventually will restore your authority over all the earth and then expand your realm. What Satan meant for evil, God will use for good, because man's final state will be greater than the original. That is how God works.

In the interim, every human knows that somehow he is supposed to rule. Something in your nature says you should have authority. You are a natural ruler, because God created man to rule. The problem is that self-centeredness motivates you to dominate others and control your environment. You long for the authority that was your origin and will be your destiny. Being powerless to achieve that, however, you substitute your own form of authority: control and manipulation. Every human being wants to be in control of his environment, himself and others. This is the basis of almost all relationship problems: each person wants to be in control. That is the sinful version of the spiritual authority man received from God.

Your nature and abilities still resemble God's, even considering the effects of sin. Part of that resemblance is your aptitude for ruling. Your work consists of using the authority and power God delegated to you to conduct His business; that it is the essence of ruling.

Jesus quoted a verse from Psalm 82 that states, "You are 'gods'; you are all sons of the Most High" (Ps. 82:6). You are a god in the sense that the Most High has delegated to you godly power and authority. Both the Old and New Testaments acknowledge the God-likeness of redeemed man. God has endowed you with His nature and empowered you with His authority so you can perform His work effectively. God's work associate—that's what you are.

Conclusion

You are God's dwelling. He has not left you alone on this planet; his Holy Spirit lives within you, sustains you, helps develop you into God's image and empowers you to do God's work. Therefore, God Himself works through you to conduct His business, providing the necessary power and authority, and developing you into His image so you can perform His work effectively. God created mankind to rule and it is still part of your nature to be in charge and do whatever needs to be done. As you rely on God within you, you can do that successfully.

Personal Study

1.   Considering our relative ignorance about spiritual matters, it is essential that we rely on the Holy Spirit to guide us.

   • How has your worldly mindset caused you to be ignorant of the spiritual realm?

   • What part of you most strongly resists the guidance of the Holy Spirit, and what can you do about it?

2.   If the Holy Spirit is "a deposit, guaranteeing what is to come," it is important that we benefit as much as possible from Him now to prepare ourselves for "what is to come."

- Explain how you can learn to trust and cooperate with the Holy Spirit, and therefore learn as much as possible from Him.

3. God has chosen to make your sin-corrupted body His sacred temple, although its desires are totally opposed to His.

    - What significance does that give to the following statement by Paul? "I beat my body and make it my slave so that after I have preached to others, I myself will not be disqualified for the prize" (1 Cor. 9:27).

    - To which of your body's appetites and desires should you be especially alert? How can you prevent them from corrupting your integrity, single-mindedness and purity?

16

Personal Initiative

I strongly suspect that many of our desires and life-long ambitions have come from God. Consider the following: "I thank God, who put into the heart of Titus the same concern I have for you" (2 Cor. 8:16). It seems likely the Holy Spirit would plant a concern or desire in your spirit and allow you to nurture it with time. Then at the right moment, after you have nurtured it to maturity and it has become your own intense desire, God causes the work to be done so "your" desire is fulfilled. It is consistent with God's nature and way of doing things.

It also is consistent with God's promises to do what we ask, within the parameters of His will being done and our asking in Jesus' name. It is consistent with the Holy Spirit's role of revealing kingdom matters to us. And it is consistent with the doctrines of God's sovereignty and your free will. It explains one way God's will can always be done through people with free wills.

While we are speculating on how God might do this, let us develop our hypothesis a little more. First, He gives you a personality that provides the necessary aptitudes, interests and attributes you will need to do His will effectively. You enjoy using your abilities because they are fulfilling and rewarding; you can use them effectively and you get good results.

God then arranges a significant event or circumstance in your life that sparks a desire, which draws your attention and causes you to focus on a specific need. At first, you might only watch others who are active in that area, then you might help them or begin doing a little something on your own. It may seem like a hobby to you, just something you "play around with." But as time progresses, so does your interest. Eventually the matter becomes a significant part of your life and you may even make it your career. It was God's intent all along for you to do it, and now you have chosen to make it a major part of your life.

There is an important kingdom principle called synergy: two or more ingredients combining and producing greater results than they would separately. A scriptural example is one causing 1,000 to flee and two causing 10,000 to flee (Deut. 32:30). Instead of simply adding their individual efforts to get a combined result of 2,000, the combined power compounds their efforts to produce 10,000. That is synergy.

I am convinced this principle applies to your relationship with God and the results you get when doing His work. God simply has chosen to do His work through cooperative human beings. God places a desire in you and you cultivate it, think about it, talk about it, ponder it and plan for it. The desire grows and becomes a major part of you; you might even become preoccupied with it. The power of your spirit joins with the power of God and the result is the fulfillment of your desire. I believe that is how creative faith works, for example. You and God work together to bring your desire into existence. How else can you reconcile "your kingdom come, your will be done" with "I will give you the desires of your heart?"

In no way am I suggesting that every desire or idea you have is from God or conforms to His will. You still have self-centered interests that motivate you to work everything out for your own pleasure and benefit. But I am saying this is one way God works in you and through you.

To me, this says a lot about the importance of using your own initiative. We may have a certain limited autonomy in matters of kingdom business. I am certain this would be dependent on your spiritual maturity and skill in performing God's will.

Take the case of Peter and the lame man in Acts chapter 3. Peter did not pray for the man's healing, nor did he ask others to agree with him in prayer. He simply said, "In the name of Jesus Christ of Nazareth, walk." Then Peter took him by the hand and helped him up. He clearly stated that he was acting in Jesus' behalf—in the name of Jesus—and he did what needed to be done.

Paul exercised the same authority on several occasions. Once a slave girl who had a demon by which she predicted the future was following Paul and creating a disturbance. Paul finally become so troubled he spoke to the spirit, "In the name of Jesus Christ I command you to come out of her!" (Acts 16:18). Notice that Paul became personally troubled and then took action in the name of Jesus.

On another occasion, Paul was preaching so long that a young man sitting in a window sank into a deep sleep. He fell out of the third story window to the ground and died. Paul did not publicly pray or ask others to pray. He "threw himself on the young man and put his arms around him" (Acts 20:10). The young man came back to life and presumably stayed awake for the remainder of Paul's teaching. This is very similar to the Old Testament prophet who laid on top of a dead child and brought him back to life.

There is the incident of a man, lame from birth, who was listening to Paul. "Paul looked directly at him, saw that he had faith to be healed and called out, 'Stand up on your feet!' At that, the man jumped up and began to walk" (Acts 14:9-10). Paul simply observed the situation and responded to it.

Think for a moment about how Jesus administered God's work. He did not pray to the Father or the Holy Spirit for them to perform the healing; He spoke and healing occurred. "Be healed." "Your faith has made you whole." "According to your faith it is done." To the wind and waves, "Peace. Be still." To demons, "Be silent and come out of him."

You might be thinking, "Yeah, but I'm not Jesus." Well, in a sense you are. You are legally part of His Father's kingdom, a child of God, and Jesus' brother or sister. You have the same Holy Spirit within you. Jesus has authorized you to act in His behalf and perform the same functions He did. He said you should follow Him, which means copy what He did. He commissioned you to do kingdom business, as He did on earth. Maybe technically you are not Jesus

Himself, but for all practical purposes there should be no difference between your results and His.

I am not suggesting you should not pray for people or ask God to heal someone. Scriptures are full of examples and instruction on how to pray and how to ask God. Maybe you cannot accept this yet, but I believe there are situations and maybe even a stage at which you stop asking God to do something and begin acting in the authority He gave you.

Let me show you an Old Testament incident in which God rebuked someone for praying instead of acting with authority. God had commissioned Moses to lead the Israelites out of Egypt. After the plagues, the people followed Moses to the sea and then discovered the Egyptian army was pursuing them. The people cried out to Moses, who appeared to be exercising great faith in God when he responded to them.

"Do not be afraid. Stand firm and you will see the deliverance the Lord will bring you today. The Egyptians you see today you will never see again. The Lord will fight for you; you need only to be still" (Exod. 14:13-14).

Sounds great, doesn't it? A wonderful statement of faith in what God will do! The only problem was that God expected Moses to deliver the people! So He immediately spoke to Moses. "Why are you crying out to me? Tell the Israelites to move on. Raise your staff and stretch out your hand over the sea to divide the water so the Israelites can go through the sea on dry ground" (Exod. 14:15-16). God expected Moses to direct the people, to stretch out his hand and divide the water. There is no record that God told Moses ahead of time that He would divide the water.

Maybe God showed Moses what would happen and Moses didn't want to believe that he was responsible for doing it, but God chose not to record that part of the incident in Scripture. This would be an important point since God later reprimands him for not acting, so it seems unlikely God chose not to record it.

Another possibility is that God expected Moses to do whatever was necessary to deliver the people, including such unprecedented acts as dividing the water and immediately drying the sea floor. I think this is the only reasonable conclusion.

The third and fourth chapters of Exodus show that God's original statement to Moses was, "I am sending you to Pharaoh to bring my people the Israelites out of Egypt" (Exod. 3:10). It was only after Moses resisted that God told him details about how to address Pharaoh and about various signs he could use. Eventually, God became angry with Moses for stubbornly insisting on having so many answers before he would agree to go. Even in this extended dialog, however, nothing was said about crossing the Red Sea, which remains an awe-inspiring miracle thousands of years later.

God's role was to harden the Egyptians' hearts so they would follow the Israelites into the sea. The rest was up to Moses, including dividing the Red Sea and directing the people to cross over. God had given Moses authority and responsibility for delivering the people and He would not let Moses abdicate.

I believe God is equally upset with us if we reject the responsibility for telling people the Good News of the kingdom, driving out demons and healing the sick. Should you expect a revelation from God, a booming voice, an electric jolt or goose bumps before you tell someone about Jesus? Or command a demon to leave? Or administer healing? Of course not. You do not need a degree in theology to know what to do. Simply read the Bible to see what Jesus did, then go imitate Him.

If you discover that someone doesn't know Jesus, introduce them. If they don't believe God exists or cares about people, explain what He has done for you. If they have a need, take care of it. This is all kingdom business. This is what God authorized, equipped and commissioned you to do. No excuses.

How often do we abdicate by praying for God to do something? God did not say, "Moses, stretch out your hand and I will perform a miracle." Instead, "Moses, use what I gave you and do the job." Likewise, God gave *you* power and authority over demons. God told *you* to heal the sick. God told *you* to tell everyone the Good News of the kingdom. God told *you* to make disciples. He expects *you* to do it in His behalf. He has given *you* the keys to the kingdom, so unlock the kingdom resources and use them to conduct kingdom business.

The Old Testament provides glimpses of what was to come in the New Testament. So you do not think that God's expectation of

Moses was an isolated instance, let me draw your attention to a few others. My purpose is to show that even in the Old Testament, God expected people to use their own initiative in doing God's work. If that were true in the old covenant, in which people worshiped God from a distance, it certainly is true in the new covenant, in which we are God's children and representatives and clearly directed to do God's work.

When Samuel anointed Saul as king, he told him some events that would happen as confirmation of God's choice. Then Samuel said, "The Spirit of the Lord will come upon you in power, and you will prophesy . . . and you will be changed into a different person. Once these signs are fulfilled, do whatever your hand finds to do, for God is with you" (1 Sam. 10:6-7). Notice the sequence: 1) the Holy Spirit will come on you with power, 2) your nature will change and 3) do whatever your hand finds to do, because God is with you. The same process occurs with you in the new covenant: 1) the Holy Spirit comes on you at salvation, 2) your nature begins to become like Jesus' and 3) use your initiative, because God will produce the results.

Why did David go to battle against Goliath? Because he was upset at the pagan's display of contempt for God and His people. There is no indication that God spoke to David about combating Goliath. Instead, the Bible shows that David was aggravated and volunteered to fight the giant.

To be fair, I must point out that David did consult the Lord for direction at other times. For example, he consulted God twice about attacking the Philistines who were plundering an Israeli city (1 Sam. 23:1-6). God provided implements the priests were to use to discover God's will, but He also honored people's initiative when they chose to act in God's behalf by simply doing what the situation called for.

When Kind David talked to Nathan the prophet about building a temple, Nathan gave an interesting reply: "Whatever you have in mind, go ahead and do it, for the Lord is with you" (2 Sam. 7:3 and 1 Chron. 17:2). In this particular case, God spoke to Nathan later about David's son building the temple. But Nathan's initial response reveals their understanding that God honored people's initiative. It is significant that God did not rebuke David for being presumptuous; God honored David's initiative but changed David's plan. This incident also shows that if you use your initiative and violate God's plan, He will let you know. As long as you commit your ways to Him and try to be sensitive to His direction, you need not worry about taking the initiative because God can handle it.

When King David was about to die, he charged Solomon to obey God and walk in His ways, "so that you may prosper in all you do and wherever you go" (1 Kings 2:3). David did not say that God would bless Solomon's efforts only if He told him specifically what to do. He said, "in all you do and wherever you go."

In the very first Psalm, David describes a man who delights in serving God. Of such a man David says, "Whatever he does prospers" (Ps. 1:3).

King Solomon wrote, "Commit to the Lord whatever you do, and you plans will succeed" (Prov. 16:3).

As we have seen, the word "whatever" is very significant when we act in God's behalf. Consider some key New Testament verses where the word occurs.

"I will give you the keys of the kingdom of heaven; whatever you bind on earth will be bound in heaven, and whatever you loose on earth will be loosed in heaven" (Matt. 16:19; 18:18).

"I tell you the truth, if you have faith and do not doubt, not only can you do what was done to the fig tree, but also you can say to this mountain, 'Go, throw yourself into the sea,' and it will be done. If you believe, you will receive whatever you ask for in prayer" (Matt. 21:21-22).

If we were to stop here, it would be easy to conclude that God is little more than a genie in a bottle. "Whatever you wish, I will do." Do you honestly believe that God would enslave Himself to your sinful attitudes and indulge your selfish desires? That would be ridiculous! He expects you to deny your worldly thinking and put it to death.

Then what do these verses mean? One more "whatever" verse shows us. "And whatever you do, whether in word or deed, do it all in the name of the Lord Jesus" (Col. 3:17). That is, do everything as if you were Jesus. Do it in His behalf, as His representative. This shows the importance of the sequence we see in both the Old and

New Testaments: 1) the Holy Spirit comes on you, 2) your nature changes and 3) everything you do is successful.

If you are a Christian, the Holy Spirit has come upon you and you are in the process of changing your nature. We understand the concept of a learning curve and the relationship between learning and success. Similarly, you can expect that the more you become like Jesus, the higher your success rate will go.

One of the ways sin perverts God's intent is by taking matters to an extreme, and that is certainly possible with this topic. At one extreme, it is possible to believe it is your power that performed the work and then accept credit for it. Or you might believe that God actually performed the work, but He could do it through you because you were such a godly person. The self-centeredness and pride in these attitudes are obvious. The other extreme would be to believe you have nothing worthwhile to contribute, so you merely wait for God to do everything. This is an attitude of disbelief and disobedience. The correct position is between these extremes: Use the abilities God gave you to do His work, then expect His power to produce results. It is your duty as a believer to use kingdom resources to do kingdom business.

So what if you take the initiative and nothing happens? Is "failure" evidence that you missed God's will? I think such a question springs from some invalid assumptions. First, it incorrectly assumes you are responsible for results, which you are not. You should be faithful; it is God who gives the increase. It is not your might nor your power that produces results, but God's Spirit.

A second invalid assumption is that if you do all the right things, you will get the desired result. This ignores the free will of everyone else involved. Remember that God did everything right, but Adam and Eve still sinned. It also is possible you missed God's will, or that Satan has interfered. In any case, be sensitive to God and let Him show you how to respond.

So what if nothing happens? Keep in mind that in heaven you will be rewarded for faithfulness, not penalized for failure. God values perseverance and expects you to keep trying in the face of apparent failure. "For though a righteous man falls seven times, he rises again, but the wicked are brought down by calamity" (Prov. 24:16). The only person who really fails is the one who gives up.

It is important to realize that God has chosen to conduct His business through cooperative people. Faith is an example. Seldom does God act contrary to your faith. Only occasionally will He heal when you don't expect Him to, for example. Your beliefs and state of mind are critical to receiving or participating in God's work. Repentance—changing your mind—is essential. Whether your mind is a catalyst or actually works synergistically with God is unclear. It is clear, however, that God expects you to conform your thinking to the reality of His kingdom so He can work effectively through you.

So keep working on the way you think, making every thought obedient to Christ. Change your priorities, perspective, attitude and standards. Do everything in the name of Jesus and expect everything you do to be successful. It really is as straightforward as it sounds.

Consider an analogy for a moment. Assume you have a young child in school and their class is presenting a special program. As a dutiful and civic-minded parent, you volunteer to help out.

Each child in the program is to wear a vest and bow tie provided by the school. Your job is to see that each child has a vest and tie, and is wearing them properly (which is the hard part). A teacher has shown you where they stored the vests and ties.

Now, you find yourself backstage as the children are arriving for the program. What do you do? You have authority to perform a specific task and you know where the resources are, so you start to work. On your own initiative, you begin looking for a child without a vest or tie. Having located such a child, you help them put the items on. If you see a child whose tie is undone or whose vest is crooked, you help straighten them up.

You don't need for the school staff to assure you it really is okay for you to do this task; your instructions and authority are clear. If one of the children objects to wearing a tie, you have no reason to question whether he should wear it. It does not matter whether the child's parent is a single mother or the state governor, your duty is the same. You are responsible for the task, you have the authority and resources to perform it, and you use your own initiative to do so. And if you are good at your job, you will see that every child is wearing a vest and bow tie, unless one of the school staff tells you otherwise.

Emulating Jesus

I had a Panasonic printer on my computer system that emulated an Epson printer. That means if my computer software could not work directly with my Panasonic printer, I could tell it to perform as if it had an Epson printer. The program generated data for an Epson and my Panasonic processed it as if it were an Epson. My computer did not know the difference.

To emulate a person is to equal them by imitating them or copying their performance. Jesus taught that His disciples were to emulate Him. He said, "If anyone would come after me, he must deny himself and take up his cross and follow me" (Matt. 16:24). To "come after" Jesus means to commit yourself to what He represented, being willing to do whatever is necessary to fulfill God's will for your life. Denying yourself means rejecting your self-centered desires. A cross in this context is a circumstance that has the potential for great harm or for revealing your carnality. The main purpose of a "cross" is to create or hasten a crisis, in part by revealing your inadequacy. And to follow Jesus is to imitate or emulate Him, to perform as if you were Jesus Himself. You emulate Jesus by doing what He would do in your situation. That requires exercising initiative and deciding what you should do. Duplicate His performance and His nature.

Jesus emulated His Father. He said, "Anyone who has seen me has seen the Father" (John 14:9). He came in His Father's name, acting in His behalf (John 5:43). He performed miracles in His Father's name (John 10:25). He said He only did what He saw His Father doing (John 5:19). He did only what the Father taught Him (John 8:28). He taught what the Father wanted rather than speak on His own (John 7:17). He said only what the Father told Him to say (John 12:50). He came down from heaven to do His Father's will (John 6:38). He sought to please His Father rather than Himself (John 5:30).

God sent Jesus to conduct specific business for the kingdom. Jesus came to earth as God's representative, did what His Father wanted and acted in His Father's behalf. You and I are now taking Jesus' place. You are now God's representative and you are to do your Father's work in His behalf. This does not mean you need a divine revelation for every task you perform. It means you should know what your task is and perform it as Jesus would.

At this point you might object, "I can't do what Jesus did. I have a full-time job and a family to support." So consider how Jesus responded to interruptions and other brief encounters. He was walking down the road, traveling from one place to another, and a blind man cried out to him. Jesus stopped, healed him and went on His way.

On another occasion, Jesus was going somewhere and He saw a man who had climbed a tree to get a look at Him as He passed by. Jesus called him down, went to his house and offered him salvation.

He was talking with a group of people in someone's home one day when four men lowered a paralyzed man down to Him from the roof. Jesus told the paralyzed man his sins were forgiven and then healed him.

When a rich young man came to Jesus and asked Him how to get eternal life, Jesus told him to obey the commandments. He said he did. Then Jesus told him to make a radical lifestyle change, but the man was unwilling to do it and went away.

One day Jesus saw a man who had been an invalid for 38 years. Jesus asked him whether he wanted to get well and then healed him.

How long did these encounters take? How much effort did Jesus have to make? Can you not set aside a few minutes in your busy schedule to change someone for eternity? If not, then you are too busy doing the wrong things.

You can emulate Jesus, because He told you to and gave you the authority and resources to do it. When you see someone who needs God, take the initiative to introduce them to Him and meet their need. It really is that simple.

Conclusion

God has chosen to conduct His business through cooperative people. He has transferred you to His kingdom, commissioned you to do kingdom work, begun developing godly character in you and put His Spirit within you to make you effective. Now He expects you to use what He has given you and exercise initiative to do His work.

God alone can produce the desired results, but He can only produce results as you give Him opportunity. At some point, you need to stop asking God to do everything and begin using the resources He gave you.

Personal Study

1.   Identify a strong desire or dream you have.

   • Is it possible God gave you that dream?

   • Which of your skills and abilities could you use to fulfill that dream?

   • List as many reasons as possible why God may want you to fulfill that dream.

   • List as many reasons as possible why He may not want you to do it.

   • If it seems a good thing to do, what steps can you take to prepare yourself or actually give life to the dream?

2.   Consider a typical incident in which you could use your skills and abilities to help someone.

   • How do you think Jesus would have responded if He were in that situation?

- In what ways might your worldly desires resist helping the person?

- How might your taking the initiative enable God to do even more in that person's life?

3. Identify a recent opportunity you had to tell someone how Jesus could help them.

- If you had that same opportunity now, what fears might prevent you from talking to them about Jesus? What would be an appropriate response to those fears?

- If you were to begin talking to the person, how might the Holy Spirit help you?

- If you talk to someone about Jesus and they are not interested, how should that affect your willingness to talk to someone else? What could you do to prepare yourself for the next person?

17

Kingdom Business

In the previous chapters, we have considered kingdom values, legal matters, logistics and personal initiative. We have seen that God values character that is like His. We have observed that God has legally transferred you to His kingdom and commissioned you to act in His behalf. We have also discovered that He has already done everything necessary for you to be effective in His kingdom, including equipping you with a personality suitable for the work He has for you, and empowering you with His Holy Spirit. And finally, we have shown that He expects you to use your personal initiative in doing His work.

Now let us consider the work itself. What exactly does He expect you to do?

Two of the Gospels record what we call "The Great Commission," a concise statement of your responsibilities as a kingdom representative. The Scriptures state that after Jesus' resurrection and before His ascent into heaven, He appeared to His disciples and gave them specific directions.

> *"All authority in heaven and on earth has been given to me. Therefore go and make disciples of all nations, baptizing them in the name of the Father and of the Son and of the Holy Spirit, and teaching them to obey everything I have*

commanded you. And surely I will be with you always, to the very end of the age" (Matt. 28:18-20).

The Book of Mark records Jesus' statement as follows. "Go into all the world and preach the good news to all creation. Whoever believes and is baptized will be saved, but whoever does not believe will be condemned" (Mark 16:15-16).

Between these accounts, we can compile the following list of responsibilities: preach the Good News, make disciples, baptize them and teach them to obey everything Jesus commanded. This is your general job description.

Now Mark's account includes a list of "signs" that will accompany you; these are evidences that you are conducting kingdom business. While you are going about your business, you will have opportunities to drive out demons, speak in unknown languages, be protected from harmful snakes and poisons, and heal the sick. These are a few kingdom benefits; some of these benefits you will receive and others you will administer to others. As important as these signs are, they are primarily evidence you are doing kingdom business; they are not the business themselves. Kingdom business consists of spreading the Good News, making disciples, baptizing them and teaching them obedience.

What does it mean to preach the Good News? First, we need to identify the "good news." Most people consider good news to be something that makes them happy; the weather will be better tomorrow, they just got a raise at work, the problem they dreaded has been resolved.

To understand the Bible's meaning of "good news," we must look at the world from God's perspective. God recognizes the world as under the destructive power of Satan's kingdom, so the good news is we can transfer to God's kingdom, experience His blessings and be relieved of the oppression of Satan's kingdom. That is good news. And "preaching" this good news is nothing more than telling people about it in your own words as opportunities come up.

Does God expect everyone to do this? If you were to look at the relevant Scriptures, you would see that Jesus does not qualify His commands. He does not limit "preaching" to those with ministerial license or seminary degree. Every believer is responsible, everywhere he goes, to be ready to tell everyone. It really is not that big a deal. If you had just eaten a delicious dinner at a restaurant, you would tell others so they could go and enjoy it, too. Or if you heard about a sale at a popular department store, you would tell all your friends. If you can spread the good news about such incidental matters, how vitally important it is that you spread the good news about eternal matters!

You are responsible for spreading the news; you are not responsible for whether people accept what you tell them. You are to deliver the message, not drag people into the kingdom against their will or trick them into saying the sinner's prayer. Honor their free will, as God does. Be as effective as possible in spreading the good news, then allow people to respond as they choose.

After someone has entered God's kingdom, they need to be discipled. Jesus said, "If anyone would come after me, he must deny himself and take up his cross and follow me" (Matt. 16:24). The first step in becoming Jesus' disciple is to deny yourself, to reject your sinful attitudes and self-centered desires. This requires a change in your behavior, but more important is the change in the way you think. You must help other Christians repent, especially new ones; help them change their perspective, their priorities, their standards, their attitudes.

Discipling someone for Jesus includes helping them take up their cross. Those situations that cause discomfort, pain and potentially even great harm, also have potential for great benefit. They cause us to get serious about God, our relationship with Him, and our own maturity. They help us keep everything in perspective and set right priorities. As a muscle only strengthens when exercised and even pushed to its limits, we develop only when stretched beyond our comfort zone.

Following Jesus means to emulate Him. Do what He would do in your situation. After all, you are His representative, conducting His business in His behalf. Teaching others to do so is part of the discipling process.

To make disciples requires that you tell them the Good News of the kingdom and encourage them to accept Jesus as their Lord and

Savior. Once they are in the kingdom, you disciple them by teaching them to repent, reject the ways of their former sinful nature, use their difficulties as opportunities to grow, and do what Jesus would do.

None of this requires that you be a minister or have professional training. You cannot teach someone something you do not know yourself, however, so you need to be further along in the process than the person you are discipling. Notice, also, that you can do this regardless of your personality type or character. Just as every healthy human can bear and raise children regardless of their character, you can make disciples. You may not do it the way other Christians would, but you can and must do it.

Having made someone a disciple, you should baptize them "in the name of the Father and of the Son and of the Holy Spirit." Again, you do not need to be a minister to baptize someone in water. Although our human government considers such acts as water baptism typical responsibilities of clergy, God expects all His people to be ready to do His work. And as we discovered in an earlier chapter, to do something "in the name of" someone is to act in the authority they gave you and in their behalf.

The final part of the Great Commission is to teach disciples, other believers, to obey everything Jesus commanded. We could consider this part of discipling, too. I have learned that when I teach, I do not need to know everything about my subject; I only need to know more than my students. I also have learned to rely on the Holy Spirit to teach me and help me make the material relevant to my students. Every parent can teach their children; likewise, you can teach others to obey what Jesus commanded. No teaching certification is required.

As you perform your kingdom duties, you will have opportunities to drive out demons, speak in unknown languages, heal the sick and be protected from harm. These are signs or evidence of doing God's work, convincing proofs to both believers and unbelievers that God's kingdom is real and powerful.

When you drive a demon out of someone or heal them, they will experience relief from their suffering. It is important to remember, however, that your purpose is not to relieve people of their suffering; it is to demonstrate the power of God and glorify Him by overcoming

Satan's work. You must be kingdom-centered, rather than focusing on people's needs. Your goal is not to make people feel better, have a better self-image, have better relationships, or be more effective and fulfilled. These are all side effects or fringe benefits. As a kingdom representative, your purpose is to advance God's kingdom.

People are inherently selfish and concerned for their own well-being, so they are attracted by kingdom benefits. God recognizes this. In the Old Testament, He offered Israel a choice between blessing and curse, between life and death. The choice was theirs, and God honored their free will. They were free to choose to receive the benefits of right relationship with Him, or profound problems resulting from a lack of such relationship. His purpose was not primarily to make them healthy, wealthy and wise; He wanted relationship with them. He wanted them to be His people and Him to be their God. The blessings and curses were the results of their choice.

Everyone on earth receives some of God's blessings, whether they acknowledge them as such or not. God "causes his sun to rise on the evil and the good, and sends rain on the righteous and the unrighteous" (Matt. 5:45). The consistency of the days and seasons is part of God's blessing on His creation. After God destroyed the unrighteous with a flood, He told Noah He would never do it again and promised him seasonal continuity. "As long as the earth endures, seedtime and harvest, cold and heat, summer and winter, day and night will never cease" (Gen. 8:22). Since that day, the righteous and unrighteous alike have benefited from God's blessing of consistent seasons.

This is not true of all God's blessings, however; only the most basic ones, those essential to human life. The greater blessings God reserves for those who love Him. It is those blessings we are to offer as expressions of God's nature and evidence of His kingdom. We need to see the big picture. God did not set up His kingdom simply to make people better off; nor does Satan's kingdom exist primarily to make people worse off.

God's kingdom exists because of who He is—almighty God, the eternal one, all-powerful creator of all things. God is God, therefore His kingdom exists. Satan's kingdom exists because he wants to be God. Man is only in the picture because God created him.

Satan chose to get at God through His creation, so he enticed man through his free will and won a temporary victory. Since that event, mankind's entire existence has been on the front lines of the battle between God and Satan. The battle involves us, but is not about us.

Every human since Adam and Eve's fall has been born into Satan's kingdom and has experienced the results: total consumption with self, rebellious nature, conflict with everything and everyone around him, relative ineffectiveness and powerlessness. Every time a person chooses to transfer citizenship from Satan's kingdom to God's, Satan loses some influence and God's angels celebrate. When a person enters God's kingdom, he receives the benefits, which include freedom from his bondage to sin, wholeness and intimacy with God. God's plan of redemption will restore creation to His intent, except for those beings who choose not to be restored. God wants His creation to experience His benefits and blessings. He offered Israel a choice between blessing and curse, and He urged them to choose blessing; that was His desire for them. He takes the same stance in the New Testament. He offers His kingdom to everyone, draws them to Himself, and extends kingdom benefits to non-citizens, so to speak, so they will become interested; yet He honors their choice.

God, however, would be God without a single Christian. He was God before He created the first angel or human. He is complete in Himself. He wanted to share Himself and His glory with others, so He created them. He then had a kingdom, because a king must have subjects to be a king. God's kingdom does not exist for the benefit of His subjects; that would make angels and humans the center of the kingdom. Instead, God is the focus. We exist for His benefit; the function of the kingdom is to serve and honor God. Every kingdom benefit we experience is simply a result of our citizenship.

Satan originally urged Adam and Eve to be concerned for themselves; the original sin was Eve's concern that God might be holding back something of benefit—the knowledge of good and evil. She then used her free will to choose what she believed was best for her, resulting in an act of disobedience. Concern for ourselves, or self-centeredness, has been the trademark of humanity ever since.

God acknowledges that and appeals to our self-interest by drawing us with the benefits of His kingdom. Even as Christians, we continue to be self-centered, so it is difficult for us to consider being a part of God's kingdom for any reason other than receiving its benefits. In our own perspective, we remain the center of the universe; what benefits us is most important to us.

Developing godly character and changing the way we think has an interesting effect on our perspective, however. We begin to realize the awesomeness of God and the insignificance of ourselves. One result of this new perspective is that we consider the kingdom benefits to be inconsequential compared to the king.

Each of us advances the kingdom differently with our own style. Doing kingdom business requires a broad range of activities, and we all are generally responsible for doing all of them. Due to our specialized natures, however, each of us will be more skilled at different tasks.

Consider the analogy of being an adult in today's American culture. To be a functional adult, you need a broad range of skills. You need to dress yourself, practice personal hygiene and feed yourself. You need to perform basic math for a wide variety of tasks—determining what combination of dollar bills and coins to use to purchase an item, or balancing your checkbook, or knowing how many more chairs to put at the table for your guests, for example. You need basic reading skills. You must be able to drive or find other means of transportation. To be effective as an adult, you need a broad range of skills.

From experience, we know that some people are better at certain skills than others. Take math, for example. Some people struggle to balance their checkbook while others seem to solve all kinds of math problems easily in their heads. Consider driving skills. With some people driving, you feel perfectly safe as a passenger; but with others you would almost prefer to walk. It should be clear that not everyone does everything equally well.

The same is true in God's kingdom. We all must pray, but some people really *pray*. We all must read the Bible to understand our relationship with God and His expectations, but some people seem to fully understand everything they read in the Bible and explain it to others. God intends for all of us to spread the Good News of the kingdom, but we each do it in our own way and with differing results.

Each of us is responsible for making disciples. Some of us are good at bringing new converts into the kingdom. Others are more effective at helping new converts grow up, and still others are most effective at caring for the converts and helping them address the issues in their lives.

Each of us is to drive demons out. Some of us greatly dislike conflict and therefore are reluctant to engage in spiritual warfare. Others of us feel very comfortable using authority or confronting antagonists, so may be eager to find another demon to drive out.

Each of us is responsible for all of the Great Commission. How you fulfill your commission and the effectiveness of your efforts will depend in part on your character.

Imagine this scene. You are driving along a residential street, following another car. A small child suddenly runs into the street and the car in front of you hits him. You run to the child and observe blood on his face, a bruise and swelling on his forehead. The child is in great pain.

What thoughts are likely to go through your mind? "I'm going to throw up"? Or maybe you are the take-charge type, so you direct everyone to stand back, you cover the child up, tell someone to find the parents and someone else to call 911.

At some point, your thoughts might turn to God. "Oh, God! What should I do? What if I pray and nothing happens? There are so many people around and I'd be humiliated if nothing happened!"

Would you expect God to totally and immediately heal the child if you prayed? What if the child were dead—no pulse and no breath? Would you expect God to bring the child back to life and heal him if you prayed?

Does God heal today? Is He any less interested in healing people today than in the past? Do you see opportunities for God to heal people today? Does God heal people through you on a regular basis? Why not? I suggest one of the biggest hindrances to God healing others through you is that you do not expect him to.

A brief look through the Scriptures shows that healing is as much a part of God's plan as salvation, in both the Old and New Testaments. All of God's covenants with Israel included both redemption and healing. "Praise the Lord, O my soul, and forget not all his benefits. He forgives all my sins and heals all my diseases" (Ps. 103:2-3).

At the beginning of His ministry, Jesus read the following from Isaiah: "The Spirit of the Lord is on me, because he has anointed me to preach good news to the poor. He has sent me to proclaim freedom for the prisoners and recovery of sight for the blind, to release the oppressed, to proclaim the year of the Lord's favor" (Luke 4:18-19). After reading this, Jesus announced, "Today this scripture is fulfilled in your hearing." Notice that healing was as important as preaching the gospel and freeing those oppressed by Satan. Even before His famous Sermon on the Mount, "Jesus went throughout Galilee, teaching in their synagogues, preaching the good news of the kingdom, and healing every disease and sickness among the people" (Matt. 4:23).

Jesus empowered His followers to do the same. "When Jesus had called the Twelve together, he gave them power and authority to drive out all demons and to cure diseases, and he sent them out to preach the kingdom of God and to heal the sick . . . . So they set out and went from village to village, preaching the gospel and healing people everywhere" (Luke 9:1-2, 6). This was still early in Jesus' ministry, so the disciples were very inexperienced. They were little more than green recruits, but their job was to preach the gospel of the kingdom and heal the sick, and they did it.

"After this the Lord appointed seventy-two others and sent them two by two ahead of him to every town and place where he was about to go . . . . 'Heal the sick who are there and tell them, "The kingdom of God is near you."'" (Luke 10:1, 9). As soon as Jesus selected the 72 additional disciples, He immediately sent them out to announce the arrival of God's kingdom and to heal the sick. These people were virtual "green-horns," but they went out and were successful doing what Jesus told them.

Are you beginning to see that extensive training and great faith are not necessary to spread the Good News, drive out demons and heal the sick? Keep in mind that the disciples did these even before they received the Holy Spirit.

Does the Great Commission apply today as much as it did in the first century? Sure, it does. Are you not better equipped to fulfill your commission than first century believers? Yes, you are.

Consider the sacrament of communion, and the elements of bread and juice. The bread represents Jesus' body and the healing it brings to us. According to Isaiah, "by his wounds we are healed" (Isa. 53:5). The juice represents His blood, "which is poured out for many for the forgiveness of sins" (Matt. 26:28). Every time you celebrate communion, you acknowledge both salvation and healing.

Sickness and problems with demons are part of the curse of sin. It is your duty as a kingdom representative to promote God's kingdom and combat the effects of Satan's kingdom.

Consider an analogy for a moment. Assume it is an election year and you volunteer to help your favorite political party. You are assigned the task of registering voters. Let's say hypothetically that in addition to working at a voter registration table in a local shopping center, you can also carry registration forms with you and register people anywhere. You have the authority and the resources to perform your task at will.

Let's assume you are fairly civic-minded and really want people to vote in the election. As you go about your normal business, your civic-mindedness causes you to be alert to any clue of someone's interest in the election. The more enthused you are about the election, the more likely you are to raise the subject in conversation.

If someone is angry at politicians in general or your candidate in particular, you do not take it as a personal offense. If they are completely indifferent about the election, even after you try to persuade them, you do not consider it a personal failure. In both cases, you honor the person's freedom to choose. If they question your ability to register them on the street corner, you assure them it is legal. You know what your task is, you know you have the authority and resources to perform it, and you perform the task whenever you identify a need for it.

This is a pretty straightforward analogy, and you should not have much difficulty applying it to God's kingdom. You have the task of offering the benefits of God's kingdom to the world around you. It is your responsibility, you have what you need to do it, and you exercise your own initiative to perform the task whenever you identify a need for it. Could it be any simpler? The two specific kingdom benefits you are to offer people are salvation and healing. And everyone you meet who is not already in the kingdom needs its benefits.

Conclusion

Every believer is a member of God's kingdom and is responsible for spreading the news of the kingdom, making disciples, baptizing them and teaching them to obey all that Jesus taught. We recognize that not all of us will be equally effective at all these tasks, yet each of us should be ready to do kingdom business.

Personal Study

1. Consider the main responsibilities Jesus listed in the Great Commission: 1) spread the good news of the kingdom, 2) make disciples, 3) baptize them, and 4) teach them to obey. How could people with the following spiritual gifts fulfill the Great Commission, and what are they likely to emphasize?

   - Teacher: enjoys researching, learning, and showing others.

   - Administrator: good at organizing and coordinating.

   - Healing: offers spiritual, mental, physical health to those who need it.

   - Server: performs specialized tasks for whoever needs them.

   - Helper: dedicated to an individual, does whatever they need.

- Craftsman: creates an excellent product.

- Generosity: offers resources to those in need.

2. People are inherently self-centered, so the Good News of the kingdom appeals to them when they recognize its benefits.

   - At what point should they be told about denying their sinful nature?

   - Explain your answer, using Jesus as an example.

3. A disciple is one who embraces the disciplines advocated by his teacher and learns to follow his example.

   - What kind of help do most people need to become disciples of Jesus?

   - What specific help do you need to become a better disciple of Jesus?

   - What changes can you make that would help you become a better disciple?

   - Which of your skills and abilities might you use to help others become disciples?

Information about
books, articles and other materials
by Larry Fox
is available online at Fox Ventures
(www.foxven.com).

CPSIA information can be obtained
at www.ICGtesting.com
Printed in the USA
FFOW03n1426311017
41754FF